SELF-ADVOCACY IN THE LIVES OF PEOPLE WITH LEARNING DIFFICULTIES

Disability, Human Rights and Society
Series Editor: Professor Len Barton, University of Sheffield

The *Disability, Human Rights and Society* series reflects a commitment to a particular view of 'disability' and a desire to make this view accessible to a wider audience. The series approach defines 'disability' as a form of oppression and identifies the ways in which disabled people are marginalized, restricted and experience discrimination. The fundamental issue is not one of an individual's inabilities or limitations, but rather a hostile and unadaptive society.

Authors in this series are united in the belief that the question of disability must be set within an equal opportunities framework. The series gives priority to the examination and critique of those factors that are unacceptable, offensive and in need of change. It also recognizes that any attempt to redirect resources in order to provide opportunities for discriminated people cannot pretend to be apolitical. Finally, it raises the urgent task of establishing links with other marginalized groups in an attempt to engage in a common struggle. The issue of disability needs to be given equal significance to those of race, gender and age in equal opportunities policies. This series provides support for such a task.

Anyone interested in contributing to the series is invited to approach the Series Editor at the Department of Educational Studies, University of Sheffield.

Current and forthcoming titles

F. Armstrong and L. Barton (eds): *Disability, Human Rights and Education*
M. Corker: *Deaf and Disabled, or Deafness Disabled? Towards a Human Rights Perspective*
M. Corker and S. French (eds): *Disability Discourse*
D. Goodley: *Self-advocacy in the Lives of People with Learning Difficulties*
M. Moore, S. Beazley and J. Maelzer: *Researching Disability Issues*
J. Read: *Disability, the Family and Society: Listening to Mothers*
A. Roulstone: *Enabling Technology: Disabled People, Work and New Technology*
C. Thomas: *Female Forms: Experiencing and Understanding Disability*
A. Vlachou: *Struggles for Inclusive Education: An Ethnographic Study*

SELF-ADVOCACY IN THE LIVES OF PEOPLE WITH LEARNING DIFFICULTIES
The politics of resilience

Dan Goodley

Open University Press
Buckingham · Philadelphia

Open University Press
Celtic Court
22 Ballmoor
Buckingham
MK18 1XW

email: enquiries@openup.co.uk
world wide web: www.openup.co.uk

and
325 Chestnut Street
Philadelphia, PA 19106, USA

First Published 2000

A catalogue record of this book is available from the British Library

ISBN   0 335 20526 7 (pb)   0 335 20527 5 (hb)

Library of Congress Cataloging-in-Publication Data
Goodley, Dan, 1972–
    Self-advocacy in the lives of people with learning difficulties: the politics of resilience / Dan Goodley.
        p.   cm. – (Disability, human rights, and society)
    Includes bibliographical references and index.
    ISBN 0-335-20527-5 – ISBN 0-335-20526-7 (pbk.)
    1. Mentally ill – Great Britain – Political activity.   2. Discrimination against the handicapped – Great Britain.   3. Self-help groups – Great Britain.   I. Title.
    II. Series.
    HV3008.G7 G66 2000
    362.3'0941–dc21   00-039966

Typeset by Type Study, Scarborough
Printed in Great Britain by St Edmundsbury Press Ltd, Bury St Edmunds, Suffolk

This book is dedicated to Elaine Hogg and her friends and comrades who have taken up where she left off.

Contents

Series editor's preface

The Disability, Human Rights and Society series reflects a commitment to a social model of disability and a desire to make this view accessible to a wide audience. 'Disability' is viewed as a form of oppression and the fundamental issue is not one of an individual's inabilities or limitations. but rather a hostile and unadaptive society.

Priority is given to identifying and challenging those barriers to change, including the urgent task of establishing links with other marginalized groups and thus seeking to make connections between class, gender, race, age and disability factors.

The series aims to further establish disability as a serious topic of study, one in which the latest research findings and ideas can be seriously engaged with.

I am delighted to be able to include this book on self-advocacy in the series. In a most readable, informative and challenging analysis, Goodley clearly demonstrates the importance of the topic and the need to engage seriously with the issues involved. The book provides a wealth of ideas, insights and questions and draws on a wide range of sources as well as original material from the author's own ethnographic research.

In a socio-historical account the crucial question of defining self-advocacy, delineating the varied practices covered by the term and the range of functions they serve, are key aspects of the analysis. Questions concerning how self-advocacy within groups works, what impact they have on the lives of people with learning difficulties in terms of individual and collective identity and solidarity, are viewed as matters of crucial importance.

Self-advocacy is complex and multi-faceted and is a response to the experience of discrimination, exclusion and prejudice in both institutional and attitudinal forms. Adding to the quality of the book are stories of particular self-advocates whose resilience and activism is presented in ways that do not romanticise their achievements.

The fundamental importance of the social model of disability is firmly established throughout the book. Essential to an effective appraisal of self-advocacy is 'An awareness of the socio-historical, cultural and political bases of disability' (p. 26). Goodley identifies some particular criticisms of the model whilst arguing for an 'inclusive' social model that benefits from including 'literature that views learning difficulties as a social construction' (p. 26). Thus, negative, individualistic and medicalized discourses and conceptions are critiqued through an approach which advocates as its starting point a '"capacity" rather than "deficiency" stance with respect to people with learning difficulties and their self-advocacy' (p. 36).

This is a book of major importance and I am sure it will stimulate increasing debate and dialogue and contribute to encouraging further explorations of both a theoretical and empirical form of this extremely significant topic. It will appeal to a wide readership, one which hopefully will begin to listen more effectively to the voices of people with learning difficulties and to work with them in the struggle for change.

Professor Len Barton
Sheffield

Preface

> Until I started going to a self-advocacy group, which set me free, I
> couldn't put my views across, tell people what I thought of them,
> tell the DHSS, tell anyone. I couldn't tell the staff where they were
> going wrong.
>
> (Patrick Burke, Chapter 5 of this book)

This book emerged from listening to stories from people, such as Patrick, who
informed me about their experiences of discrimination and their attempts to
rebuff such inequalities. This book examines a particular form of exclusion
that exists in British society at the start of the twenty-first century. This mar-
ginalization of a certain section of the population is justified by inadequate
anti-discriminatory legislation, is enforced through an ever-growing 'care
industry' that puts paternalism before partnership and is theoretically
informed through increasingly specialized 'knowledge' about abnormality.
People with the label of 'learning difficulties' – what used to be called 'mental
retardation' – are encouraged to exist on the boundaries of social life: other,
different, lacking and victim. Interest in 'them' is fuelled by 'our' voyeuristic
fascination with deficiency. What causes their 'disorder'? How can we help
'them'? Could a cure be found for their 'illness'? Any talk of change in their
lives is so often intertwined with the image of individuals adjusting to their
unfortunate and tragic incomplete human conditions. These discourses
inform the contemporary socio-political landscape.

Fortunately, the future is not so bleak. People with the label of learning
difficulties are pushing for interpersonal and social change through their
involvement with 'self-advocacy'. This rather abstract term captures people
with the label of learning difficulties attempting to unravel the discrimination
they face, contesting the assumptions of deficit that are pinned to their very
identities and stating what they want to happen to them in their lives. Self-
advocacy is about people with learning difficulties embracing positive self-
perceptions and shifting their position from the outskirts to the centre of
society. While the British Disability Civil Rights Movement has enjoyed publicity and impact within political, legislative and public life, contributing
to radical social theories of disability in the academy while also informing
professional practice and service provision, the self-advocacy movement,
self-advocacy groups and individual self-advocates continue to be ignored.

This book aims to challenge this ignorance – to examine this quiet revolution on the part of people with learning difficulties.

The role of other societal members in supporting the challenges posed by self-advocates requires immediate investigation. Service systems, their providers, professionals and policy makers involved in 'user empowerment' initiatives all need to reconsider their roles in relation to the challenges now being posed by self-advocacy. Likewise, researchers, students and teachers of the human and social sciences need to question how the challenge of self-advocacy informs their theories, methods, analyses and research programmes. Specifically, disability researchers and writers need to draw on the potential of self-advocacy to contribute to the development of a social theory of disability, to challenge a disabling society and to destabilize naturalized notions of impairment. One tangible influence of the self-advocacy movement can be seen in the choice of terminology. Hence, the term learning difficulties is used in this book to describe people who have been labelled at some point in their lives as requiring specialist 'mental handicap services' (Walmsley 1993: 46), and this term is chosen instead of other synonyms, such as 'mental handicap', 'mental impairment' or 'learning disabilities', because it is the term preferred by many in the self-advocacy movement. As one self-advocate puts it: 'If you put "people with learning difficulties" then they know that people want to learn and to be taught how to do things' (quoted in Sutcliffe and Simons 1993: 23). A number of publications by British self-advocacy groups demonstrate this preference (see Huddersfield People First n.d.; People First Liverpool 1996; publications by People First London, including (all n.d.) 'Making It Easy First', 'Outside but Not Inside . . . Yet', 'Your Right to Housing and Support', 'Safer Sex Pack', 'Oi! It's My Assessment' and 'Laws about Our Rights – Civil Rights (Disabled Persons) Bill').

This book appraises the self-advocacy of people with the label of learning difficulties through an examination of the narratives and actions of self-advocacy groups and their members. Previous work on self-advocacy has illustrated the importance of the self-advocacy movement (and the groups within) to self-advocates (group members with learning difficulties), noting the problematic connections that exist between self-advocacy groups, professionalization, service provision and policy making. This book illuminates self-advocacy as resilience in the face of a society that continues to exclude people on the basis of their purported and reported inadequacies. Through the life stories of self-advocates and a qualitative attention to the dynamics of self-advocacy groups, it is argued that self-advocacy is a continuously evolving living practice. Self-advocacy informs the construction of identities. Self-advocacy occurs even in the most disabling environments. Self-advocacy emerges through the not unproblematic relationship between people with learning difficulties, their peers, professionals, supporters and allies. Self-advocacy takes many forms, individually and collectively, from speaking out in a supportive context, informing others of one's rights, recognizing self-worth, commonality and difference, through to consultation with professionals. With reference to a social model of disability – and disability politics generally – this book makes a case for taking seriously the personal and political significance of self-advocacy as enacted by people with learning difficulties in and outside of their groups, with and without the support of others. Their politics of resilience merits our attention and support.

Acknowledgements

Many people have supported me during the time of writing this book. Thanks to Tim Booth for his supervision of the project and literary criticism of the original text on which this book is based; for the critical commentaries of Dorothy Atkinson and Alan Walker; to Wendy Booth, Michele Moore, Patrick McGhee and Derrick Armstrong for spaces to talk; to Len Barton for his insightful analyses of drafts of this book; and to Anya Souza, Jackie Downer, Lloyd Page, Joyce Kershaw, Patrick Burke, Rebecca Lawthom, Kath Sutherland, Kevin Fehin, Mike Oliver and The Beatles for inspiration.

Love and respect to Rebecca Lawthom, who is always there for me, and of course to my Mum, Dad and our Matt.

Most of all, I owe a great deal to the self-advocates (and their supporters) who let me into their lives. Their consideration, warmth and openness continued, and continue, to blow me away. Most of all they reminded me that it is all still too easy to assume incompetence on the part of others on the basis of limited, biased and discriminatory information. They are the real disability experts and may they continue to change their worlds. I hope the people around them are watching, listening and reacting in ways that they should.

Dan Goodley
Holmfirth

PART I

SETTING THE AGENDA

 **1**

Introduction

Over the past thirty years a new social movement has emerged. Often this movement has been ignored. Often it has been usurped by proponents of fashionable terms like 'user empowerment' and 'participation'. Sometimes it has been understood as a consequence of well meaning professional intervention or training, or taken up as an innovative approach to 'user consultation'. In addition, self-advocacy has been recognized by a minority as a 'new' political activity, comprised of a number of groups, constituting a movement, with the potential to challenge disabling society (Browning *et al.* 1984). This book delves into this movement to understand its impact, its workings and some of the stories of its players.

Self-advocacy can be seen as a counter-movement to state paternalism, wherein people with the label of learning difficulties conspicuously support one another to speak out against some of the most appalling examples of discrimination in contemporary British culture. The self-advocacy movement has invited people with learning difficulties to revolt against disablement in a variety of ways, in a number of contexts, individually and collectively, with and without the support of others. The movement captures resilience in the face of adversity. Hitherto, a number of studies have examined self-advocacy (e.g. Shearer 1972, 1973; Hanna 1978; Crawley 1982, 1988, 1990; Williams 1982; Williams and Shoultz 1982; Worrel 1987, 1988; Simons 1992; Sutcliffe and Simons 1993; Hampson 1994; Dybwad and Bersani 1996; P. Mitchell 1997; Shoultz 1997a, b, c). However, a contemporary critique of what the movement means to people involved has until now been lacking: 'Thus far there has been little independent evaluation of citizen, professional and group advocacy for their respective or collective effects upon service users [*sic*] . . . sufficient to indicate the best way forward at the present time' (Grant 1992: 75).

This need for a contemporary appraisal is further justified by a number of problems with previous literature. First, the movement's diversity and the literature's deficiency in accounting for recent developments (Miller and Keys 1996) has meant that a multitude of existing philosophies and practices remain unearthed. As Crawley (1988: 47) put it, we cannot assume that the increase in the frequency of so-called self-advocacy groups directly relates to an increase in opportunities for meaningful self-advocacy. Second, what these developments mean to people with learning difficulties has yet to be extensively assessed (Page and Aspis 1997). As the movement has grown, its relationship to the empowerment of people with learning difficulties becomes increasingly opaque. While literature by self-advocacy groups and their research allies fills this conceptual gap, these critiques often get lost in wider concerns of policy, professionalism and service provision (Simons 1992). What self-advocacy means to a member of a self-advocacy group in terms of identity, selfhood, personal biography and personal ambition requires exploration (Atkinson and Williams 1990). Third, as the politics of disability develop, tensions exist about the role of people with learning difficulties in the British and international movements (Campbell and Oliver 1996). Indeed, the social model of disability – the British disability movement's big idea (Hasler 1993) – has been criticized for excluding people with the label of learning difficulties (Chappell 1998). A consequence of this is that self-advocacy is not afforded the same political weight as other forms of activism and self-help.

This book examines the ways in which people with learning difficulties or 'self-advocates' – members of self-advocacy groups – individually and collectively advocate for themselves. The subsequent appraisal pitches analysis in broad considerations of professional support, service and advocacy innovations, disability theory, disability politics, story and action. Two questions are posed. First, how do self-advocacy groups impact upon the lives of people with learning difficulties? Second, how do self-advocacy groups work? A number of sources and methods are drawn upon to examine the self-advocacy movement, some groups within it (ethnography) and individual self-advocates' life experiences (life stories). Moreover, in developing an 'inclusive' social model of disability, links are made between the social model of disability (e.g. Finkelstein 1981; Abberley 1987; Barnes 1990, 1991; Oliver 1990, 1996; Morris 1991, 1996; BCODP 1992; Campbell and Oliver 1996) and social theories of learning difficulties (e.g. Dexter 1956, 1958; Edgerton 1967, 1976; Hunt 1967, Dingham 1968; Bogdan and Taylor 1976, 1982; Atkinson and Williams 1990; Booth and Booth 1994, 1998). The book is divided into four major parts.

In the remainder of this part – on setting the agenda – Chapter 2 reviews the literature on self-advocacy of people with learning difficulties, concluding that self-advocacy constitutes a personal and political activity with potentially massive impacts upon the lives of people with learning difficulties and, therefore, deserves appraisal. Chapter 3 sets out what is termed an 'inclusive' social model of disability, the theoretical perspective that guides this book. It is argued that an appraisal of self-advocacy that is grounded in the experiences and actions of people with learning difficulties will draw upon, and in some small way build upon, an inclusive social model of disability. Chapter 4 critically evaluates the methodologies, methods and analyses that were employed to answer the two questions.

Part II – on living self-advocacy – marks the start of a deep appraisal of self-advocacy. Chapter 5 presents the life stories of five 'top self-advocates' with learning difficulties: narrators who have been involved with the self-advocacy movement from its early days in England (1980s onwards). Their stories are chosen to illuminate the movement's history and the impact of group involvement upon life experiences. Chapter 6 draws out broader themes from the narratives: pointing out the struggles of narrators throughout their life courses and signifying how self-advocacy groups enhance self-determination.

Part III – on self-advocacy in action – moves away from narratives of self-advocacy to the group dynamics of four self-advocacy groups. Drawing upon ethnographic study, Chapter 7 describes and appraises self-advocacy in action inside each group and Chapter 8 takes further the appraisal by focusing on the 'support' offered by advisors and self-advocates across the four groups.

The final part of the book revisits self-advocacy and the social model of disability. Chapter 9 draws the book to a close by revisiting self-advocacy in the light of the empirical findings. A number of analytical connections are pulled together from the empirical sections of the book and a number of questions that remain unanswered are posed, therefore pointing ways forward for future research. Finally, some lessons for advisors, policy makers, service providers and professionals are outlined. Three appendices are provided to give more insight into the doing of the research.

 **2**

Self-advocacy and people with learning difficulties

> Once upon a time I wouldn't speak out at all. I used to be told to shut up. Now that I've been around a self-advocacy group I have learned to say what I want to say.
> (The views of a member, People First Liverpool 1996: 2)

This chapter reviews previous literature on self-advocacy. First, individual and collective self-advocacy are defined. Second, because the literature usually considers collective self-advocacy as occurring formally in self-advocacy groups, and these groups have been identified as forming a 'new social movement', the origins of the movement are traced. Third, the components of groups are presented and some of the controversies inherent in the different ways in which self-advocacy groups are organized are discussed. Finally, it is concluded that self-advocacy constitutes a political activity with potentially massive impacts upon the lives of people with learning difficulties and, therefore, deserves appraisal.

Defining self-advocacy

> Self-advocacy enables us to make choices and make our decisions and control the way that our lives should be made.
> (Gary Bourlet 1988, a self-advocate with learning difficulties and a former president of People First London)

Sutcliffe and Simons (1993) observe that 'self-advocacy' is difficult to define. It means so much to so many and has grown in complexity over the years. It is different from advocacy, where someone else speaks up and represents another (Crawley 1988; Flynn and Ward 1991). Instead, as Williams and Shoultz (1982: 159) put it, self-advocacy is speaking or acting for oneself. It means deciding what's best for you and taking charge of getting it – standing up for your rights as a person. Paula Mitchell (1997) suggests that 'self-advocating' is congruent with 'acting like an adult'. This points immediately to the problematic nature of the term: after all, how many adults without learning difficulties talk about 'self-advocating'? Therefore, following Bhavnani

(1990), the term self-advocacy has been applied to account for the self-determination of minority groups who have historically been denied a 'voice' and has been increasingly recognized over the past three decades (Miller and Keys 1996). Self-advocacy is expressed by other terms, such as 'speaking out', 'talking up', 'shouting up for your rights' and 'self-help' (Crawley 1982; Williams and Shoultz 1982; Cooper and Hersov 1986; Worrel 1988; Amans and Darbyshire 1989; Simons 1992; Sutcliffe and Simons 1993; People First Liverpool 1996; Huddersfield People First n.d.; Miller and Keys 1996; Kennedy 1997; O'Brien and Lyle O'Brien 1997). In all definitions, the self-determination of people with learning difficulties is emphasized and members of this labelled group are referred to as *self-advocates*.

Self-advocacy can 'be done' by a person individually or in a group (Williams 1982: 3; Williams and Shoultz 1982; Mittler 1984; McKenna 1986; Crawley 1990; Brooks 1991; Sutcliffe and Simons 1993; Hampson 1994; Greasley 1995; Shoultz 1997a, b, c). In the former case, Simons (1992: 5) refers to self-advocacy as: 'A process of individual development through which a person comes to have the confidence and ability to express his or her *own* feelings and wishes.' According to Clare (1990), Sutcliffe (1990) and Sutcliffe and Simons (1993), among others, self-advocacy on an *individual level* can refer to expressing thoughts and feelings in an assertive way, being able to make choices and decisions, having a clear knowledge about your rights and being able to make changes to your lifestyle. This may appear in formal contexts, such as individual programme plans (IPPs: see Sutcliffe and Simons 1993; Greasley 1995), career interviews, educational settings (Sievert *et al.* 1988; Clare 1990; Phillips 1990), day centres, homes and hospitals (Crawley 1982, 1988; Brooks 1991). In addition, self-advocacy appears to be associated with informal relationships with others: whether it is with friends (Taylor and Bogdan 1989; Goode 1992) or family (Simons 1992; P. Mitchell 1997) in childhood and adulthood (Daniels 1982).

Much of the literature appears to suggest a mutually inclusive relationship between individual and *collective* self-advocacy. The link between sticking up for yourself on your own *and* with (and for) others is highlighted in the comments of a number of informants in Simons's study (1992, quotes taken from pp. 18–20). Simons found from his informants that self-advocacy meant self-expression ('It's sticking up for yourself'), highlighted the ability to represent self and others ('helping people worse off than yourself') and gave a context for self-development ('it gives you confidence – and then people have confidence in you'). Informants collectively voiced and acted upon complaints ('We talked about the lack of seat-belts in the minibus'), explored issues of integration ('The main issue is community living') and gave a place to appraise service provision ('Talking about things that could be done in Centres . . . how we could all make things better. It's a ceaseless battle to get more houses'). According to Hanna (1978) and Worrel (1987, 1988), among others, this collective aspect of self-advocacy is most clearly observable in *self-advocacy groups*. Previous literature has tended to focus on the doing of self-advocacy in the formal context of groups.

As with the generic term of self-advocacy, groups go under many names, such as 'speaking out', 'trainee committees' and 'working groups' (Crawley 1982, 1988). One of the most common labels in the literature is that of People First (see, for example, Hanna 1978; Worrel 1987, 1988; Crawley 1990; Dybwad and Bersani 1996). People First Liverpool (1996) provide a useful introduction to their group:

> We are a group of People with Learning Difficulties, who are learning to speak out and trying to help other people to speak out for themselves. We have meetings every fortnight, where we talk about whatever people want to talk about. We elect a chair, a secretary, a treasurer and a vice-treasurer. We employ two people to support us. We run training courses about self-advocacy . . . we also do evaluations of services and talks in colleges. We run training courses for staff on how staff should treat us, they should treat us with respect. We go to meetings with bosses and speak out about how the service users feel, and how they should be treated.

Self-advocacy within groups, as will be shown below, can serve many functions and is organized in different ways (Simons 1992; Kennedy 1997). For now it would prove useful to trace the history of these groups, who make up what is known as the self-advocacy movement.

The history of the self-advocacy movement

> Empowerment is a process. Power is not given to people nor is it earned. It happens as a result of a constructive, meaningful activity that leads people to be more knowledgeable, skilful, informed and aware than they were before.
>
> (Worrel 1988: 7)

The self-advocacy movement is a living testament to the group activity of people with learning difficulties in challenging institutionalized prejudice and oppressive hegemony within society (Williams and Shoultz 1982; Bramley and Elkins 1988). It is impossible to ascertain when self-advocacy started. As Campbell and Oliver (1996) point out, in their historical account of the British disability movement over the past 30 years, disabled people were self-organizing long before the 1960s. The same can be said about people with learning difficulties. Instead, the few accounts of the history of self-advocacy appear to start from the time when 'self-advocacy' was formally recognized and defined by people without learning difficulties some 30 years ago. As Potts and Fido (1991) put it, people with learning difficulties have consistently had their histories written for them by others: 'from careworker and psychologist to historian and social scientist'.

So to the beginnings of the movement. According to Crawley (1982), Williams and Shoultz (1982), Browning *et al.* (1984), Bersani (1996), Dybwad (1996), Hersov (1996), Perske (1996) and Shoultz (1997b, c), the origins of the movement can be traced back to documentation in the late 1960s. In Sweden, a small group of people with learning difficulties developed a list of requests about how their services should be provided (Shoultz 1997b). They gave this list to the parent organization that supported them. Whether or not the requests were acted on remains unknown (*ibid.*), but something unprecedented and previously undocumented had occurred. Perske (1996: 20–1) describes another similar episode:

> STOCKHOLM, SWEDEN, November 8, 1969. Ten persons with mental retardation [*sic*] and six university students – all good friends – came together for a special adventure . . . [They meet in a club and go to the theatre.] The sixteen went to a coffee shop and discussed all that they had experienced. Everyone decided that they wanted to see the play at a later date. So, they began making a checklist of preparations. As they left, the group decided not to return to the club. They agreed to break up at this new and strange location and each find his or her own way home.

Perske (1996) suggests that Bengt Nirje, a principle writer of normalization principles (along with Wolfensberger 1972b in the USA), used the scenario presented above in formulating ideas about 'risk-taking' for people with learning difficulties. Early normalization principles and the beginnings of self-advocacy appear to have been initially complementary (see O'Brien 1987; Lawson 1991, Brown and Smith 1992a, b). Being more of an ideology than a service technique (Brown and Smith 1992b: xv), normalization appeared to mark a radical departure in terms of professional and policy values with respect to people with learning difficulties. Nirje, alongside proponents such as Wolf Wolfensberger (in North America; see Wolfensberger 1972a, b, 1987) and John O'Brien (in Britain; see O'Brien 1987), argued for a model of 'empowerment' that made a 'normal life' for people with learning difficulties throughout their experiences of housing, education, working and leisure conditions (Emerson 1992).

The early 1970s saw a number of attempts to make available patterns of life and conditions of everyday living that were as close as possible to the regular circumstances of life in society. Moreover, normalization was championed as a method for assessing service systems that were in tune with the needs of disabled people (via the PASSING programmes). Later, O'Brien's 'five major service accomplishments' aimed to provide a starting point for putting normalization into practice (O'Brien 1987). O'Brien's philosophy was that if services were to 'empower' they must have ensured that their users were *present* in the community, support the *making of choices*, ensured that users' *competence* in community environments were enhanced and encouraged mutual *respect* and *participation* within the community. As Wolfensberger asserted: 'We should assist a person to become capable of meaningful choosing for himself among those normative options that are considered moral and those that are not. If a person is capable of *meaningful choice*, he must also risk the consequences' (1972b: 238; cited in Goode and Gaddy 1976: 10).

Nevertheless, as these 'professional-practice' models of normalization were doing the rounds so too were 'client-focused' approaches to empowerment (Dalley 1989: 201). Associated more with civil rights and new social movements than with service consumerism (Beresford 1992), self-advocacy's beginnings can be traced back to the First and Second Swedish National Conferences of Retarded Adults in 1968 and 1970. According to Crawley (1982: 70), the staging of these conferences reflected a social climate, inside and outside of services, wherein the views of people with learning difficulties were starting to be formally recognized. Around the same time, two conferences in the USA contributed substantially to public visibility of adults with learning difficulties (Dybwad 1996). The first, the 35th Spring Conference at a school in Massachusetts, entitled 'Outlook for the Adult Retarded', debated the social impact of the increasing life spans of people with learning difficulties. The other, the 'Golden Anniversary White House Convention on Children and Youth', saw one of the first questions to be publicly raised over the legal status of adults and children with learning difficulties. These were among the earliest documented conferences in which the experiences of people with learning difficulties were of primary interest. In 1969, at the 'Third National Youth Conference on Mental Retardation in Miami', a panel of young adults with learning difficulties discussed their personal reactions to work programmes. This kind of overt participation represented a radical new departure from advocacy to something which appears to have seriously embraced the experiences as accounted for *by* people with learning difficulties (Dybwad 1996; Shoultz 1997b).

These events in Sweden and the USA (and Canada, see Shoultz 1997c; and for Australia see Bramley and Elkins 1988) inspired what became known as Participation Events in the UK (Crawley 1982; Hersov 1996; People First Liverpool 1996). The first one, Our Life (in June 1972), organized by the Campaign for Mentally Handicapped People (CMH), brought together a number of residents from long-stay hospitals to talk about where they would like to live in the future. When written up (Shearer 1972) it was the first publication in the UK to be wholly made up of the comments by 'mentally handicapped' people about the services they received (Hersov 1996). The following year another conference took place: *Listen* (see Shearer 1973). This considered relationships, choices and independence, with another workshop on participation occurring soon afterwards (see William's report in 1973). According to Crawley (1982), the next two in 1974 and 1975 had delegates discussing experiences of employment. Hersov (1996) states that these events had an immeasurable impact upon the UK self-advocacy movement. *Listen* (1973), for example, cites delegates articulating views on aspects of life including relationships (with each other, family and staff), and choice and independence. For Shearer (1973), the CMH meetings taught those professionals and researchers who were present about the sharp perceptions held by delegates with learning difficulties, their entirely realistic desire to share experiences and the ways in which disabilities are imposed by society's preoccupation with impairment. In the

Listen conference report, Shearer's concerns and ambitions typify many feelings prominent in the early days:

> 'Listen' and 'Our Life' have shown the potential for development and have indicated the waste if this potential is neglected. It is now up to others to ensure that the future is one of development and not neglect. It is up to everyone concerned with services to mentally handicapped people to pick up and build on the work that all the delegates put into 'Listen' and to do them justice and show that something lasting was achieved at the conference.
>
> (Shearer 1973: 34)

Shearer suggests that delegates also shared these concerns, with scepticism being expressed with regard to staff reactions in hospitals ('The staff won't do anything like that . . . every time you do it [speak out] they don't like it'), and in hostels ('I wouldn't bet on it . . . Very few speak . . . people don't want to listen'). Furthermore, many delegates felt that the one-off nature of the CMH conferences was inadequate: 'we should have a meeting once a month'. Fortunately, CMH's American links culminated in Paul Williams and Bonnie Shoultz co-writing the book *We Can Speak for Ourselves*, reviewing international developments (Williams and Shoultz 1982). This highlighted the variety of groups that were taking off in the UK and the USA, fitting the United Nations Declaration of the Rights of Human Persons (1975, cited in Campbell and Oliver 1996: 19), which asserted that: 'Organisations of disabled persons may be usefully consulted in all matters regarding the rights of disabled persons' (Section 3447.12).

Groups continued to grow in dance companies, sport and recreational clubs, through to adult training centres and hospitals. According to Hersov (1996), in the UK two of these set-ups, the MENCAP London Division's Participation Forum and City Lit, grew in stature in the early eighties (reflecting strong financial support gained through charity funds). In 1984, they sent representatives to the First International Self-advocacy Leadership Conference in Tacoma, USA (see O'Brien 1985 for conference report). By this time the movement had grown markedly in the USA, with the People First organization holding its first convention for North American members as early as 1974 (Dybwad 1996). By 1975 there were 16 People First chapters formed in 12 cities (Crawley 1982). According to O'Brien and Sang (1984), the links between English and American self-advocates continued to be productive. Things were starting to take off.

At the First International People First Conference in 1984, a number of English delegates were inspired to set up People First of London and Thames. This self-advocacy group was independent of a service base, with members attending voluntarily, and by 1997 had a number of paid independent supporters. It has continued to be one of the most influential collectives within the movement (Hersov 1996). Another significant year for UK self-advocates was 1988. The Second International People First Conference was held in Twickenham, entitled 'A Voice of Our Own – Now and in the Future'

(Wertheimer 1989). In 1993, the Third International Conference took place in Toronto, Canada, with many UK People First groups attending. The fourth was held in Alaska in 1998.

While the UK movement has grown in strength internationally, it has also made some links with the larger disability movement in the UK. Hersov (1996) records how the well known self-advocate Gary Boulet represented People First London on the 1992 national council of the British Council of Organisations of Disabled People, as it was then known (now the British Council of Disabled People, BCODP). More recently, Simone Aspis, previously Campaigns Officer at People First London, has maintained links with the BCODP and was the self-advocacy movement's only representative in Campbell and Oliver's (1996) account of the British disability movement. Moreover, self-advocates have become involved in formal studies of services (see Whittaker *et al.* 1991, Downer and Ferns 1993; People First London publications), appeared on TV and in the broadsheets and taken part in civil rights demonstrations:

> In the last decade, there have been important landmarks in the growth of self-advocacy throughout the country . . . There is every reason to believe that the [movement] . . . will continue to gain new members and widespread support, and that it will reach even greater heights in the future.
>
> (Hersov 1996: 139)

For some the People First movement *is* the self-advocacy movement (see, for example, Dybwad and Bersani 1996). However, the foundations of the British movement are not found solely in People First (nor the London groups focused on by commentators like Hersov). The movement's origins can be traced back not only to 'independent' (People First) groups but also to the growth over the past three decades of *trainee committees* in adult training centres, social education centres, hospitals, long-stay institutions and group homes. Bronach Crawley's thesis in 1982, and her 1988 survey of trainee committees, documented the rush of self-advocacy issues into centre curricula (Crawley 1982, 1988). Similarly, Paul Williams's (1982) paper on participation and self-advocacy reflected some small-scale translation of self-advocacy issues into service decision making (participation). He argued:

> Handicapped people have a lifetime of experience of being controlled and dominated by others. They are denied experiences of equality with others and control over their own affairs . . . Participation seeks to provide handicapped people and others with experiences of equality and sharing. Self-advocacy enables handicapped people to take their own decisions and exercise control over their own affairs.
>
> (Williams 1982: 3)

In terms of recognizing diversity, it is clear that the doing of self-advocacy in service bases fits the user participation and community care discourses in government policy that have proliferated since the mid-1980s in Britain (see Menolascino and Eaton 1980; HMSO 1990). In 1991, the Health Minister Virginia Bottomley observed that: 'The challenge is to ensure that we provide a seamless service based entirely around the needs and wishes of the users of care and their carers' (HMSO 1991).

As learning difficulties services experience a transition from public sector organizations to private sector management, and a shift from residential to community bases, self-advocacy appeals to those promoting service innovation in a market economy (Braddock 1994). For Crawley (1982: 78), where People First has succeeded through its independent organization, formality and the impetus of members, the medium of service-based collectives has merged self-advocacy with user empowerment initiatives promoted by community care policies. She cites, for example, the work of the AVRO Centre in Southend, Essex. In 1981, they campaigned to change the term 'trainee' to 'student' and rallied against the 25 pence per day centre charges, gaining publicity in the *Guardian* later that year (30 November 1981). Here, then, is another side to the movement: 'The rapid growth of the number of committees in the last few years, and the spontaneous nature of this development, is indicative of an awakening to the need to consult with the 'consumer' of the services that Adult Training Centres provide' (Crawley 1982: 94).

Furthermore, the diversity within the self-advocacy movement has intensified through the input of *citizen advocacy* schemes (Wolfensberger 1972a; Flynn and Ward 1991; Hampson 1994). Advocacy constitutes a particular type of helping relationship and has been celebrated as an independent alternative to the support of service-affiliated professionals (Biklen 1976). For example, Smiley and Craik (1972) described a programme initiated by social workers that located and screened citizen advocates to act as big brother, friend, social worker and legal counsellor to people with learning difficulties. Taken further, Schapiro (1976) reports on a programme where 20 senior citizens were paid to support deinstitutionalized adults, with an increase in the adults' capabilities for independent living being reported. While many individual advocacy relationships appear to have developed in line with the demands of the 1981 United Nations Declaration of Rights of the Mentally Handicapped, the impact of citizen advocacy upon the self-advocacy movement is yet to be understood (Flynn and Ward 1991). In 1979, Herr recognized that advocacy was necessary in championing the legal rights of people with learning difficulties. However, there are concerns that if citizen advocacy remains accountable to service systems then its impact upon self-advocacy, both individual and collectively, will be stifling rather than empowering (Flynn and Ward 1991; Tyne 1994). For Daniels (1982: 25), the move from parent and professional advocacy to self-advocacy mirrors the developmental task of growing up and marks the recognition that people with learning difficulties are adults with their own agendas. Gilbert and Specht (1976) found that professionals saw citizen advocacy as undermining their professional ethics and the interests of their clients, while both Ross (1972) and Wise (1973) recognize that the relationship between professionalism, advocacy and self-advocacy is one marred by struggles. Finally, Paula Mitchell (1998) notes that the influence of parents and carer groups upon the development of self-advocacy is still ill-considered if not ignored. The self-advocacy movement is complicated, a container for a variety of struggles and a context not so easily understood as relating directly to the self-empowerment of its main players – self-advocates with learning difficulties.

The movement's diverse nature suggests that self-advocacy has developed, branched off and grown in a multitude of ways. As a consequence of these developments, Bersani (1996: 265–6) argues, with reference to Tom Shake-speare's (1993) commentary, that the self-advocacy movement now consti-tutes a *new social movement* in its own right, characterized by a number of key points, though questions still abound:

- *Members go beyond typical roles*: here people with learning difficulties, 'self-advocates', transcend typical positions of client, trainee, patient and user. Some have striven to change their own and others' lives, some represent their peers in centres, others are paid advocates as part of (citizen) advocacy initiatives. However, exactly how do others without learning difficulties support or stifle the transition to the role of self-advocate?
- *Representation of a strong ideological change*: a change from the term 'mental handicap' to 'learning difficulties' and claims that there has been a growth in the number of independent self-advocacy groups free from parental and professional organizations can be seen as indicators of change. There have also been more general demands for ideological change: 'We believe that people with disabilities should be treated as equals. That means that people should be given the same decisions, choices, rights, responsibilities and chances to speak up to empower themselves as well as to make new friend-ships and renew old friendships just like everyone else' (Self-advocates Becoming Empowered organization, USA, paraphrased by Kennedy 1997: 1). Meanwhile, self-advocacy in service settings calls into question client–staff relationships and the professional ethos (Crawley 1982). Yet, how are societal structures, professional practices and political understand-ings implicated in this move away from 'retardate' to 'self-advocate'?
- *Emergence of a new identity, often drawing upon a characteristic formerly seen as weakness*: slogans such as 'disabled and proud', 'label jars not people' (used by People First), 'rights not charity' and 'piss on pity' (appropriated from the larger disability movement) may be seen as reflecting a new found posi-tive identity. Questions remain as to whether or not these new identities are resistant to dominant discourses which, for example, position people in terms of their purported 'handicaps'.
- *Relationship between the individual and movement is blurred*: this is apparent in the definitions of self-advocacy offered by self-advocates presented above. Individual and collective self-advocacy appear to be inseparable. Even so, is the movement, the formal group context and the support of others that important to individual self-advocates' life experiences?

While self-advocacy may appear to constitute a new collective movement, recognized by others with(out) learning difficulties, delving further into the literature unearths problematics. Typical of previous examinations, Bersani's (1996) above account focuses predominantly on People First groups. As noted above, the movement is actually made up of many factions (Browning *et al.* 1984; Bramley and Elkins 1988; Crawley 1988), yet some observers have argued that any deviation from the People First group poses a threat to the very doing of self-advocacy. These observations are considered in the following section.

Understanding the self-advocacy group

Now we can dig deeper into this 'new social movement'. Much of the literature that has explored self-advocacy has done so with reference to the self-advocacy group (Hanna 1978; Siegel and Kantor 1982; Williams 1982; Williams and Shoultz 1982; McKenna 1986; Worrel 1987, 1988; Crawley 1990; Brooks 1991; Simons 1992; Dowson and Whittaker 1993; Sutcliffe and Simons 1993; Hampson 1994; Shoultz 1997a, b, c). Observers have focused on contexts where self-advocacy can be seen as formally taking place:

> When many people think of self-advocacy, they think in terms of self-advocacy groups and the activities of their members. Although this perspective does not exclude the idea of individual self-advocacy, it focuses primarily on people who have consciously decided to 'speak out' or who associate themselves with groups that have taken up that standard. Hence it is possible to talk in terms of a broad movement that falls squarely in the self-help group tradition, and has strong parallels with other alliances (for example the British Coalition of Disabled People and Survivors Speak Out).[1]
>
> (Sutcliffe and Simons 1993: 36).

The next section reviews literature to examine the composition of groups and the reasoning that is employed to justify a number of structural and organizational forms. In addition, controversies associated with group components and typology will be presented.

Speak for Ourselves of Newcastle has produced a video called 'Start! How to set up and run a successful self-advocacy group' (1993). Speak for Ourselves functions independently of service, advocacy and parental agencies. Members come along voluntarily, supporters have no service ties and activities are financed by money from voluntary organizations (and the sale of the video). Group members with learning difficulties (self-advocates) and people without learning difficulties that support the group (supporters or advisors) front the video. Typically, Speak for Ourselves gets together for a weekly meeting. At the meeting, a chairperson (a self-advocate) is responsible for keeping the group in order and bringing in people who have something to say. Often topics for discussion are decided at the start of the meeting, which are returned to later, although members are encouraged to speak up freely. Experiences, good and bad are divulged, opinions are shared and in some cases action is taken by the group for and with members. Speak for Ourselves argues in the video that self-advocates themselves can and should be involved as far as possible in the setting up of their *own* groups. A number of steps to follow are offered:

* *Get people interested*: tell centre users, hostel flat-mates and work colleagues what they will get out of being in the group, by word of mouth, leaflets or posters.
* *Find a meeting place*: someone's house or a community centre makes an ideal setting, while an ATC could be used if nowhere else is available.
* *Organize transport*: so members can get to meetings. This is helped when a self-advocate takes on the role of 'transport officer'.
* *Find an advisor*: this is a person (usually without learning difficulties) who helps the group, 'Someone who gives support especially in the early days', but who, 'Shouldn't run your group but help you to run it'. Speak for Ourselves suggests getting in touch with the Council for Voluntary Services. It is 'Better to find someone who doesn't work at the Day Centre.' Later, 'You will have to decide if your advisor is to be paid or volunteer.'
* *Elect a committee*: officers mentioned include chairperson, secretary, treasurer and transport officer. Officers may be chosen on a nomination and election basis or members may take turns in the various positions.
* *Raise money*: through sources such as charitable trusts, health authorities and local councils, or payment may be accrued if self-advocates help to train people who work with people with learning difficulties.
* *Make the group aware of what it can do*: members of Speak for Ourselves give their own experiences, 'Talking about improving services, write letters to the council, plan conferences, invite guests, right to get engaged, have a boyfriend and get married, have parties and discos.'

Consequently, a number of specific points come out of the video. First, self-advocates themselves are the significant parties. Right from the start, and in activities from then on, the group is centred on the interests of the members. Second, interested people are required. A voluntary basis to group membership is prescribed, with self-advocates themselves determining their own group membership. Finally, the need for clarity by the advisor of his or her role is argued for, mirroring Paul Williams argument: 'Most groups have an advisor. This person is there to help when, and only when, required; the advisor is not in control of the group' (Williams 1982: 3). However, while the members of Speak for Ourselves of Newcastle have a clear outline of how their group is run, other groups in the movement run along very different lines. While the basic components of advisors and self-advocates remain, ways of organizing self-advocacy take a number of forms (Bramley and Elkins 1988).

People First of Washington State described four models or 'types' of self-advocacy group that exist in the movement. This typology has been employed in a number of studies (see, for example, Crawley 1982, 1988, 1990; McKenna 1986; Simons 1992; Dowson and Whittaker 1993). The pros and cons of each type are presented in Table 2.1.

In the literature the 'ideal' autonomous group type is generally regarded as potentially the most empowering (see, for example, Hanna 1978; Daniels 1982; Worrel 1987, 1988; Crawley 1990; Dowson and Whittaker 1993; Speak for Ourselves of Newcastle 1993; Tyne 1994; People First Liverpool 1996; Huddersfield People First n.d.). By contrast, the service-system model has received the most damning criticism. For Bill Worrel (1987: 30) self-advocacy is a growing force and an essential part of this process is learning to be an independent organization. When service systems get involved with self-advocacy the ability of a group to promote self-determination is threatened (Worrel 1988). As a high profile self-advocate in Canada, Pat Worth, puts it: 'Being involved on a one-to-one basis with people with handicaps, as People First is, helps to deal with the issues directly. Associations delivering services may find this difficult to achieve' (quoted in Yarmol 1987: 28). Tyne (1994: 250) argues that service-based sponsorship of (self-)advocacy limits and sometimes subverts it altogether. For Downer and Ferns (1993: 145–6) a contradiction emerges. They argue that while positive steps must be taken to make sure that self-advocacy happens in residential and daycare establishments, there is also a need to help people to set up groups without taking them over and making them part of services. For Hanna (1978), Crawley (1982, 1990) and Worrel (1987, 1988) to understand the paradox of service-based self-advocacy, and the potential of autonomous groups such as People First, we need only to look at the roles of those who support self-advocates.

In examining group structure, previous literature has tended to deal with the role of the advisor (Hanna 1978; Worrel 1987, 1988; Clare 1990; Sutcliffe 1990; Simons 1992; Sutcliffe and Simons 1993; Dowson and Whittaker 1993). Going back to what Speak for Ourselves of Newcastle (1993) has to say, the advisor should be 'Someone who gives support especially in the early days', but who *'shouldn't'* run your group but help *you* to run it.' Speak for Ourselves goes further to suggest that it is better to find someone who doesn't work at the day centre, and later the group 'will have to decide if your advisor is to paid or volunteer.' As Barnes and Wistow (1992c: 94) acknowledge, for many people who have had little experience of being able to exercise control over their own lives, learning to participate in comparatively safe environments may be an important first step. This is where the advisor comes in: 'Once you have shown that you respect the members as equal human beings, that you're not like the rest of society, you have built the basis for a strong working relationship with the group' (Worrel 1988: 55). Dowson and Whittaker (1993: 44–7) forewarn advisors to be clear about their roles, to be honest about doubts they may have inside the group, to express opinions, but clarify that they are opinions not facts: 'Be a supporter not a spokesperson – don't take on others' responsibilities.' The first step in understanding the advisor role is to understand the members. This awareness leads to another key point: that the advisor may need to withdraw when the group wants it, when he or she is not needed or when someone else would do better in the job. The advisor should aim to work himself or herself out of a job (Dowson and Whittaker 1993: 44).

Ideally a reciprocal relationship forms. As the group increases in autonomy

Table 2.1 The pros and cons of the four models of self-advocacy group

Model	Advantages	Disadvantages
1 The 'autonomous' or 'ideal' model		
For example, People First, Speak for Ourselves of Newcastle	These groups are independent in terms of time, organization and finance from professional services or parent bodies	Groups must support themselves from the beginning
	Advisors are independent of services	Financial struggles and lack of resources are a problem
	Group members are free from 'conflicts of interest' with professionals or parents, so can feel free to voice opinions without fear of embarrassment or recrimination	
2 The 'divisional' model		
Arises out of existing parent or professional organizations for people with learning difficulties, e.g. MENCAP executive committees, advocacy organizations	There is easy access to a range of resources (meeting places, money, administrative support)	Potential 'conflict of interests' can occur between the demands of self-advocates and those of parents and professionals
	Advisors can be well-trained in advocacy skills	Risks of self-advocates being overpowered and relegated to a back seat are ever-present as the concerns of the organization take precedence

3 The 'coalition' model Arises out of a larger group for disabled people (or other minority group), e.g. independent living organization, council of disabled people, community initiative	Self-advocacy along with other disabled people increases the strength of the group and makes links with the larger disability movement. A strong and positive disabled identity is encouraged Advisors can be well-trained and disabled Adds legitimacy, increases political power and improves ability to generate funding.	Risk of being overpowered and relegated to a back seat as more articulate and politically strong disabled members take over
4 The 'service-system' model Self-advocacy group located in a service delivery system, e.g. trainee committee in ATC, SEC, patients' forum in hospital, residents' panel at group home	No need to recruit members as a meeting place is instantly provided Transport problems are minimal, as is access to a range of resources and provisions	Constant threat of 'conflicts of interest' between self-advocates and service if group challenges service system May be nothing more than an extension of existing training activities and becomes a token gesture rather than 'real' self-advocacy

then the advisor's input decreases proportionally. Many self-advocates have urged advisors to keep this relationship in mind. As Capitol People First of Sacramento, California demands: 'we need teachers not keepers' (quoted in Booth and Booth 1992: 67). Advisors are important but not always needed (Worrel 1988: 73): 'Maybe in the future there will be no need for advisors. Our goal should be that as a group develops the skills and the links with the community, to be able to use the many advisors in the community that we all use in our lives' (*ibid.*). For Worrel (1988: 35) all advisors should be asking themselves how they *use* their power in ways that empower or disempower members. Similarly, Hanna (1978: 32) asserts that:

> There is an underlying philosophy that anyone who wants to become an advisor to a People First organisation must embrace. The philosophy is consistent with the goals and purposes of the organisation, 'that people are people, no matter what their abilities or limitations might be' . . . they may have limitations but everyone has limitations of one sort or another.

Previous literature has identified a number of controversies associated with the *status of advisors*. For example, when advisors are staff or professionals, particularly in service systems, problems arise. For Clare (1990) there is an undeniable paradox in professionally led self-advocacy. Staff members of service systems are necessarily located in positions of power (Oliver 1990, 1993, 1996). Their descriptions, assessments and evaluations, as well as their knowledge of available opportunities, are called upon to determine the course of a disabled person's life: 'Their professional identity, and certainly their professional accreditation, will be based on their control of knowledge about disability' (Clare 1990: 24). Consequently, staff-advisors are placed in a seemingly impossible role (Hanna 1978: 31). While their existence is testimony to the fact that many professionals were instrumental in supporting early self-advocacy groups (Crawley 1982; Worrel 1987: 31), their impossible position may be largely put down to a conflict of interests. Conflicting motivations between facilitating self-advocates' independence and maintaining service goals is a common and underlying dilemma of professional advisors in service-based groups. For Worrel (1987: 35; also see 1988: 38) groups that avoid controversy often have advisors who are affiliated with service organizations. In these groups, supporting members is hindered by rules of operation such as: 'Don't bring your problems to the meetings.' This may be translated into: 'Don't rock the boat by raising real problems in your life that the members of the group might identify with. We may have a revolt on our hands!' (Worrel 1987: 35). Sutcliffe (1990: 27) elaborates on this point. If groups are to provide an independent voice, then being advised by staff members whose loyalties are split may seriously undermine the development of self-advocacy. Members may be intimidated by the advisor's accountability to the services they use, and may feel uneasy complaining about the services that they are offered:

A conflict of interest occurs when the advisor is paid by the agency that serves the members. If a group wants to criticise the way the workshop is run, the advisor may have trouble supporting the group while being a staff person at the workshop.

(Worrel 1988: 38)

For Williams (1982: 4) self-advocacy is not simply fun, sport or entertainment, it has a serious purpose. However, groups that meet as part of the week's programme in a SEC or ATC may soon resemble another activity implemented by staff and the potentially radical impact of groups upon members' lives is lost. Moreover, for advisors to work themselves out of a job seems impractical when that support is part of the working week. It would seem that the general principle of 'letting go' directly opposes the very philosophy of professional intervention (Barker and Peck 1987: 28; cited in Flynn and Ward 1991: 132). The answer to these problems, then, is the 'ideal autonomous' group, where advisors are free from service accountability and the group can progress without a conflict of interests (Hanna 1978; Williams 1982; Williams and Shoultz 1982; McKenna 1986; Worrel 1987, 1988; Crawley 1990; Flynn and Ward 1991; Simons 1992; Downer and Ferns 1993; Dowson and Whittaker 1993; Sutcliffe and Simons 1993; Hampson 1994; Shoultz 1997a, b, c; P. Mitchell 1998).

Scrutiny of the typology and advisor roles presented in the literature above ensures that types of self-advocacy other than the autonomous group type, supported by the independent advisor (People First), are given short thrift if not rejected altogether. Yet to adopt this rejection of certain group types would appear to make an appraisal of self-advocacy highly selective and ignore the prevalence, and influence, of other group types. The typology literature suggests that self-advocacy is not synonymous with People First. As Crawley (1982, 1988) observed, the spread of self-advocacy groups throughout adult training and social education centres as well as group homes and hostels has contributed much to the growth of the movement. Recently, as Flynn and Ward (1991) and Tyne (1994) recognize, the input of citizen advocacy constitutes another development. Moreover, there may be contradictions inherent within People First groups. For example, a group that is financially independent of services, but has staff advisors who come into the group in their own time, problematizes the simplistic understandings of 'good' and 'bad' self-advocacy presented in previous literature. In 1992, Simons estimated that there were approximately 500 self-advocacy groups in the UK (Simons 1992). A recent postal survey of 134 of these groups illuminates further the diverse nature of the self-advocacy movement and the complicated characteristics of groups (Goodley 1998c: 85–112). Moreover, it would appear that the typology literature has dated as the movement has matured.

This postal survey invited a reassessment of the typology of groups developed by People First of Washington (1984). Three rather than four distinct 'types' emerged: autonomous, service-based and divisional/coalition (the last type being a composition of two distinct types because of the impossibility of separation and the lack of coalition groups). It was found that the responses obtained resisted being slotted into categories. Only 60 of the 134 groups (48 per cent) were accounted for by the typology literature, with 74 defying classification. The organizational, financial and structural components of groups made 'pigeon-holing' difficult, perhaps impossible (Goodley 1998c: 103–10). The following example in relation to the 'ideal' autonomous self-advocacy group illustrates these difficulties (see pp. 103–5).

People First of Washington State (cited in Crawley 1990) defines the *autonomous group* as retaining 'complete financial and organisational autonomy from any parent or professional advocacy organisation as well as from the service delivery systems'. Crawley (1990: 98–9) continues:

> This type of group avoids any conflict of interests. Its members and their advisors can feel comfortable in taking any position without fear of recrimination. It is also seen as being independent and self-reliant from the outset.

To identify these 'ideal' groups in the 134 postal survey responses required setting criteria. Following Hanna (1978), Worrel (1987, 1988) and Shoultz (1997a), it was decided that a group could potentially fit the autonomous model when it fitted three criteria (Goodley 1998c: 103–5):

- *Criterion 1: supporters are independent* – either voluntary independent(s) (independent person offering support voluntarily, e.g. a student is accepted by a local group as advisor) or paid (by group) independent(s) (the group pays an independent person to be the advisor, e.g. the group receives money from a charity and employ a support worker to help them in their activities). Only 23 of the 134 (17 per cent) groups had *only* these supporters.
- *Criterion 2: independent settings for meetings where groups are not attached to services* (see Simons 1992: 6) – including the group's own office or a room away from the centre (and other services). Fifteen of the 23 said they met in these places, two met in homes, one in a charity office, another in an independent organization and, perhaps most surprisingly, four in day centres. Most groups (15/23) got together monthly, four fortnightly.
- *Criterion 3: financial and organizational autonomy* (Crawley 1990, Sutcliffe and Simons 1993) was examined with reference to funding sources cited by the groups. The 15 groups that fitted criteria 1 and 2 explicitly reported the following funding details: ten (66 per cent) local authority support; four (27 per cent) health authority money; six (40 per cent) charity money; seven (47 per cent) self-funded. Asked about other funding, two said they were financially supported by policy initiatives, two gave the response 'many', while one group cited fund-raising, handouts from local businesses and money from charities. These numerous funding sources suggest that the 'ideal' state of non-accountability to professional, parent and service delivery systems (Shoultz 1997b) is beyond many groups. Nevertheless, those groups that received no indirect service sponsorship for their advisors

(because they were volunteers or groups paid for their support themselves out of existing funds and they had no job affiliation with services), were deemed to fit the third financially autonomous criterion, thus emphasizing their independence from service providers (Simons 1992: 9).

Placing all three criteria together, the following was concluded from the respondents who gave sufficient information:

> Only 11 per cent (15) of the 134 groups are strictly *autonomous* in that – supporters are only voluntary or paid by the group and therefore 'independent'; meetings take place in own offices or in rooms away from services; support is not directly funded by local or health authorities or bodies which have parent, professional or advocacy affiliation, therefore boasting financial autonomy.
>
> (Goodley 1998c: 105)

From this analysis it would appear that People First of Washington's 'ideal' self-advocacy has become lost in Britain. Indeed, a number of characteristics emerged in the data set that were not encompassed in the 'ideal' group type detected by the criteria used above, though the groups saw themselves as independent:

- Voluntary staff supporting groups in meetings away from services (five groups), e.g. a care assistant from a local hostel for people with learning difficulties supports a group on Wednesday evenings at the Dog and Partridge Pub.
- Those who have voluntary independents or paid-by-group independents and others as well (nine groups in addition to the 23 cited above), e.g. a group is supported by an advocacy worker but also has its own support worker that it pays out of its funds.
- Meetings of People First groups taking place in centres (14 groups), e.g. a People First group hires the canteen of the local day centre.

The rigidity of criteria in identifying the 'ideal group' may ignore many other set-ups that hold autonomy at the centre of their aims but have seemingly non-autonomous structural elements. Furthermore, just because a group fits all the autonomous criteria, this may not causally relate to the promotion of 'ideal' self-advocacy. To classify using the typology literature appears to lose the richness of the group's structure. A typology provides a useful starting point, but the strengths in a typology's simplicity are also its weaknesses.

When a group is identified as 'service-system' based (as 21 per cent of the groups were; Goodley 1998c: 106–7) there are problems in applying the assumptions that are tied to that category. Downgrading a group because of its purported stifling structure supposes that services have no worth at all (McKenna 1986) and pitches understandings at a surface level. Consequently, the political ambitions, aims and actions of supporters and, more importantly, self-advocates go unrecognized, hidden behind a negative label. These survey findings capture a snapshot of the movement at large. They reflect some of the diversity, developments and variety in what some have described as the last civil rights movement (T. Shakespeare 1993; Bersani 1996; Campbell and Oliver 1996). Some of the concerns of self-advocates were highlighted, from plans to get married, living independently, wanting a job through to political protests. Moreover, the dilemmas of support were illustrated in the many roles and statuses held by advisors. The personal impact of being in a self-advocacy group and the actual workings of self-advocacy groups were not illuminated by its findings. The movement's insiders who responded to the survey were lost in the search for an overview.

When groups are penned into a structural typology members' actions are hidden by the specifications of that model. In the literature these types are not described as neutral concepts. If a group is service-based it is limited, if it is autonomous it has great potential (see, for example, Crawley 1990). If advisors are staff members they are in an impossible position (Hanna 1978), if they are independent of professional status they can properly facilitate self-advocacy (Worrel 1987, 1988). Although structural constraints upon empowerment are undoubtedly important (Tomlinson 1995), it should be remembered that the actions of people with learning difficulties in the disabling environments of the 1970s gave rise to the birth of the self-advocacy movement in the first place. Previous literature, including the postal survey cited above, run the risk of ignoring everyday self-empowering acts of people with learning difficulties. In conclusion, it would appear that the movement's heterogeneity counters the imposition of classifications and categories presented in the literature (e.g. Hanna 1978; Worrel 1987, 1988; Crawley 1990; Sutcliffe 1990; Flynn and Ward 1991; Simons 1992; Downer and Fearns 1993; Dowson and Whittaker 1993). While this postal survey provides a useful account of the movement's complexity, questions remain about the life experiences and actions that go on under the banner of self-advocacy.

Questions about self-advocacy: where does this leave us?

Two broad questions remain unanswered in the overview provided in this chapter.

How do self-advocacy groups impact upon the lives of people with learning difficulties?

Carabello and Siegel (1996: 238) ask: who are the leaders in the movement, whom do they represent and are they people with disabilities? A turn to the perspectives of self-advocates would uncover what members gain from groups. As Worrel (1988: 78) asserts: 'We have to try to look at life through the eyes of the person who has been labelled, understand what it means to be labelled, and why self-advocacy is important.' When Safilios-Rothschild (1981: 11) argued that the reluctance of professionals to relinquish extensive power and control over their clients is something that cannot easily be broken, she was unable to foresee the challenges that were to be posed by disabled people and their organizations (Brisenden 1989: 218). Indeed, the significance of the role of non-disabled people in self-advocacy groups has been questioned: 'The most well-meaning, helpful, sensitive and committed advisor will never be able to do the job of empowerment as effectively as a well-prepared, well-trained self-advocate' (Worrel 1988: 13).

For Fairclough (1989, 1992), Ferguson *et al.* (1992a, b, c), Goode (1992), Ferguson and Ferguson (1995) and Skrtic (1995a, b, c), the resistance of disabled people has ensured that they themselves have, historically, been self-organizing. Self-advocacy is nothing new, though recognition is (Crawley 1988: 47). Part II of this book uncovers some of the links between self-advocacy group membership and life experiences.

How do self-advocacy groups work?

There appears to be a tendency in the literature to sweep under the carpet certain group types or advisor roles because they epitomize 'bad self-advocacy'. It remains to be seen whether or not groups other than People First are any good, or, for that matter, that bad (Crawley 1988, Sutcliffe and Simons 1993). After all, as Worrel (1988: 40) recognizes, most advisors today are faced with conflict of interests and the first essential step for advisors is to be sensitive to this issue of power. If some groups do provide 'real' opportunities for self-advocacy (Crawley 1988), as the literature suggests, then in what ways do they provide these 'real' opportunities (and indeed what is 'real')? Do types of group and status of advisors so causally relate to the promotion or relegation of self-advocacy, as suggested by previous literature? Or are other group processes influential? Part III examines further the organization of groups and dynamics of self-advocacy.

The need for a contemporary appraisal

The self-advocacy movement boasts complexity. As we enter the decade of the citizen (Dahrendorf 1990), how are people with learning difficulties faring? A contemporary appraisal of self-advocacy seems timely. This book appraises self-advocacy in the lives of people with learning difficulties by focusing on the questions posed above, with a particular theoretical perspective in mind. This perspective is considered in the next chapter.

Note

1 For a useful introduction to the struggles of mental health users, see Chamberlin (1990).

 **3**

Self-advocacy, impairment and the social model of disability

It means no one will hire me on a job unless they hear from a rehab counsellor or social worker. Get what I mean when I say it's hard for handicapped people to find a job?
(Larry on what learning difficulties means in Langness and Turner 1986: 71)

The reintegration of individuals is currently largely determined by others who have power . . . there is only one guaranteed way to regain our power and therefore control of our own lives . . . That way is through self-advocacy and self-help.
(Lawson 1991: 69)

This chapter introduces an 'inclusive' social model of disability, the theoretical perspective that guides this book. First, the contrasting perspectives of individual and social models of disability will be presented. It is suggested that the former model reflects dominant understandings of disability that are held in society. Any appraisal of self-advocacy theoretically underpinned by this model would undermine the self-advocacy of people with learning difficulties (Goodley 1997). In contrast, the social model of disability holds the self-empowerment of disabled people at its core and is a theoretical ally to the actions of disabled activists. In addition, it is argued that the model benefits from the inclusion of literature that views learning difficulties as a social construction. Finally, it is concluded that an appraisal of self-advocacy grounded in the experiences, stories and actions of people with learning difficulties will draw upon, and in some small way build upon, an inclusive social model of disability. An awareness of the socio-historical, cultural and political bases of disability is a prerequisite for an appraisal of self-advocacy.

'The tragic person with disabilities': an individual model of disability

The word 'retarded' is a word. What it does is put people in a class . . . There's always going to be people who are going to hold it to

the ground. We're on one side of the wall and the stone throwers
are on the other side.

(Ed Murphy, cited in Bogdan and Taylor 1982: 77)

From the mid-seventeenth century onwards, one of the major projects of
modernity was being realized. The victory of scientific rationality over expressions of the divine purpose (Kumar 1978) further enforced humanity's search
for technological supremacy and control over nature (Branson and Miller
1989). Intellectual and societal progress went hand in hand and the immature
academic paradigms of the social sciences blossomed. Around the start of the
twentieth century, dominant understandings of society's 'defectives' were
influenced by the work of Charles Darwin. His 1859 book, *On the Origins of
Species*, was seen by many as an indicator of how far scientific understanding
had progressed (Barnes 1991). By providing a direct relationship between
human beings and other animals, with terminology denoting survival of the
fittest and natural selection, Darwin's theories of evolution fitted the scientific
project of modernity (Turner 1990). Consequently, earlier concepts of idiocy,
previously located within the realms of religion, were now positioned within
a scientific Darwinian framework. Crudely, as Hunt (1993) puts it, idiocy was
transformed. Mental deficiency was attributed to genetic mutation – the
unfortunate result of inappropriate breeding on the part of defective parents
(Sarason and Doris 1969). The views of an eminent theorist around this
period highlight the impact of Darwinism on intellectual thought:

> The feeble-minded are a parasitic, predatory class, never capable of self-
> support or of managing their own affairs . . . they cause unutterable
> sorrow at home and are a menace and danger to the community. Feeble-
> minded women are almost invariably immoral, and if at large usually
> become carriers of venereal disease or give birth to children who are
> defective as themselves . . . every feeble-minded person, especially the
> high-grade imbecile, is a potential criminal . . . the unrecognised imbecile
> is a most dangerous element in the community.
>
> (Fernald 1912, lecture given to the Massachusetts Medical Society;
> quoted in Sarason and Doris 1969)

Societal hopes for the prevention of such individual defects soon became
immersed within celebrated notions of *social Darwinism*[1] (Barnes 1991). A
rational and powerful ideology was provided where the control of 'mental
defectives' could be efficiently devised (Fido and Potts 1989). According to
Barnes (1991), the perceived scientific authenticity provided by frameworks
of understanding such as Darwinism appealed to a society dominated by a
relatively small elite of property owning individuals, who welcomed any
opportunity to justify their newly acquired wealth, status and power. 'It was
quickly adapted from the biological domain to apply to human societies'
(p. 19). The implications of this grounding of scientific and socio-political concerns were devastating. Social Darwinists were instrumental in forming the
eugenics movement. One proponent of eugenics, a 'founding father' of psychology (Hunt 1993), Francis Galton (Darwin's cousin), argued:

> Eugenics is the science of improving stock, which . . . takes cognisance of all influences that tend in however remote a degree to give to the more suitable races or strains of blood a better chance of prevailing speedily over the less suitable than they otherwise would have had.
>
> (Galton 1869; cited in Hunt 1993)

The eugenics movement advocated selective breeding from one generation to another and expected a subsequent increase in the proportion of people with better than average hereditary endowments (Taylor and Bogdan 1992). The 1903 American Breeders Association championed numerous policies concerning the regulation of particular individuals' rights to conception (Stratford 1991). In turn, institutionalization provided an effective way of separating defective people from society, thus reducing 'breeding opportunities'. Sterilization was addressed as an additional remedy, with the first mandatory sterilization law being passed in the USA in 1907 (Stratford 1991). The logical conclusion of the eugenics movement was realized with the rise of fascism in the 1930s and the extermination of more than 300,000 'mental defectives' (Wolfensberger 1981).

In 1946, an ex-member of the British Eugenics Society, who had worked for six years with the 'feeble-minded', concluded that such labelled people: 'Show such a variety of virtues – generosity, altruism, good will, sweet temper – that I began to think that a world peopled by mental defectives might be an improvement on the present one' (cited in Morris 1969: xix). Townsend (1969) and Lawson (1991) observe that by the 1950s eugenic beliefs had been discredited for a number of reasons. First, it became more and more obvious that genetic variation was far more complex than had originally been thought, with *social factors* being implicated in understandings of subnormality. Second, the anticipation that a residue of 'feeble-minded' within the population would lead to national degeneracy had not been confirmed. Third, the formation of an 'unholy alliance' between various governments' commitment to decreasing public expenditure and an increasing body of literature denouncing institutionalization prompted moves towards intensive deinstitutionalization (Banton *et al.* 1985). However, old ideas such as social Darwinism take a long time to die (Wright and Digby 1996).

Foucault's (1970, 1975) conception of 'genealogy' is useful here. Knowledge, archaic, ridiculous, unbelievable as it may be, can become buried and disguised in what is considered rational, common sense or 'the truth': 'Truths are illusions of which one has forgotten that they are illusions, worn out metaphors' (Hekman 1990:27). As Jenkins (1993: 18) argues, ubiquitous taken-for-granted concepts of normality do two things at once: they describe as normal those human characteristics which are most typical and then assert that they are the way things ought to be. For Brechin and Walmsley (1989: 9) the scandals of the 'institutionalized years' can so easily be repeated if care is not taken to prevent them. Even in the 'humanitarian' epoch of community care, institutionalization exists as the only option available to some people with learning difficulties (Potts and Fido 1991). Ferguson (1987: 51) observed that in the USA alone, over 125,000 people with labels of 'retardation' remained incarcerated in large, segregated public institutions. In the UK, the OPCS surveys showed that 422,000 disabled people, 20 per cent of whom were below retirement age, still lived in 'communal establishments' or institutions (Martin *et al.* 1989). Beliefs, whether they are about biological inferiority or segregation of 'defectives', burrow themselves into contemporary rhetoric and practice:

> Many of the fundamental attitudes and prejudices which led originally to the establishment of colonies remain virtually untouched. Assessment and classification still abound. So too does arbitrary removal from home, whether this home is with the family or friends or is a group home, hostel or hospital . . . Just as the inmates were forced to fit into the colony, so today people have to accommodate to available places. If they do not fit in or object to their placement, the label of 'problem behaviour' is likely to be applied.
>
> (Potts and Fido 1991: 133)

Like it or not, we are heirs to past attitudes, beliefs and current practices (Stratford 1991: 5). Old structures and vocabularies persist (Taylor and Bogdan 1992: 85), and practices which appear to be universal and commonsensical can often be shown to originate in the dominant class or dominant bloc, and to have become naturalized (Fairclough 1989: 33): 'Most definitions we use to interpret the world are learned from others and are sufficiently imbedded in the cultural heritage to make it difficult to extract and objectify them for analysis' (Mercer 1973:1). To find out what these beliefs are, Parker *et al.* (1995), along with Fairclough (1989), assert that the commonsensical must be rendered strange. Over the past 30 years, a proliferation of writings has done exactly this: rendered everyday understandings of disability as strange.

Oliver (1990, following the UPIAS's 1976 *Fundamental Principles* document; see below) was one of the first (disabled) writers to label dominant appendages of knowledge about disability (Berger and Luckman 1987). These, Oliver asserts, reflect an *individual model of disability* or 'personal tragedy perspective'. For Barnes (1991), in these dominant discourses lie social Darwinism, the medicalization of disability and assumptions of pathology associated with impairment. Consequently, for Shakespeare and Watson (1997) well regarded 'professional' and 'expertly' defined models of disability are steeped in the characteristics of the individual model. The World Health Organization's (WHO 1992) definition of disability is a good example: 'Disability is the *effects of* the impairment on everyday activities' (italics added). For learning difficulties, The West Midlands Regional Health Authority's definition shows similarities with WHO's: 'A learning disability is an impairment of intellectual functions, which occurs before adulthood and *results in* significant disabilities in day to day life' (italics added; cited in Ford 1996: 57). Finally, the 1995 Disability Discrimination Act (DDA) reifies the individual model when it defines disability as: 'Either a physical or mental impairment, which has a substantial and long-term adverse affect on a person's ability to carry out normal day-to-day activities' (HMSO 1995: section 1.1).

These definitions say something very simple: that impairment, whether it be physical or 'of mind', results in and creates disability. Hence impairment and disability are synonymous, inseparable concepts. Following this, 'impaired thought' *leads to* a myriad of disabilities: disabled thought, disabled learning, disabled interactions with others, disabled personal relationships, disabled sex lives and disabled parenting.[2] The emerging image of the person with learning difficulties or physical impairment, then, is one not of autonomy but of a loss of wholeness and a personal tragedy that renders the individual the focus of professional intervention (Morris 1991, 1993b). Barnes (1990) argues that this results in disabled people being assigned a position in a *culture of dependence*. Their social ineptitude, reified by the dominant discourse, renders them as burdens to their families and to society at large. They are conceptualized as any other minority group and treated and reacted to as a category rather than as people (Brechin *et al.* 1981). They represent a challenge, a problem at the level of everyday intercourse (Thomas 1982). As the antithesis of the norms, disabled people no longer represent the collective values of the status quo (Morris 1991), delineated by prevailing cultural politics (Corbett 1991).

Prior to Oliver's (1990) identification of the individual model, Abberley (1987: 18) suggested that an individualized concept of disability:

> By presenting disadvantage as the consequence of a naturalised 'impairment' . . . legitimates the failure of welfare facilities and the distribution system in general to provide for social needs, that is, it interprets the effects of social maldistribution as the consequence of individual deficiency.

In the light of the literature discussed in Chapter 2 it is difficult to see how self-advocacy, empowerment and self-determination of disabled people can be formed upon understandings of disability that assume individual inability (Finkelstein and Stuart 1996). Indeed, Morris (1991) observes that when disabled people step out of the passive role assigned by society, and take up roles as *activists* (or self-advocates), disabling culture is unable to deal with unfamiliar shows of dissent. Unfamiliarity in this case breeds contempt, and at the root of this contempt is an unwillingness to listen to disabled people, either as individuals or through their representative bodies (Brisenden 1989: 218). Self-advocacy, self-help, collective action and disability politics are incongruent with an individual model of disability (Oliver 1996), antithetical social processes to a culture of disablement. Instead, a more embracing perspective is needed to build a 'New World' which rejects historically oppressive discourses such as social Darwinism (Zarb 1992; Finkelstein and Stuart 1996). The next section introduces an alternative model of disability that appears to fit more readily with the self-empowerment of disabled people.

'The disabled self-advocate': the social model of disability

> My day's going to come through . . . I'm going to tell them the
> truth. They know the truth. All this petty nonsense.
>
> (Ed Murphy, cited in Bogdan and Taylor 1982: 77)

Redefining disability as a political category has been at the heart of the disability civil rights movement (Schlaff 1993). According to Finkelstein and
Stuart (1996), Campbell and Oliver (1996) and Shakespeare and Watson
(1997), in the 1970s a number of disabled people started to articulate an
emancipatory alternative to the individual model. This other way of viewing
disability has been termed the *social model of disability* or social oppression
model (Abberley 1987; Oliver and Zarb 1989; Oliver 1990). As the disability
movement's 'big idea' (Hasler 1993), a key component of the social model is
the distinction between impairment and disability. The Union of the Physically Impaired Against Segregation (UPIAS) was among the first to provide
such a distinction in its 1976 *Fundamental Principles* document:

> Impairment – lacking part of or all of a limb, or having a defective limb
> organism or mechanism of the body.

> Disability – the disadvantage or restriction of activity caused by a con-
> temporary social organisation which takes no account of people who
> have physical impairments and thus excludes them from mainstream
> social activities.
>
> (UPIAS 1976: 3–4; quoted in Oliver 1990: 11)

These definitions, by contrast with dominant discourses that locate disability
in the realms of individual impairment, direct the social model to uncover the
ways in which society disables. Impairment and disability are not synonymous terms (Oliver 1990; BCODP 1992; Barnes 1993; Morris 1996). Instead,
disabled people are just that – people disabled by a contemporary social, economic, cultural and political climate on the basis of their purported impairments.

A number of studies exemplify the concerns of a social model. In 1981,
Finkelstein illustrated the disablement of modern culture by describing an
imaginary community where wheelchair users were the majority. In this 'disability culture', as opposed to disablist, able-bodied people were marked by
bruises from banging their heads on lowered entrances and suffered backache
from stooping down. They were helped by able-bodied equipment such as
helmets, neck braces and, 'best of all', limb amputation, and money was collected for them in up-turned helmets with 'Help the able-bodied' imprinted
upon them (Finkelstein 1981). Barnes (1990) examined the effects of daycare settings on disabled people. He concluded that not only were disabled
children assigned a position of dependency (the 'cabbage syndrome'), but
when they challenged such a condition this contrasted sharply with the positions allotted to them in the professionalized climate. Jenny Corbett (1991)
denounces notions of abnormality that are fundamentally located in white,

middle-class, male, able-bodied definitions of 'otherness' – step out of the 'disabled role' and you flout the rules. Barnes (1993) examined the media representations of disabled people. He found that in most cases two general images emerge. First, disabled people are 'super-cripples', overcoming their impairments at all odds (heroes in a tragic tale). Second, tragedy figures are well represented (victims of impairment). In the latter case, impairment gets the better of human resources – distress, bitterness, anger or pathetic reactions being expressed. He observes that on television news reports disabled people might get a mention, if they are lucky, for bravery (e.g. wheelchair race in the London marathon) or for pity (e.g. fighting against impairment through new drug trials).

Literature of the social model not only examines the ways in which society excludes, discriminates and stigmatises people with impairments. It also suggests ways forward for emancipation that do not mean having to overcome one's impairment (see, for example, Corbett 1991; Oliver 1993). Instead, freedom comes with a change in society (Oliver 1990, 1996; Campbell and Oliver 1996). Protests by disabled people have appeared in the British Council of Disabled People (BCODP), the Direct Action Network (DAN), independent living schemes and, of course, the self-advocacy movement. As Campbell and Oliver (1996) document, these organisations *of* disabled people present a challenge to disabling society. The *Rights Not Charity* newsletter of the BCODP and journals such as *Disability and Society* continue to parallel in theory and writing many of the actions of political activists. Hales's (1996) edited collection explores the care and support of disabled people in terms of a social model where, for example, a new type of welfare system is presented, reflecting a disability culture rather than a disabling culture (Finkelstein and Stuart 1996; see also Morris 1993b).

As the social model matures, calls for types of social change become more diverse (Finkelstein 1993; Oliver 1996).[3] Campling (1981), along with Morris's (1991) *Pride against Prejudice* and (1996) *Encounters with Strangers*, links politics with theory in ways that are sensitive to feminist issues. In the latter study, Morris writes about feeling excluded by both feminists and the male-dominated disability movement (see also Wendell 1996). Similarly, Stuart's (1993) focus on 'double oppression', being black and disabled, argues for a 'race' sensitive social model, while Zarb and Oliver (1993) show how similar practices pathologize both ageing and disability. Even in view of this diversity, all proponents of the social model assert that to enable emancipation, society must no longer disable.

The social model of disability is not reserved for people with physical impairments, although it may often seem that way (Ferguson 1987). As early as 1956, Dexter (see also Dexter 1958) argued: 'We need to see mental defectives in terms of the general theory of social problems' (Dexter 1956: 10–11). While Dexter's terminology is a reflection of its time, his plea pre-empted a whole collection of literature that was to emerge over the next 40 years, conceptualizing learning difficulties as a social creation of a disabling society. Examples included the following. Taking further Goffman's work (1961, 1963), Edgerton's (1967) ethnographic relationships with 'mentally handicapped' patients illustrated the stigmatization of labelling and institutionalization. Similarly, Morris's (1969) *Put Away* and Braginsky and Braginsky's (1971) *Hansels and Gretels* uncovered the experiences of adults and children with learning difficulties in institutions. Bayley's (1973) exploration of 'mental handicap' in the community noted the social limitations of support and debilitating effects on community memberships (as did Mercer's *Labeling the Mentally Retarded*, which came out that same year). O'Donnell's (1976) assessment of resident rights highlighted the concerns that even the most institutionalized demand. Brechin *et al.*'s (1981) *Handicap in a Social World* and Brechin and Walmsley's (1989) *Making Connections* piece together the experiences of people with physical impairments and learning difficulties (see also Kurtz 1981). The anthropological studies of Turner (1980), Koegel (1981, 1986), Langness and Levine (1986), Langness and Turner (1986), Whittemore *et al.* (1986) and Groce (1992), examine the cultural formations of learning difficulties.

Furthermore, just as people with physical impairments have written about disability from their own perspective, so the accounts of people with learning difficulties have clarified the socially constructed nature of disability. Examples include *The World of Nigel Hunt* (Hunt 1967), Ed Murphy's story by Bogdan and Taylor (1976; see also 1982), *Tongue Tied* by Joey Deacon (1974), Kaufman's (1988) account of mother and disabled daughter and Atkinson and Williams's (1990) anthology of prose, artwork and poetry. Korbin (1986) presents the life course of Sarah, a child labelled with Down's syndrome, to show the impact of social factors on development, and Lea (1988) refutes pathologizing clinical definitions via the poetry of people defined by such criteria. Potts and Fido (1991; see also Fido and Potts 1989) collected the oral histories of a number of long-term residents in an English mental hospital, and Oswin (1991) uncovered the experiences of bereavement of people with learning difficulties. Cheston (1994) provides accounts of 'special education leavers', while Angrosino (1994) talks of how he collected life stories 'on the bus with Vonny Lee' and Booth and Booth's (1994) *Parenting under Pressure* explores the personal stories of parents with learning difficulties.[4]

Similar to the controversies in the social model, the multiple identities of people with learning difficulties have been highlighted. Downer and Ferns (1993) have argued that black people with learning difficulties have double identities that need to be addressed. A piece by Powerhouse (1996), a refuge for women with learning difficulties, takes diversity even further, with disabled women with learning difficulties calling into question the dominant male, physically impaired focus of the social model (Morris 1996). Dingham's quizzical statement in 1968 pre-empted much of the literature presented above:

What should concern us is the mystifying fact that so many social scientists . . . do not regard mental retardation as a social and cultural phenomenon. I say mystifying, because nothing in the probabilistic world of social scientific reality is more certain than the assertion that mental retardation is a socio-cultural problem through and through.

(p. 76)

Perhaps Dingham will be reassured by developments that have taken place since. In view of the literature presented above, many researchers now recognize the social nature of learning difficulties. Take, for example, Bogdan and Taylor's (1982: 15) statement:

> Mental retardation is, in fact, a socio-political not a psychological construction. The myth, perpetuated by a society which refuses to recognise the true nature of its needed social reforms, has successfully camouflaged the politics of diagnosis and incarceration.

However, differences can be observed in the literature, as revealed in the following assertion by Levine and Langness (1986: 191):

> If there is one firm conclusion to be made . . . it is that *mild* mental retardation is as much or more a social and cultural phenomenon as it is a medical – genetic or cognitive – psychological one . . . The definition of retardation, then, and some of the consequences of being thus labelled are concomitants of social life [italics added].

This quote highlights two things. First, learning difficulties, just like disability in general, can be understood as a social phenomenon – a creation of culture, politics and society (Morris 1969; Korbin 1986). To find the origins of learning difficulties, we are encouraged to turn attention away from a focus on prescribed incompetence, on to a society that excludes, discriminates and stigmatizes people so labelled (Mercer 1973). However, a second point emerges. Levine and Langness (1986) exemplify a sociology of learning difficulties that focuses on the social construct of 'mild' learning difficulties. While Groce (1992; following Edgerton 1967; Scheiner and Abroms 1980) estimates that 75–85 per cent of all 'retarded' individuals are considered 'mildly retarded', this still leaves the disabilities of a number of individuals unaccounted for by sociological analysis.

As Ferguson *et al.* (1992c) and Watson (1996) argue, it would appear that where 'impairment' is 'less' then it is easier to frame a social theory of learning difficulties. This attention to, and perhaps preoccupation with, the notion of 'impairment' has wide implications for an understanding of disability as a social phenomenon (Shakespeare and Watson 1997) and appraisals of organizations of disabled people (Campbell and Oliver 1996). People with learning difficulties may be excluded from a socially grounded understanding of disability on the basis of their purported impairments. As Simone Aspis of People First London candidly writes:

> People with learning difficulties face discrimination in the disability movement. People without learning difficulties use the medical model when dealing with us. *We are always asked to talk about advocacy and our impairments as though our barriers aren't disabling in the same way as disabled people without learning difficulties.* We want concentration on our access needs in the mainstream disability movement.
>
> (Quoted in Campbell and Oliver 1996: 97; italics added)

Pat Worth, a Canadian self-advocate, expresses similar misgivings: 'People see our disability only, they don't see our ability. We may have a handicap but *we're* not the handicap' (quoted in Yarmol 1987: 28).

A preoccupation with naturalized impairment may ignore fundamental components of a social model of disability: self-help, collective and political action and self-advocacy (Oliver 1996). In addition, naturalized views of impairment take no account of learning difficulties literature that has examined impairment as a social construction. The knock-on effect of such ignorance is that disability becomes, in effect, a synonym for physical disability and people with learning difficulties are excluded (Ferguson 1987: 53). The next section draws together the social model of disability and literature that examines learning difficulties as a social and cultural artefact. Consequently, a theoretical basis is provided for an appraisal of self-advocacy in this book.

Impairment difficulties: towards an 'inclusive' social model of disability

> Oppression is extreme. Their [people with learning difficulties] major handicap is the straitjacket of isolation imposed on them by society. The result is a lack of life experience and self-confidence.
> (Worrel 1988: 6)

Using UPIAS's (1976) distinction between impairment and disability, on which the social model of disability was formulated (according to Oliver 1990, 1996; BCODP 1992; Finkelstein and Stuart 1996; Shakespeare and Watson 1997), people with learning difficulties can be encompassed in the definition of *disability*:

> Disability – the disadvantage or restriction of activity caused by a contemporary social organisation which takes no account of people who have physical impairments [or learning difficulties] and thus excludes them from mainstream social activities.

However, learning difficulties problematizes the UPIAS's definition of impairment. The social model represents impairment as opposite in character to disability, the former not being seen as socially produced (Hughes and Paterson 1997: 329). At this stage, in conceptualizing the impairment of people with learning difficulties, two available options can be identified. The first involves an acceptance of 'learning difficulties' as having some organic basis, but arguing that people with such an impairment should not be excluded and their difference should be celebrated. The second option – one strongly proposed by Paul Abberley in 1987 – involves questioning the naturalized notion of impairment. The 'difference' of people with learning difficulties, understood as being located in some biological deficit, individualizes their very humanity: ripping them out of a social context, placing them in the realms of pathological curiosity. The stance of this book is that while we can accept that people with learning difficulties do themselves recognize that they may be 'impaired' and 'different' (see Worth, cited above), the social model of disability can only include people with learning difficulties when it recognizes the social origins of 'learning difficulties' and 'difference'.

The complexity of learning difficulties has long been recognized in socio-logical literature on learning difficulties (Watson 1996). As presented below, the social bases of impairment, with respect to learning difficulties, have been demonstrated by deconstructing dominant clinical criteria that are used in diagnosing an 'impairment of mind'. Reviewing diagnoses of 'mental retarda-tion', Ryan and Thomas (1980, later 1987) observed three diagnostic criteria: low intelligence, social incompetence and maladaptive functioning. While these criteria are assumed to originate within the individual (as indicative of impairment), by contrast, the historical, political and socio-cultural bases of these criteria have been demonstrated (Levine and Langness 1986). Whereas the social model has, in effect, exiled impairment from sociological consider-ation (Hughes and Paterson 1997: 329), a whole body of literature has demon-strated the socio-cultural and political nature of criteria used in diagnosing and hence constructing learning difficulties. It is suggested below that an 'inclusive' social model of disability can be forged from drawing upon literature associated with the sociology of learning difficulties. This literature destabilizes accepted embodied notions of 'impairment' and pushes us towards an understanding of people with learning difficulties that recognizes their resilience in the face of arbitrary, so-called scientific categorizations, which threaten to deny their humanity altogether.[5] In this sense, then, an 'inclusive' social model of disabil-ity takes as its starting point a 'capacity' rather than 'deficiency' stance with respect to people with learning difficulties and their self-advocacy (see Booth and Booth 1994): impairment is resocialized, culturized and politicized; regained from individualistic, psychologizing and medicalizing discourses which have maintained its essentialist difference and deficiency. Consequently, the phenomenon of 'learning difficulties' is placed in a socio-political land-scape, ripe for analysis by the sociological imagination.

Criterion 1: The social creation of a 'lesser intelligence'

Korbin (1986: 20–1) asserts that the discrepancy between chronological age and exhibited competence in people with learning difficulties questions rather than clarifies the embodied origins of low intelligence. Among many others, Townsend (in Morris 1969) criticizes intelligence tests on the basis that they measure only a limited number of abilities, crudely approximate scores which can quickly increase following short-term educational intervention, and dis-criminate against certain class, cultural and ethnic groups. Moreover it would appear that the very presence of low intelligence is a direct product of disabling society:

> The educational system can be said to *produce* mentally handicapped people . . . Despite the fact that they develop slowly, their education – by

contrast with that of many 'normal' children – stops short at sixteen. It is therefore hardly surprising that some handicapped people complain that they were never given adequate opportunity to learn to read and write.

(Ryan and Thomas 1980: 22)

Numerous studies have demonstrated the socio-political origins of lowered intelligence (e.g. Bayley 1973; Mercer 1973; Turner 1980; Whittemore *et al.* 1986). One of these, Mercer's (1973) *Labeling the Mentally Retarded*, accessed what Townsend (1969: xvii) termed the 'strong social element in the identification of handicap'. For Mercer (1973), a 'social system perspective' explains the origin of learning difficulties, and in doing so, deconstructs individualistic clinical criteria.

It is often assumed that a low score on an intelligence test is a symptom of impairment. There is a tendency to assume that 'minimal brain dysfunction' exists, even when it cannot be detected, 'because of the inadequacy of present diagnostic tools' (Mercer 1973: 8). However, Mercer outlines a number of stages in children's schooling that lead to the diagnosis of low intelligence and hence 'mental retardation'. The origins of learning difficulties can be found not in 'minimal brain dysfunction', but in the employment of IQ testing and discriminatory referral processes by teachers and professionals, where tomorrow's playground insults are foretold by today's professional diagnoses (Ferguson 1987: 51).

For Mercer, the process of 'labelling the retarded' [*sic*] starts with the administering of IQ tests. Stage 1, 'enrolment in public school', recognizes immediate class and race biases in the discovery of 'the retardate' [*sic*]. No students in the private school Mercer appraised were subjected to IQ testing and they were not, therefore, drawn into the diagnostic trap. However, for public school students entering stage 2, 'normal students in the regular classroom', the labelling process continued and here 'primarily the expectations of the teacher determine who will be identified and referred as a possible candidate for the status of retardate' (Mercer 1973: 103). Assessment procedures were tied up in an ethos that reinforced the norms of the school, rewarding intellect and punishing failure. All but two of the 71 students placed in special education classes were recommended by their teacher. This critical period in the classification of otherness (52 of the 71 were defined as 'mentally retarded' before the fifth grade) was dependent upon teachers' subjective criteria, justified by reference to 'valid', 'reliable' and 'scientific' intelligence testing procedures. By stage 3, 'the retained student status', those labelled were retained for a grade or more. Already non-Anglo students were well represented in this remedial population. Stage 4, 'referral by the principal' for psychological assessment, occurred if the student, caught up in a vicious cycle of failure and punishment, continued to under-achieve. For many this led to stage 5, 'psychological testing and evaluation', where the IQ test reappeared: 'Once tested a child's IQ becomes the most critical variable determining whether he retains the status of normal student or moves closer to the status of the retardate' (p. 114).

However, the key to a diagnosis of low IQ (and therefore handicap) appeared to lie in the referral process. Those pupils referred by a teacher or principal were most likely to be tested (76 per cent); the remainder who were not referred by professional authority 'escaped the risk of being assigned the status of mental retardate' (p. 113). Moreover, the reasoning behind referrals highlights further the social bases of diagnosis. Most children were referred, tested and hence labelled when they were perceived as having 'academic difficulties' (seven out of ten tested). Only four out of ten testees were referred because of 'behavioural difficulties'. Academic success, so highly valued in society, impinges directly on diagnosis. In this stage, 'As soon as the intelligence test was used, the higher failure rate of children from lower socio-economic backgrounds and from minority homes produced the disproportions characteristic of classes for the mentally retarded' (p. 115).

This discrimination continued in stage 6, 'the labelling', and stage 7, 'the labelled', where non-Anglo, working-class children were statistically more likely to be placed in special schools even when their IQs were not significantly lower than those not recommended for placement. In stage 8, 'vacating the status of retardate', a final chance for graduating from the status of 'retardate' was permitted. Those that did graduate were those deemed to have a 'high' IQ and a low probability of neurological deficits (i.e. they were 'physically educable'). Mercer concludes:

> On the basis of our social system epidemiology of mental retardation in the community, that institutionalized Anglo-centrism is a recurring pattern in the labeling process, a pattern that is closely linked with the statistical definitions of 'normal' and the IQ test.
>
> (p. 123)

Identifying the sociological and cultural bases of inability appears to be important: 'Any conceptualisation of "intelligence" that does not allow for these factors (and for racial attributions, culture and gender) is fatuous; conversely, one that does make allowances would be so weak as to have relatively little content' (Borthwick 1996: 408).

Miles (1992), considering the socio-cultural construction of 'mental retardation' in Pakistan, notes how the nation's high rate of non-literacy creates a very different population of 'retarded' [*sic*]. In a climate of social Darwinism, the development in late nineteenth-century Britain of a national school system brought to light those who could not be accommodated in that system (Townsend 1969: xxii). So occurred an expansion in the proportion of those in society who were identified as 'mentally handicapped'. In today's system, people with learning difficulties continue to be disabled of skills and hence intelligence throughout childhood (Korbin 1986). People are forced to adapt to inadequate practices and disabling educational systems (Apple 1982; Bratlinger 1985; Oliver 1996). Skrtic (1995c: 212) notes that even when the needs of a disabled client do not match the professional's repertoire of skills, there is still a tendency to force the client artificially into available standard

practices – deskilling them thus. Low intelligence, a facet of learning difficulties, appears to have social origins.

Criterion 2: The creation of 'social incompetence'

Guskin (1963) observes that people with learning difficulties are expected to
play a generalizing and all-encompassing role. As Kurtz (1981: 14) puts it,
'acting like a retarded person can soon become second nature.' As Barnes
(1990) points out, social incompetence within a social order that emphasizes
the dependency of disabled people may be no more than a reflection of the
paternalistic role of the state: 'The level of incapacity accepted for special
attention and care depends on the perceptions and tolerance of families, peer
groups, *the community and bureaucracy*' (Townsend 1969: xx, italics added).

In deconstructing the notion of social incompetence, literature tends to focus
upon ideological, structural and bureaucratic practices. For example, Koegel
(1986) pinpoints a number of prevalent assumptions that shape the socializa-
tion of people with learning difficulties, potentially augmenting their incompetence. These include that they remain children (never reach adulthood), that
they are the same (homogeneous group), that their impairments affect all their
actions (the reductionist cause and effect reasoning for Mercer 1973) and that
'they' are more different than 'us'. Yet, for Morris (1969), people are labelled
and defined not because they are of subnormal intelligence or are incapacitated
but because they are deemed incomplete and deviant. Ryan and Thomas (1980:
26) point to societal structures that phrase people in terms of their lacking
capacities. There is a tendency to attribute behaviour to individual inability,
while failing to examine the deficiencies within the person's environment
(Oswin 1991). 'Implicit in these statements is the assumption that the condition
characterises the individual and that the condition exists as an entity regardless
of whether the person is aware of its presence or aware of others recognizing
his pathology' (Mercer 1973: 7). Such assumptions have implications. For
example, a zoo on the Isle of Wight refused entry to a group of people with
learning difficulties (*Guardian* 6 July 1996: 4). The manager argued:

> It was in the best interests of the zoo and the poor people in the group . . .
> the adults were severely disabled and I was very concerned they may
> harm the animals. One even had a fit . . . and was trying to bite. Nobody
> but an idiot would have let them in.

Taking the point further, Gunn (1990) outlines a number of legal deficiencies
which position people with learning difficulties as incompetent. These include
ineligibility for jury service, the imposition of limits on sexual relationships, a
lack of adequate sex education (Brown 1994) and exemption from paying
community charge. Social incompetence is the legal requirement of people
with learning difficulties (Hudson 1988).

As basic rights are withheld, so the possibilities for taking on socially com-
petent roles are limited. Ferguson found in 1987 that 50–80 per cent of disabled people are unemployed. In 1989, although estimates were conservative

(Barnes 1991), Martin *et al.* found that only 34 per cent of disabled people under pension age living at home were working. The 1995 Disability Discrimination Act (HMSO 1995) does not appear to improve matters.

The Act legitimates forms of exclusion that will continue to decrease the life chances of disabled people (see Barnes 1996b). This is apparent in the Act's position on employment (Part II), where employers may justify discrimination. An employer can reject a disabled job applicant if an individualized assessment of the 'risk', carried out by an expert, taking into account the feasibility of 'reasonable adjustments' (that is, adjusting the work environment to accommodate another's impairment), designates that applicant 'unemployable' (Gooding 1995: 18). Barnes (1996b) argues that this focus upon individualized assessments reinforces the power imbalance between disabled applicant and expert assessor, with disabled people having to prove themselves worthy of consideration for employment. The job interview starts sooner for disabled applicants than for non-disabled applicants. Furthermore, significant sections of the workforce are excluded from the provisions of the Act. These include small businesses (fewer than 20 employees). The detrimental effects upon people with learning difficulties are potentially massive in the light of the many small workshops and businesses that employ people so labelled. The Department of Trade and Industry (DTI 1996) brought out a pamphlet on small businesses with the headline cover, '96% of all firms employ fewer than 20 people'. Social incompetence appears to be prescribed constitutionally, and organizational forms reinforce 'handicapped behaviour' (Townsend 1969: xxi).

Criterion 3: The creation of 'maladaptive functioning'

Hot topics for practitioners, particularly in psychology, are the 'challenging' or 'maladaptive behaviours' of people with learning difficulties,[6] which can be defined as:

> Culturally abnormal behaviour(s) of such an intensity, frequency or duration that the physical safety of the person or others is likely to be placed in serious jeopardy, or behaviour which is likely to seriously limit use of, or result in the person being denied access to, ordinary community facilities.
>
> (Emerson 1995: 4–5)

Ideologically such behaviours are seen as reflecting some underlying 'impairment'. Assumptions find their way into expert opinion. For example, Kennedy (1996: 123) reports on a paediatrician who, on examining a child with 'hypnotonic spastic quadriplegia' [*sic*], found vaginal injuries, anal scars and a sexually transmitted disease. He reported, 'These symptoms could be due to an obscure syndrome.' In addition, Goodwin (1982) recalls the case of a paediatrician belatedly and reluctantly reporting three boys who were having sexual intercourse with their sister who had the label of learning difficulties. His 'excuse' was: 'isn't it better to save three normal boys than one retarded girl?' Similarly, Goodwin also reports the case of a counsellor's comments to a mother whose disabled son had been sexually abused: 'At least it didn't happen to one of your non-disabled children.'

Brechin and Walmsley (1989: 7) observe that because some professionals view 'problem behaviour' as normal for people with learning difficulties, the symptoms of child sex abuse are understood as the inevitable consequence of handicap. By contrast, in keeping with a sociology of learning difficulties, a number of observers have suggested that the origins of maladaptive or challenging behaviours can be found in cultural, social and political structures. Shearer (1981a) suggests that maladaptive behaviours reflect outwardly the management of 'spoilt identities' (Goffman 1963), the impact of other social actors' responses:

> At any given time for any given individual it may not be possible to differentiate between behaviour that is a consequence of the retardation and behaviour that is a consequence of behaving as one thinks the expectations of others define proper behaviour.
>
> (Kurtz 1981: 14)

According to Ferguson *et al.* (1992a), in 1973 the entire category of 'borderline retardation' was dropped from the Manual of Terminology of the American Association on Mental Deficiency. What constitutes 'maladaptive behaviour' varies from decade to decade. Indeed, for Emerson (1995: 5) many challenging behaviours may actually be functionally adaptive responses to exclusive environments. Often the most apparently irrational maladaptive behaviours are themselves forms of resistance. Genealogically, perceptions of (ab)normality become misshaped over the years. For example, the term 'idiot' comes from the Greek word 'idiote', meaning 'private person'. Privacy was devalued in Ancient Greece. Later the term was applied to those very people who were deemed in need of privacy and segregation from the wider community, but ancient values remain attached (see Parker *et al.* 1995: 16).

Oswin (1991) explored the bereavement experiences of people with learning difficulties. She found that often people were not told that a family member had died for fear that, 'They were not up to such news'. Some of Oswin's informants were not told until some years afterwards. Even when the loss of a family member was disclosed, any outward display of grief by people with learning difficulties tended to be noted down by care assistants and psychologists as 'challenging behaviour': 'Any alterations in behaviour following loss are usually attributed to the original diagnosis that person has already' (French and Kuczaj 1992: 108). However, anger may be a functionally adaptive response to bereavement (heightened when the effects of institutionalization are taken into account). Nevertheless, people with learning difficulties are viewed solely in terms of their purported 'impairments'. Not only are 'patients' pathologized by the diagnostic classification itself, they are further pathologized when they do not fit criteria (Parker *et al.* 1995: 3). A response of crying on hearing the death of a loved one may be seen as overly emotional, passive and dependent, indicative of 'retardation'. By contrast, lashing out in anger is likely to be viewed as challenging behaviour. A double-bind exists; whatever the response, a diagnosis looms. 'If someone else whispers a lot during the play people might ignore it or get angry. If we whisper it is because we are retarded. It's like we have to be more normal than normal people' (Martin Levine, self-advocate, in Friedman-Lambert 1987: 15). Zetlin and Turner (1985: 575) examined the case reports of professionals. In them were many incidents of 'problem behaviour', including minor violations such as the regular use of marijuana and associated 'uppers', 'and/or the daily consumption of a sizeable quantity of beer by two sample members'! Here a professional's own sense of right and wrong becomes implicated in assessing the suitability of behaviour.

Consequently, assessment techniques for challenging behaviour are low in validity and reliability, simplistic and inappropriate (Emerson 1995: 177). Assessment also ignores the cultural and social processes that help to shape others' reactions to challenging behaviour. Rusch *et al.* (1986) found that those institutionalized people with learning difficulties defined as having challenging behaviour were most likely to be abused by staff and other inmates (indeed, a diagnosis of challenging behaviour was the major predictor of subsequent abuse). Moreover, one in 40 of ward staff in Canadian hospitals said that their typical response to patients exhibiting self-injurious behaviour was to hit them. As with Mercer's (1973) cycle of denied educational opportunities and consequent lowering of intelligence, challenging behaviours, once culturally defined, may be reconstituted and reinforced through a process of abuse.

Finally, medical abuse has been identified in considerations of the origins of maladaptive behaviour. Up to 40 per cent of community residents and 50 per cent of institutionalized people with learning difficulties receive psychotropic medication for 'challenging behaviours' (Emerson 1995: 15). In 1987, the Ohio Legal Rights Service survey reported that up to 70 per cent of people with learning difficulties were using neuroleptics. In the USA alone, over one million children are prescribed drugs to control their behaviour in schools and at home (Breggin 1993). Common drugs include Ritalin, neuroleptics and anti-depressants. There are consequences. Anti-psychotic medication affects muscle tension, sedates or 'snows' thought and decreases the rate of learning. Similarly, some evidence suggests that Ritalin causes brain damage (Breggin 1993).

Surprisingly, even when people with learning difficulties are subjected to a multitude of maladaptive environments, only a small proportion of them exhibit challenging behaviour (Humphreys *et al.* 1987: 9). For Clegg (1993: 390), professional practice must take into account: 'Important psychological issues such as coping with chronic lack of self-esteem or *surviving within damaging social environments*' (italics added). After all, people subjected to such environments are aware of the impacts, as Ed Murphy notes about his girlfriend: 'I don't think that retardation is holding her back so much as emotional problems. If she had confidence that would make the difference. I know she could build herself up' (cited in Bogdan and Taylor 1982: 74).

Too often there is a tendency to view people with learning difficulties in terms of their 'deficits' (Ryan and Thomas 1980: 82; Booth and Booth 1994). When they are allowed into the community, perfection is demanded. Any deviation from the perfect path to community membership and 'they' may be recalled, incidents of maladaptive actions being cited. However, attending to what people are able to do, even when society attempts to banish them from mainstream life, recognizes their 'capacities' and the tendency for all of us to attach significance to the 'truth' of individual impairment. Maladaptive behaviour may be a testimony to the historical exclusion of people deemed inhuman.

A social model of impairment

The social model of disability does not deny that some illnesses may have disabling consequences (Oliver 1996: 35–6). However, UPIAS's definition of impairment appears to be inappropriate in the light of the literature cited above that has deconstructed the criteria used in diagnosing 'impairment' in people with learning difficulties. Koegel (1986: 47) warns:

> However much we pay lip service to the influence of socio-cultural factors, we *do* primarily see mental retardation as a biomedical phenomenon and *do*, as a result, tend to attribute incompetent behaviour exclusively to physiological causes.

While people with the label of learning difficulties have recognized that they have difficulties learning, it is impossible to separate organic and social origins (Sleeter 1995: 162). Perhaps uncovering the causes of impairment is itself an inadequate project:

> The most relevant issue here is not what causes mental retardation – or blindness, or any other physical disability – but why some cultures regard it as seriously troublesome and others do not. About this subject, we remain almost wholly ignorant.
> (Edgerton 1976: 62–3; quoted in Oliver 1990: 15–16)

Nevertheless, it is crucial that we ask ourselves how we understand learning difficulties, as assumptions inform actions that either exclude or include on the basis of historically located discourses of disablement (Goodley 1996b). In a review of 307 research studies in learning difficulties, Kavale and Nye (1981) found little consensus regarding their individual and physical origins. A way forward is the adoption of a social model that de-biologizes and de-medicalizes both disability and impairment (Hughes and Paterson 1997: 330–1). Shakespeare and Watson (1997) assert that a social model of disability (and to that add learning difficulties) provides a model to understand disability and impairment, thus working towards a 'non-disablist culture' (see Finkelstein and Stuart 1996).

For this book, bringing together literature from the social model and the sociology of learning difficulties fields appears to provide a platform on which to conceptualize the personal and social facets of self-advocacy in the lives of people with learning difficulties. The social model reminds us that society has to change and this change will come about as part of a process of political empowerment of disabled people as a group (Oliver 1996: 37). In this sense, self-advocacy and an inclusive social model are conceptually compatible.

An 'inclusive' social model of disability and an appraisal of self-advocacy

> First, we need a sociology of those who study mental deficiency . . . second, we badly need a sociology of those who work in institutions . . . third, we need to see mental defectives in terms of the general theory of social problems.
>
> (Dexter 1956: 10–11)

This chapter has introduced two models of disability. The first, the individual model, exists in dominant practices and appears to subjugate people with learning difficulties. By contrast, the social model of disability provides a context in which self-empowerment is located. In addition, with respect to the self-advocacy of people with learning difficulties, it has been argued that a social model of disability benefits from incorporating literature associated with a sociology of learning difficulties. This literature tackles the social construction of 'learning difficulties', while recognizing the resilience of people so labelled in disabling environments.

Combining the social model with a sociology of learning difficulties may be termed an 'inclusive' social model of disability, embracing the ambitions of disabled people while being sensitive to the impact of disabling society. This book draws upon an inclusive model to appraise self-advocacy in the lives of people with learning difficulties. As Campbell and Oliver (1996: 169) point out, the disability movement has 'Succeeded in giving a voice to disabled people . . . the crucial issue for the movement over the next few years is to make sure this collective voice is not merely heard but taken notice of.' The voices of self-advocates are central to the appraisal of self-advocacy in this book. This appraisal can in some small way build upon a social model of disability through the inclusion of the perspectives of people with learning difficulties who are involved in their own self-determination. This leads on to questions of methodology, method and analysis, which are considered in the next chapter.

Notes

1 Social Darwinism is chosen from a multitude of philosophies to show the historical origins of learning difficulties and subsequent social-cultural reactions. Other philosophical and institutional beliefs implicated in society's treatment of people with learning difficulties include religious and moral tensions, medicalization, the rise of psychological assessment and Foucauldian considerations of 'the body'. For a comprehensive historical overview see Wright and Digby (1996).

2 See Oliver (n.d.) for an overview, Chadwick (1995) for an evaluation of the implications of the DDA and Walmsley (1991) for discussion about definitions of learning difficulties.

3 See Swain *et al.* (1993), which brings together many of these diverse strands within the social model.

4 See Stanovich and Stanovich (1979) for a bibliography of writings by people with learning difficulties.

5 Such a challenge parallels recent poststructuralist critiques of the body as biology. Judith Butler's (1990, 1993) Foucauldian critiques of sex and gender, and her reflections on transsexual identities, have become popular resources for feminists opposed to embodied notions of women.

6 See, for example, the many workshops, conferences and training programmes advertised in the *Bulletin of the British Psychology Society* for an illustration of challenging behaviour.

 **4**

Researching self-advocacy

> The significance of disability theory and practice lies in its radical challenge to the medical or individual model of disability. The latter is based on the assumption that the individual is 'disabled' by their impairment, whereas the social model of disability reverses the causal chain to explore how social constructed barriers have disabled people with a perceived impairment.
>
> (Barnes and Mercer 1997: 1–2)

Many disability researchers share a common opposition to traditional positivistic research. Increasingly heard are calls for models of post-positivistic research that critically engage with the existing non-reflexive positivistic conditions of research production that have reinforced the hierarchy between (non-disabled) researchers and (disabled) participants. As Clough and Barton (1995: 1) assert:

> Much of this research has been strongly influenced by positivistic assumptions. This has legitimated a form of psychological and individual reductionism which views '. . . the problem which disabled people face as being caused by their own impairments' (Oliver 1992: p. 108).

Alternative research paradigms couched in the social model have been turned to, including narrative (e.g. Booth and Booth 1994), participatory (e.g. Atkinson and Williams 1990), performative (e.g. Boal 1994), discursive (e.g. Corker 1998; Corker and French 1998); ethnographic (e.g. Vlachou 1997) and, most radically, emancipatory research paradigms (e.g. Zarb 1992), which attempt to take disability studies back into an arena of expertise populated by disabled experts who critique and challenge disablement while being politically sensitive to issues associated with impairment.[1] This book draws upon the qualitative approaches of life story and ethnographic research carried out by a non-disabled researcher alongside participants with the label of learning difficulties. This chapter critically outlines the philosophical underpinnings, methods and analyses of these two approaches, pitching evaluation within current debates about doing disability research, with the specific focus on appraising self-advocacy. Following Moore *et al.* (1998), this chapter also reflects on what was learnt, and how, from involvement with self-advocacy's experts – self-advocates with the label of learning difficulties.

Storytelling the impact of self-advocacy

Part II of this book takes up the challenge of answering the first research question, to examine the impact of self-advocacy groups on the life experiences of people with learning difficulties. Following Oliver (1992), to counter accusations of the subsequent research being a waste of time, this research question was broached by turning to the knowers of self-advocacy. Accounts were collected from insiders or 'emics' of the movement (Whittemore *et al.* 1986: 1) – self-advocates. It was anticipated that if the self-advocacy movement has a history then this history would be manifested in insiders' active engagement with the movement; and that this engagement would be illuminated through their accounts.

Bowker (1993) suggests that an age of biography is upon us. Accordingly, a current frame of reference in the social sciences is the epistemological notion that meaning and experience are constrained in texts (Potter and Wetherell 1987; Burman and Parker 1993; Parker and the Bolton Discourse Network 1999). Various approaches study texts to throw light on personal and social life. Approaches sensitive to text include interpretivism (e.g. Ferguson 1987; Ferguson *et al.* 1992a, b, c), post-structuralism (Burman and Parker 1993), social constructionism (Sarbin 1986; Berger and Luckmann 1987; Potter and Wetherell 1987; Gergen and Gergen 1988), ethnomethodology (Garfinkel 1967, 1968), ethogenics (Marsh *et al.* 1978), grounded theory (Glaser and Strauss 1967; Schatzman and Strauss 1973), critical discourse analysis (Fairclough 1989, 1992; Parker 1997), naturalistic inquiry (Lincoln and Guba 1985) and narrative inquiry (Clandinin and Connelly 1994).

Narrative inquiry is concerned with the storied nature of life (Bruner 1986, 1987). Experiences are collated, cross-referenced and reflected upon in a storied manner (Clandinin and Connelly 1994: 414). Some proponents of narrative inquiry would assert that stories are *the* central component of experience and reality (Didion 1979; Sarbin 1986; Bruner 1987; Gergen and Gergen 1988; K. J. Gergen 1988; Hoffman 1993; M. Gergen 1994). Narrative is seen as producing experience, and vice versa. People impose structure and give meaning to their lives through the use of stories (Hoffman 1993). People tell stories in order to live (Didion 1979: 11), in both the telling and the doing of self (Gergen and Gergen 1988). Some would suggest that because human beings are storytellers (*Homo narrans*) and life is story put into practice (Gillman *et al.* 1997: 680), so people are texts (Gergen 1988). Alternatively, other proponents use narrative as a medium through which to present and reflect upon some of the experiences and realities of people (Allport 1947; Parker 1963, 1990, 1994; Plummer 1983, 1995; Langness and Levine 1986; Fairclough 1989, 1992). Here, reality and narrative are not necessarily seen as synonymous. Instead, because telling stories is a large part of what people do, storytelling is used as a method to lend some insight into the experiences and realities of narrators.

Narrative inquiry deals with the collection, writing up and presentation of stories (Plummer 1983). Accounts of people with learning difficulties have taken a number of narrative forms, including autobiography (Hunt 1967), biography (Deacon 1974), life story (Bogdan and Taylor 1976), oral history (Angrosino 1994) and life history (Langness and Levine 1986). In some small way, this book adds to this narrative tradition through exploring the use of the life stories: life experiences presented in a storied form (Plummer 1983). A life story is the product of the reminiscences of one narrator that are structured together chronologically or thematically in a storied fashion (Bertaux 1981a). The life story relies on the accounts of a primary narrator, whereas a life history combines different persons' stories of an individual (Plummer 1983, 1995). Life stories can be written alone or told to others who collaborate in writing (Goodson 1992; Sparkes 1994; Hatch and Wisnieswski 1995b). An aim of this book was to write life stories collaboratively with narrators (self-advocates). The life story is suited to an examination of the impact of self-advocacy groups on the life experiences of people with learning difficulties. Drawing on Goodley (1996a), life stories boast a number of strengths:

- *An invitation to personal stories.* In an intensive literature review of narrative research in the learning difficulties field, Whittemore *et al.* (1986) revealed a tradition rich in the beliefs, perceptions and attitudes of parents, carers and professionals. The perspectives of people with learning difficulties were often not represented. According to Turner (1980), the absent accounts of people with learning difficulties reflect a general assumption that people so labelled are *unable* to articulate their own life experiences. By contrast, presenting the life stories of disabled people implies that lives exist to be recounted and addresses the absence of these lives in previous documents (Thomas 1982; Korbin 1986: 19; Thompson 1988: 2; Atkinson *et al.* 1997).
- *Addressing the abstract.* Using life stories addresses the 'disappearing individual' in the increasingly abstracted nature of social theory (Thomas and Znaniecki 1918–20; Nicholson 1928; Whittemore *et al.* 1986). Indeed, stories challenge the death of the human subject so celebrated by contemporary postmodern social researchers (see Eagleton's 1983 chapter on post-structuralism). Stories allow personal insights into social worlds (Taylor and Bogdan 1984: 7–8; Smith 1987), and theories of the social world, both 'lay' and 'academic', can be assessed from an individual standpoint (Langness and Koegel 1986). As Schutz (1964) observed, theories flounder when they fail to immerse themselves adequately in the worlds of those they attempt to understand. Yet stories not only present subjective accounts of situations but also highlight social backgrounds (Corradi 1991: 106). Bertaux-Wiame (1981: 260) suggests that stories allow readers to listen beyond the words of narrators and to tap into the speech of their social culture. Abstractions can be checked by stories (Bertaux 1981b). In this way, then, stories oppose over-deterministic (structuralist) understandings of the social world (Allport 1947).
- *Story and meaning.* Life stories investigate some of the meanings held by narrators, and also by readers (Bogdan and Taylor 1976; Smith 1987; Thompson 1988: 7–8;). A knock-on effect may be that readers' preconceptions are

re-evaluated in light of another's account (Koegel 1981, 1986); for example, falsifying the assumption that the views of people with learning difficulties do not exist (Atkinson and Williams 1990: 8). Bogdan and Taylor (1982: 16) grandly claim that life stories enable us to understand society better, specifically to understand the meaning of 'mental retardation' [*sic*].

- *Exploring the research process*. Writing stories is a reflexive venture. Consequently, the writing process, as a research exercise, can be investigated (Nisbet 1976; Plummer 1983). Some writers, like Tony Parker (1963), assert that the very exercise of writing someone else's story can expose the non-scientific and arbitrary nature of research. For others, using life stories fits a critical approach to research (Allport 1947: 127). Reflexivity in the social sciences is nothing new (Kidder and Fine 1997). In the 1930s, the Chicago School tradition in sociology encouraged researchers to provide a 'vivid sense of the research experience' (Warner and Lunt 1941: 5–6; Stott 1973). Reflexivity can be used to assess the authenticity of research methods that purport to give voices to people (Lather 1986; Oliver 1996).

Simultaneously, a number of limitations can be pinpointed:

- *Only part of the story*. Biographies are in a constant state of becoming (Turner 1991: 232–3). Today's story of a specific experience will read differently if told tomorrow. Life stories are made up of a narrator's reflections of some experiences from the past viewed at a specific time in the present. No single story can capture the range or richness of people's experiences (Bruner 1986: 143). Furthermore, when life stories are the product of collaborative, diachronic relationships (Whittemore *et al.* 1986), as they were aimed to be in this book, there is a danger that researchers suppress the disclosure of certain stories in favour of those that are of 'research interest'. Furthermore, moving from lives to text is problematic. As soon as speech is translated into prose, a story is mutilated (Thompson 1988: 230) and contaminated (Plummer 1983: 113). These effects become even more acute in collaborative life story research where the researcher primarily becomes the writer of another's oral account.
- *Bias in narrative*. Harrison and Stina-Lyon (1993) argue that the credibility of a person's narrative is the extent to which the narrative remains faithful to the reality of the narrator. However, all narrators make errors. They may ascribe intentions to actions after the event, exaggerate, rehearse stories or lie (Oakley 1981; Bruner 1987; Rosie 1993; Plummer 1995). Suggestions for overturning these sources of error include cross-checking information with other people, assessing how a person's narrative stands up against official documents and revisiting stories with narrators (Klockars 1977; Taylor and Bogdan 1984). However, it may not be appropriate to ask if participants are telling the truth (Dean and Foot-Whyte 1978, Walmsley 1993). Why people present themselves like they do may be more important. Behind the presentation of stories are intentions (Moffet and McElheny 1966, Widdicombe 1993). Stories are told like they are for a variety of reasons that we may never know about (Potter and Wetherell 1987). In

this book, no attempt is made to excavate the intentions of narrators. Therefore, life stories are constructed from the reflections of narrators and are bound together by bias. Later, as the process of writing proceeds, so another source of bias enters the fray – researcher bias. Finally, it could be concluded that all storytelling contributes to the construction of fiction within the social sciences (Banks and Banks 1998), though it remains to be seen whether this is a criticism or merely an observation of the storied nature of life.

- *Problems with relying on stories.* A preoccupation with stories may ignore the cut and thrust of contemporary political narrative and the unseen pressures of economic and structural change (Tomlinson 1995). Whyte's (1943) *Street Corner Society* was criticized by Stott (1973) on the basis that Whyte had become totally accepting of his narrators, the 'Cornerboys'. He remained uncritical of their contempt for college students, non-Italian teachers and social workers. Empathy with others' stories can prove to be a weakness as well as a strength. Moreover, debates rage over whether or not stories are good enough to 'stand alone' as markers of the phenomena under investigation (see Bogdan and Taylor 1976: 51). For Sparkes (1994) and Kidder and Fine (1997) life stories cannot stand alone and require additional analysis. If this is the case, stories presented alone may lack a theoretical punch (Allport 1947).

- *Problems with relying on story-tellers.* It is helpful to the narrative researcher if narrators are articulate (Plummer 1983: 90). A consequence of this preoccupation with articulate people has been the exclusion of those who cannot tell or have difficulties telling stories (Stott 1973: 195). While a number of imaginative strategies have been used to aid communication of people who lack articulation,[2] questions remain about whose voice is dominant in the life story. Furthermore, if the narrative researcher fails to acquire the 'necessary' skills and creative heart of the novelist, poet and artist (Nisbet 1976, Plummer 1983), writing stories is further problematized. A weakness of the life story method is that the narrative's plot and fable may be lacking from the off (Chatman 1993) – the product of narrator, writer or both.

While the life story method is thwart with tensions, it was adopted as a fitting starting point for examining the impact of self-advocacy. Chapters 5 and 6 respectively present and examine the life stories of five 'top self-advocates'. The next section considers their construction.

The informants: 'top self-advocates'

> No one person's life can be wholly representative of an entire group, for each individual is unique. Yet I feel that a detailed examination of one life may provide insight into the larger question of how mentally retarded individuals are perceived in societies.
>
> (Groce 1992: 175)

Chapter 5 presents the life stories of Jackie Downer, Lloyd Page, Joyce Kershaw, Anya Souza and Patrick Burke. These five were chosen because of their extensive experience of self-advocacy. All have been involved with self-advocacy groups for years. They are well known in the movement, some nationally, all locally. Hence my term 'top self-advocates'. Their life stories are not accounts of 'typical' self-advocates. The five narrators are high profile, experienced, articulate members of the movement, sharing extensive involvement with self-advocacy. Their stories are limited because they are not representative of the experiences of self-advocates at the morphological level; that is, the level of superficial description (Groce 1992: 175). However, following Corradi (1991: 112) and Humphreys *et al.* (1987: 8), through scrutinizing each individual story a number of general themes emerge that allow some insight into the lived experience of self-advocacy: stories from similar socio-structural backgrounds support one another to make a body of evidence (Bertaux-Wiame 1981). As Humphreys *et al.* (1987: 8) concluded when commenting on the seven life stories of people with learning difficulties involved in the NIMROD services in Wales, 'While every description is very individual in nature, issues such as the struggle for basic rights as citizens can be seen in each account.'

The life stories will be used to draw out conclusions that reflect in a generalized form what in each document is expressed in individualized form (Thomas and Znaniecki 1918–20; Corradi 1991: 110). Themes that emerge from one account will be scrutinized against other accounts (Corradi 1991: 112). Stories can contribute in some small way to an understanding of a given network of social relations (Bertaux 1981b: 40; Groce 1992: 175). In this sense, the stories exhibit the impact on life experiences of being a member of a self-advocacy group and the active engagement with the movement. Their experiences provide a starting point for understanding the influence of being a 'self-advocate' on life chances and a sense of self.

In the final analysis the stories can be refuted because they do not represent the experiences of all self-advocates with learning difficulties. Michael Kennedy, a high profile and vocal American self-advocate, offers the following response to those who say he is not talking for all people with learning difficulties:

> When people tell me that I am 'higher functioning' than the people they are talking about, I feel like they are telling me that I don't have anything in common with other people with disabilities. It's like they are putting me in a whole different category and saying that I don't have any right to speak. It upsets me because I take it that they don't want to give anyone else the opportunities I have been given, and what I say they can ignore because I am more capable.
>
> (Kennedy 1997: 1)

To say that only 'the articulate with learning difficulties' get their stories written up ignores the collaborative nature of life story research and hints at assumptions about 'articulacy'. The five life stories in Chapter 5 are not representative of all self-advocates' experiences, though how a 'typical account' is obtained is a difficult question to answer when people with learning difficulties 'constitute a broad, heterogeneous group rather than a defined, bounded category of people, fixed within the parameters of statistical norms' (Angrosino 1994: 27). The stories presented do, however, highlight some of the impacts of self-advocacy groups on the life experiences of a few.

Informants were contacted by telephone and letter. Addresses and telephone numbers were obtained from a supporter with long-term involvement in the self-advocacy movement. Access was negotiated with reference to an introductory booklet (Appendix 1).[3] As research relationships are social relationships, inequalities structured around gender, race, sexuality and disability enter the research context (Parker 1963; Oakley 1981; Bannister *et al.* 1994; Sparkes 1994). Disclosing my involvement as a volunteer to a self-advocacy group appeared to encourage acceptance: as Anya Souza put it, she 'didn't mind my sort'. Also discussed was confidentiality and the need to preserve the anonymity of others. In the end all five were proud to give their names to their life histories. Initially, Patrick Burke was to choose a pseudonym but later asked for his real name to be included.

Informants were asked for their 'life stories'. Anecdotes were presented chronologically, thematically and interspersed with opinions. Asking for stories, rather than experiences, may have invited expression (Reason and Hawkins 1988: 100). Interviews varied in length from about an hour and a half (Lloyd Page and Patrick Burke), through to two (Jackie Downer), four (Anya Souza) and five hours (Joyce Kershaw). Total contact time was longer. Interviews were carried out in a variety of places: at home, in restaurants, cafés and a group office. Audiotapes and notes of interviews were transcribed and written up as stories, and first drafts were sent to narrators. All five changed the first drafts, a number of times in some cases, until eventually accepting the finished life stories presented in Chapter 5.

Reflections on the doing of life story research

> Whether talking about disability or any other topic of social science, surely reporting research and telling stories are two very different activities. We beg to differ . . . the goals of research are perfectly compatible with the discovery of good stories.
>
> (Ferguson *et al.* 1992b: 1)

The narrative element of this appraisal of self-advocacy aimed to take up the challenge of critically examining the life story as a method for imparting the experiences of people with learning difficulties. This fits the bigger project of developing emancipatory disability research (Abberley 1992; Oliver 1992). A number of recent papers have outlined in detail the processes that led to the writing of the finished narratives presented in this book in Chapter 5 (Goodley 1998b, 1999c, 2000), though it would prove useful to consider a number of stages of narrative method that critically highlight the doing of collaborative life story research.

Part 1: Interviewing

Lofland (1971) asserts that the format and content of interviews should at all times follow the issues of significance identified by narrators. In contrast, Tremblay (1959) argues that interviewers have interests that they will want to explore in the interview. I had some questions to ask, but they were used mainly as reminders and were not needed as central themes around which to organize dialogue. All narrators spoke openly, gave extended anecdotes, reflected on past experiences and considered present situations. Their reflections were tangled up in opinions and views, which had implications later in the writing up of the interview material into life stories.

For Taylor and Bogdan (1984: 77, 94–6) the interviewer, not the interview protocol, is the research tool. Interviewers should continuously appraise the interview situation by opposing sterility, being non-judgemental, letting people talk and sensitively probing. Lloyd Page was the first to be interviewed and became the unfortunate recipient of over-enthusiastic questioning. Lowe and de Paiva (1988) have highlighted the 'tendency' for narrators with learning difficulties to reply with simple yes or no answers. Atkinson (1989, 1993b) found that frequently asked questions emphasized the researcher's interests and helped to build up trust and rapport. O'Donnell (1976), Flynn (1986) and Flynn and Saleem (1986) used direct questions to ascertain the views of people with learning difficulties. This literature was taken too literally into the interview with Lloyd Page. I was impatient, fired quick questions and gave him little time to respond. He said afterwards that he felt 'grilled like a tomato'. Field notes, written after the interview, reflect on my failings: 'Some of the literature suggests that snappy, quick questions "work best" and perhaps I had gone into the interview with such preconceptions. This assumes all interviewees with learning difficulties are the same – they're not!'

In contrast to P. Shakespeare (1993), who felt that she had acted too naturally in her interviews, Lloyd Page's interview highlights problems with literature-based interviewer posturing. Viewing Lloyd as 'a person with learning difficulties', who would respond best to a particular type of questioning, assumes that people with learning difficulties are an homogeneous group and unquestionably translates 'textbook' guidelines into the interviews (see Lawthom 1996). Good narrators are rarely found; instead they emerge in the course of one's everyday activities, not in artificially contrived research contexts (Taylor and Bogdan 1984: 86; Edgerton 1984b; Swain 1995: 86).

The four narrators interviewed after Lloyd were approached in a more 'natural' way. I tried to strike up conversations in the same way that I would with peers (when I really want to hear their opinions!). Interview transcriptions revealed many leading questions. Some literature that deals with drawing information from people with learning difficulties suggests that leading questions are inappropriate. The reasoning behind this claim is the reported tendency of people so labelled to respond affirmatively to questions regardless of their content (reflected in the huge body of work in the 1980s by Sigelman and colleagues, e.g. Sigelman *et al.* 1980, 1981, 1982; for general points see also Orne 1962).

Simons (1994) and Booth and Booth (1994) argue that assuming acquiescence on the part of people with learning difficulties unquestionably presumes deficit. When people acquiesce, perhaps this is because they feel powerless. Perhaps the narrators in this study felt in control: a testimony to their involvement in self-advocacy. Leading questions or 'probing' are a necessary part of the exchange of information between two people (Taylor and Bogdan 1984: 98). In this sense, Oakley (1981: 58) suggests that acting as 'naturally' as possible in interviews is a condition under which people come to know each other. The better 'the chat' the more leading the questions (Tremblay 1959). Furthermore, the five narrators in this study did not simply acquiesce. Joyce Kershaw ignored or spoke over some of my queries. Anya Souza presented long anecdotes that kept questions to a minimum. Patrick Burke queried questions – 'Say that again' – and asked me to say a word that he couldn't: 'Vulnerable? That's right – that's the word.' Lloyd Page had obviously got sick of my grilling and stopped the interview by turning on the TV.

Anecdotes and opinions of narrators were responded to in a value-laden way. I hope this made clear my interest in what narrators had to say (see Masson 1990; Atkinson 1993b). Nevertheless, acting naturally has implications. Narrators' words were often reactions to my leading questions and value-laden responses. These 'natural exchanges' were used in constructing narrative. Consequently, my words may have unnecessarily littered the interview material that was later used for writing stories.

Unplanned situations occurred with Lloyd Page and Patrick Burke. At their interviews other people were present, affecting how their experiences were disclosed. Interviews can benefit from the presence of others (Walmsley 1995), though interviewees may not. Lloyd Page's mother gave her opinions and reminiscences. At other times she corrected and disagreed with Lloyd. I felt tense in the interview, anxious that she was talking over Lloyd. I felt less concerned on transcribing the interviews. Her words appeared only a few times and actually added to the many passages of text provided by Lloyd. In Patrick Burke's interview, one of his supporters was present throughout. The supporter sat in the office drawing up a poster and only spoke when Patrick threw a comment her way ('Do you know we haven't got the beds in our house yet?' 'Haven't you?' (supporter)), asked her questions ('What's that woman's name?' 'What's that word I'm thinking of?' 'Where's that place we went to last week?') or was down on himself ('I'm getting there slowly.' 'You're doing a great job'). Patrick used the supporter as a resource. I am certain that Lloyd Page also appreciated his mother being present and I was the one with the anxieties. However, her attendance at the interviews, like my dominant voice, inevitably led to dilemmas when Lloyd's life story was written (see below).

Part 2: Writing stories – researcher as storyteller

> If we wish to hear respondents' stories then we must invite them
> into our work, as collaborators, sharing control with them, so that
> together we try to understand what their stories are about.
>
> (Mischler 1986: 249)

Little has been written about the writing of life stories (Hatch and Wisniewski 1995a, b). In collaborative life story research the final draft of a life story is the narrative of both narrator and writer (Ferguson *et al.* 1992c: 299). Plummer (1983: 111) encourages life story researchers to:

> Get your subjects' words, come to really grasp them from the inside and
> then turn it yourself into a structured and coherent statement that uses
> the subjects' words in places and the social scientist's in others but does
> not lose their *authentic* meaning.
>
> (Italics added.)

Two questions can be posed to explore the position of narrator and writer in collaborative narrative inquiry. First, how does the writer construct the life story of the narrator? Second, to what extent do narrators become involved in the writing of their own life story? The first question resonates with Dexter's (1956: 10) demands for 'a sociology of those who study mental deficiency'. As Atkinson (1993b: 58) notes:

> There is, however, more to telling – and hearing – people's accounts of
> their lives and experiences than simply providing a forum. The role of the
> researcher, or listener, has a bearing on how stories unfold and what they
> are about.

Researchers have spent little time examining how they move from what they collect (e.g. interview transcripts) to what they tell (e.g. stories) (Plummer 1983). More time is spent considering how information is collected (Walker 1981: 157). Therefore, examining the hand of the researcher in the writing of stories would appear to constitute a useful exercise. The second question presented above takes on a particular slant in the case of life stories which are the creation of two minds working together (Whittemore *et al.* 1986: 6). Bertaux-Wiame (1981: 264) argues that social investigation is not a matter reserved for researchers. Accordingly, how can narrators become involved in the social investigation of writing their life stories?

A number of textual strategies were used that implicated the narrators and me in the writing of the life stories. These strategies are briefly presented below to show the origins of words and to highlight some of the decisions that affected the writing process. Narrators were sent drafts of their life stories, double-spaced, in a large clear font. The stages of narrative inquiry for each narrator were as follows.

- *Lloyd Page.* Lloyd and his mother made changes to the first draft. Together they rewrote a paragraph, typed up the changes and sent them back. The second and final draft was written and accepted.

- *Jackie Downer*. Jackie reviewed the first draft alone. Changes were discussed and made during a telephone conversation, producing the second and final draft.
- *Anya Souza*. Anya and I talked on the telephone about how to include a potentially libellous passage in her account. The first draft was then written and Anya wrote down various changes before sending it back. The second draft was written up, sent back and accepted.
- *Patrick Burke*. Some weeks after the interview, Patrick and I spoke on the phone about including his experiences of sexual and physical abuse in his story. He remained as certain as he had been at the first meeting: 'I want people to know.' Written and audiotaped versions of the first draft were sent as requested. Then I received a phone call from the police. They were investigating Patrick's claims about the abuse. As he was a key witness they were concerned that his story might be leaked. I phoned Patrick to tell him what the police had said, although he already knew they were going to approach me, and he agreed that they could see his life story. Police and a social worker visited me, read the story and asked for a statement about the interview. Afterwards Patrick was adamant that his experiences were publicized, so he asked that his name and the names of the staff were changed. Legally the police could have demanded to see the story even without Patrick's consent, but they allowed me to follow through the ethical procedures that I had outlined at the start. The final draft was sent on to Patrick. His real name is now used following the court case.

Turning interview transcriptions into stories is a difficult process. Writers face problems of contamination: first, when moving from the animated spoken word to the 'frozen text' (Fairclough 1992: 229; Sparkes 1994); second, when turning disclosures into stories (Plummer 1995). For Plummer (1983), how and why words are included in stories needs to be acknowledged. To include some words and exclude others may be seen as distorting the information people give. However, any type of qualitative analysis distorts the information received. Thematic analysis, for example, is especially harsh in the way it takes, bit by bit, from the experiences told by narrators. Similarly, decisions behind the writing of stories are arbitrary, open to personal preference and specific to a given time and place. However, considering some of the decisions acknowledges incidents of 'contamination'.

- *Including self-advocates' words: writing the spoken word and elisions*. First drafts were created primarily from a review of the five transcribed interviews. Words of self-advocates were cut and pasted into narratives as unaltered text. Initially, attempts were made to fill life stories with a sense of the spoken word (see, for example, Tony Parker 1963, 1990, 1994; Potts and Fido 1991; Booth and Booth 1994). Jackie Downer said 'People with learning disability', as opposed to 'People with learning disabilities', reflecting her accent. This was kept in. Anya Souza had a tendency to finish sentences with 'basically'. A few of these were added. However, Joyce Kershaw rejected these tactics when they were employed in the first draft of 'Danny's story' (see below). Consequently, less attention was paid to presenting the spoken word in the life stories of Anya Souza and Patrick Burke. Finally, elisions of material from different parts of an interview enhance a narrative's flow, style and readability.

- *Including my words: to summarize, for grammar and for meaning.* All narratives were filled with my words. First, they were added to summarize anecdotes and to keep the narrative concise. Summarizing started early on in Jackie Downer's interview through note taking. Second, my words were added to correct syntax and grammar. Here, the written word is focused upon and the spoken voice loses out. Third, words were added to the narrative to clarify meanings within stories. Fourth, my words were used to help the story along. Putting 'So then', 'After that', 'The next day' and so on aids narrative flow, provides elisions between anecdotes and starts or concludes sentences.
- *Including my questions/assertions and narrators' answers/responses.* Sometimes questions that I had asked that were verified in the interview were added. Leading questions were common, reflecting a conversational format. There were many leading questions and short answers in Lloyd Page's interview transcription, corresponding with my impatient style. By contrast, other narrators were given more time to respond in interviews, which led to more continuous prose in their transcriptions. A number of times, narrators responded to assertions that I made with (dis)agreement and elaboration. Certain styles of questioning emerge in the narrative as if they were the words of the narrator.
- *Including others' words: aiding or stifling the words of self-advocates.* Lloyd Page's mother's words ended up in his narrative. Her obvious impact on Lloyd's life justifies including some of her words. When she once 'corrected' Lloyd this problematized the inclusion of her comments in the text:

Danny: How do you find [doctors and nurses]?
Lloyd: I must admit that I've got a bit of a negative view of doctors, nurses and professionals.
Danny: Why though?
Lloyd: You see they don't listen to us.
Mother: They're beginning to.
Lloyd: They're beginning to listen to us . . . what do we need?

In the narrative this became: 'I must admit that I've got a bit of a negative view of doctors, nurses and professionals. You see, they don't listen to us, but they're beginning to listen – what do we need.' All but one of the words in the above passage came from Lloyd but his mother's influence on what he said is not conveyed. Subtle relational interactions are lost on moving from animated interviews to written texts (Sparkes 1994). Generally, Lloyd's mother stayed in the background, though when she did intervene she was encouraging. Interviews with two or more people will result in discussion, disagreement and consultation. People tell the 'same story' in different ways (Bertaux-Wiame 1981: 259–60). A limitation of collaborative life story work is that the stories of one narrator can take second place to the stories of another narrator, and then third place to the narrative construction of the writer. However, though the words of others (including the writer) permeate the narrative, in some cases these words are directly authorized by narrators. For example, the longest paragraph of unaltered text in Lloyd Page's annotated narrative came from him reading out part of a leaflet explaining a course that he had worked on.

• *Excluding words that do not help the narrative.* Sometimes long discussions gave rise to material that did not, in my opinion, help the narrative. Words were omitted when they were trivial (for example, the exact time a person got up for work; 'early in the morning' would perhaps suffice), repetitive (when the same information was repeated later in the interview) and too detailed (giving pseudonyms to people who helped start the group – 'two staff members' is ample information). Walker (1981) recognizes that while interviewers are concerned with the accumulation of information, writers aim for simplicity and economy. However, cutting words loses personal significance that narrators attach to anecdotes.

Some general strategies emerge in the writing of life stories, though trying to write a good story ensures that the process resembles an unscientific study by an untrained observer of an insufficiently understood problem (Parker 1963). Consequently, my attempts to write good stories had to be checked by narrators.

Part 3: Writing the final drafts – collaborative ventures

Each narrator reviewed my editorial role. Changes and additions were made, during telephone conversations or from written correspondence, as directed by narrators or as a consequence of negotiation.

• *Changing names, structure and tense and adding drama.* Narrators assessed the structure of their narratives. They suggested that paragraphs were moved or taken out, tenses were changed from present to past, quote marks were added to convey a sense of critical usage of a word ('respite care') and corrections were made. Narrators stepped into the writer's role in subtle ways. The seriousness of a situation was addressed, 'The custard thrown over me was "Boiling", not "Hot".' A sense of the drama of an event was relayed. My words were also discarded if they were unintelligible or factually inaccurate.

• *Re-evaluating old stories.* Biographies are in a constant state of becoming (Turner 1991: 232–3). Jackie Downer's thoughts on England People First had changed since our interview. We agreed to keep in her initial reservations but to show how her views had changed. Lloyd Page and his mother felt that a small paragraph of the narrative implied 'sour grapes' on his part. They offered an alternative account that was written up in place of the offending passage. Anya Souza felt that what was written about her mother telling her off was too forceful. We took out this passage and added another that was less emotive. Yesterday's stories were rewritten.

- *From private stories to public stories.* Participants were reminded that their stories would become public. For one narrator, keeping her name meant that some libellous comments were taken out. In discussions (three phone calls in total), the narrator felt that a certain passage could be seen as slandering the characters of a number of people, 'That's what they accused me of before, you know.' Consequently, a general passage of prose was written that captured her feelings but lacked detail and didn't name names.

Disabled researchers have called for empowering disability research (Abberley 1992; Oliver 1992, 1996; Morris 1996; Barnes and Mercer 1997). Central to the doing of empowering research is the notion of praxis. Lather (1986) and Oliver (1996), for example, assert that participants should be involved in assessing the method, analyses and effects of research. This has parallels with Guba's (1993: iv) concept of the 'hermeneutic-dialectic', where method and results are built upon and through one another. The end product of praxis is when research 'empowers not only the researcher but also every individual in these contexts' (Erlandson *et al.* 1993: xviii).

In this study, collaborative narrative inquiry has some parallels with empowering disability research. At first, narrators disclosed experiences to a writer who became the storyteller. Then, when the first drafts were given back, narrators addressed how their experiences appeared as written stories. This method appears to make links with Lather's (1986) 'fundamental point' about empowering research: the promotion of self-reflection and deeper understanding of the research situation by the research subjects. However, whether or not the five narrators felt empowered by their involvement in the research is a difficult question to answer. Neither were their lives changed markedly by their involvement nor were they consulted about the links made between their stories and wider issues (Chapter 6), unlike recent studies which have explicitly attempted to consult people with learning difficulties in the stages of analysis (P. Mitchell 1997, Stuart 1997; Mitchell 1998). Perhaps collaborative life story research injects only one consideration into the empowering disability research paradigm. As Sparkes (1994: 180) puts it, 'There is a need for researchers to move beyond paternalistic notions of "giving" voice, towards a view of life story as an expression of solidarity with those who share their stories in the hope of creating individual and societal change.' Actually getting people with hidden lives into the research context may constitute the first step of praxis-oriented research (Ferguson *et al.* 1992c: 299). While all narrators took up the challenge of narrative inquiry, one narrator challenged the collaborative aspect of the research.

Part 4: 'Give us a say, Joyce!' The tale of a research relationship in narrative inquiry

Most time was spent face to face with Joyce Kershaw out of the five research relationships. She is the only one with two stories in this book: one that I wrote (Danny's story, Appendix 2) and the other that she wrote (Joyce's story in Chapter 5). As she put it, 'Do you know I'd been thinking about writing my story for years. It was you who made me do it – you got me so mad.' Stages involved in the writing of the two stories constitute stories in their own right. Around the time of writing 'Danny's story', I was trying to write how narrators spoke. For Joyce, in went phrases such as 'Oh they were' and 'Yer knows'. Writing was easy. Long passages of prose were cut from the transcript and pasted into the draft narrative. I thought I was letting Joyce speak to the reader as she had to me. A week after receiving her story through the post Joyce phoned me at home. She was not happy with the story. At our next meeting I read aloud what I had written. Joyce was unhappy about my writing style and asked for the first draft to be rewritten. I thanked Joyce for spending so much time with me. 'That's all right, thank you for listening to me', she replied, 'but when you're writing my story Danny – use your imagination.'

Back to the drawing board. Joyce had identified a number of problems with the first draft. My attempts to have her talking to the reader through the narrative had failed. 'It's difficult to read', she told me. There were occasions when Joyce felt that the text had not quite conveyed the significance of some of her experiences. Over the next two weeks I rewrote the narrative. On completion I felt rather pleased with myself. Together Joyce and I had written what I considered to be an illuminating life story. We had shared responsibilities. Joyce had also strengthened my position as researcher and improved my writing. In reflecting on phenomenologically grounded research, Heshusius (1987) acknowledges that: 'Research is exceedingly demanding . . . it requires one [the researcher] to be deeply interested in the lives of the persons one wants to understand . . . This approach to research requires *investment of oneself*' (in Craft 1987: 43; italics added). In addition, narrators themselves have a vested interest in the presentation of their own stories. Left at this stage of the writing process, I believed that I had reason to view the research relationship as relatively collaborative, perhaps even empowering. Joyce and I had developed a similar research relationship to the one Sparkes (1994: 170) had with a narrator: 'What might have been defined as an impediment (our differences) in terms of the development of collaboration has been used as a resource to enrich the collaborative nature of the interaction.'

The story stopped here for four of the narrators. With Joyce Kershaw there was a further twist in the research tale. I had posted the second draft to Joyce some days before we met up in a local café. As Joyce came in from the cold, she greeted me with a whack around the head from her scarf. 'I'm fed up with you', she said with a glint in her eye, 'I thought blow it – I'll write me bloody own.' She produced my story from her handbag, and placed it on the table. I turned over the bound sheets and saw that she had handwritten her own story on the back. 'There's twelve pages in all, I wrote it over the weekend.' 'That's great', I acknowledged. 'You writing your own.' I surveyed her story. It was marvellous. But what did she reckon to mine? Joyce told me that she had only read the first few pages and found that certain parts were 'not quite right', and she still did not approve of the narrative style: 'If you write it, then you've got to write it like *I do.*' I asked Joyce what she thought we should do with the two stories. I told her that she could do whatever she wanted with mine; still use it, use bits of it or get rid of it altogether. I reminded her that there were things she had told me in the interview that were in my story but absent in her story. She replied: 'Well, use mine and add bits from your story but *write it like I would.*' I told Joyce that I couldn't write like her. I could try but ultimately it would still be my story. She thought for a while and then suggested, 'Okay, I tell you what. Put your story first – "Danny's story" – then "Joyce's story" after it.' This seemed like a fair compromise. I then asked her, 'What would you like to tell the reader?' Joyce's answer now appears as a statement presented before her life story in Chapter 5.

I had to talk with Joyce about including my story in the book. Joyce shifted the locus of power from researcher to participant, then back to me again. My role was clarified through our discussions. However, following Sparkes (1994: 169), my assumption of the need for a collaborative relationship underscored my perception of Joyce as disempowered, disregarding her power to determine the nature of the relationship. Plummer (1983: 106) grandly asserts that life story researchers need 'to turn to the tools of the novelist, poet and the artist'. However, to paraphrase Joyce Kershaw, narrative inquiry may benefit further by supporting narrators to 'write their bloody own stories'.

Analysis of life stories

Chapter 6 explores what the life stories reveal about the lived experience of self-advocacy. However, the position of analysis in narrative research raises controversies. 'In the course of the critical review of the interface between life events and their personal interpretation, the researcher comes to understand the individual in a way that the individual him or herself probably cannot' (Whittemore *et al.* 1986: 7).

First, let us examine the pro-analysis camp. The meanings of a narrative arise out of the interaction of story, storyteller and audience (Reason and Hawkins 1988: 86). What audiences do with stories is often unclear. Consequently, an argument may be made for analysis that points out to readers themes within stories. Goodson (1992) suggests that analysis should increase the wider benefits of narratives by opposing unsympathetic, conservative or hostile readings. Analysis attempts to throw into sharp relief a range of structural constraints that shape narrators' lives (Sparkes 1994: 165). The emic view of the narrator and the analytical and reportorial skills of the researcher are combined to draw out broader socio-structural, cultural, political and theoretical points (for example, see Levine and Langness 1986: 192–205). Drawing out points of convergence in a number of stories shows the relevance of a few accounts to many similar others (Denzin 1970, 1992). Stories cannot stand alone (Kidder and Fine 1997). Analysis strengthens stories. However, in the other camp, some contrasting arguments are presented: 'The problem of analysis is hence the extent to which the researcher progressively imposes his or her "theory" upon the understandings of the participant' (Plummer 1995: 61).

If stories constitute 'the perfect sociological material' (see Thomas and Znaniecki 1918–20; Shaw 1931) then why analyse them? Analysis theorizes over the stories of oppressed people, takes away ownership and places abstract interpretations on personally significant stories (Freire 1970). Simone Aspis (1997), formerly Campaigns Officer for People First London, argues that when researchers draw conclusions from the stories of people with learning difficulties, then stories become secondary to researchers' 'expertise' (see also Whittemore *et al.* 1986; Goode 1992). The subversive character of stories should not be underestimated. As people rewrite their own stories this con-stitutes an important political step forward (Williams 1989: 225; Humphreys *et al.* 1990), as narratives extend each reader's sense of what it may mean to be human (Turner 1991: 230). Allport (1947: 40) argues that social progress may come about through the employment of vivid stories of personal experi-ence – just as it came about through socially orientated novels of the order of *Uncle Tom's Cabin*, *Oliver Twist* and *The Grapes of Wrath*. For Bertaux (1981b), life stories constitute an excellent discloser of underlying socio-structural relations and clarify decontextualized abstractions of structuralist theories (Sparkes 1994: 178). Here analysis is viewed as an unnecessary preoccupation of researchers.

> The best stories are those which stir people's minds, hearts, souls and by doing so gives them new insights into themselves, their problems and their human condition. The challenge is to develop a human science that more fully serves this aim. The question then is not, 'is story-telling science?' but 'can science learn to tell good stories?'
>
> (Mitroff and Kilman 1978: 83)

The arguments presented by both camps are accepted in this book. Life stories stand alone in Chapter 5 and can be viewed without reference to Chapter 6, which explores my reading of what I think can be learnt from the stories about being in self-advocacy groups. The nature of my commentary is twofold. First, analysis is story-driven. Themes that emerge in stories will be used to make sense of the lived experience of self-advocacy, in turn high-lighting points in the literature associated with self-advocacy and the social model of disability. Second, this literature will be used to highlight anecdotes in the life stories.

Self-advocacy groups in action

Part III moves on from addressing the impact of self-advocacy group member-ship upon life worlds. An appraisal of self-advocacy turns to how self-advo-cacy groups work, how they are organized, what processes occur, what support is offered and what self-advocates get out of involvement. While the life stories are of members of People First groups, a turn to action embraces four groups that capture diversity of organization and typology in the movement. Ethnography was chosen to access the qualitative richness of group dynamics.

Ethnographic study has been used to examine the processes and actions in various social contexts (Edgerton 1967; Edgerton 1976, 1984a, b; Marsh *et al.* 1978; Spradley 1979). Ethnography is a useful technique for discovering beliefs, practices and meanings within a culture. Social settings can be seen as having cultures – a set of traditional ways of acting, feeling and thinking (Edgerton 1984b: 501). To get at these cultural artefacts, ethnography employs a whole host of qualitative methods, including participant observation (Marsh *et al.* 1978), in-depth involvement (Edgerton 1984b), interviews (Spradley 1979) and story collection (Angrosino 1994). In this book, the ethnographic project relied mainly on participant observation and qualitative description in field notes, although group discussions were conducted later. The form of observational method adopted in ethnography requires interaction with a social group, becoming part of the group's processes, to understand the symbolic nature of meaning within social action (Sidell 1993: 109). The strengths of ethnography are clear.

- *A bottom-up and grounded appraisal.* The ethnographic study in this book aims to ground understandings of self-advocacy in the actions of insiders with learning difficulties (Becker 1963). Ethnographers attempt to grasp the native's point of view, their relation to life and their vision of their world (Edgerton 1967: 84; 1984b: 498; following Malinowski 1922). This involves getting to know people by being there, alongside them, during ordinary days, to try to capture their experiences at first hand (Atkinson 1993b: 59). Corbett (1998) describes ethnography as an immersion within the deep culture of a social group that attempts to find hidden treasures and submerged dangers. In theory, ethnography is committed to representing the actions of insiders. Ethnography has been used in studies that have tried to ground their analyses in everyday realities of social groups (e.g. Lincoln and Guba 1985; Erlandson *et al.* 1993). These studies can also be seen as examples of 'bottom-up' research (Atkinson and Williams 1990). According to Spradley (1979), ethnographic study aims to observe behaviour, but goes beyond it to inquire about the meaning of behaviour. The artefacts and natural objects of a culture are described but also considered in terms of the meanings that people assign to these objects. These 'grounded theory' analyses start with data and remain close to data (Glaser and Strauss 1967; Lofland 1971; Charmaz 1995). Moreover, emotional states are observed and recorded, but the ethnographer goes beyond these states to discover the meaning of fear, anxiety, anger and other feelings to cultural members. In theory, then, ethnography's links with grounded theory and bottom-up analyses fit the aims of examining self-advocacy in action from the inside.
- *The study of 'new social movements'.* Ethnographic study appears to lend itself to the study of new or marginalized cultures. First, ethnography provides a

technique for studying those groups that in some ways run counter to the larger institutional culture (Edgerton 1967, 1976, 1984a; Edgerton and Bercovici 1976). Understandings of action 'known' in dominant institutional practices may be reappraised through immersion in settings that are different, other and subversive. Second, ethnography appears to suit the study of 'new social movements', wherein we could place self-advocacy, as part of the 'new' disability movement (P. Shakespeare 1993; Bersani 1996; Campbell and Oliver 1996). Knowledge cannot only illuminate the lived experience of progressive social groups but also be illuminated by the struggles that occur in these groups (Lather 1986: 262).

- *Ethnography and empowerment.* The ethnographic enterprise addresses a number of issues associated with empowering research. Walker (1981: 148) suggests that people rarely emerge from studies as people with their dignity intact. Proponents of the social model of disability have drawn attention to research that is grounded in the experiences of disabled people (see Chapter 3). Ethnography appears to offer a method for considering participation and praxis. First, gaining access to new cultures requires couching research aims in accessible ways that are appropriate to that culture: participatory methods (see Bashford *et al.* 1995; DIY Theatre Company and Goodley 1999; Goodley 1999c). Second, being let into a culture for an extended period of time increases expectations of reciprocity where participants get something out of research (see Reason 1988, 1994; Reason and Hawkins 1988). In-depth involvement requires a reframing of the research exercise (Schatzman and Strauss 1973).

- *Reflexivity.* Ethnography requires outsiders to formulate understandings of insiders that are in tune with the interests of the research population as well as those of the researcher (Peberdy 1993: 54). Consequently, Halfpenny (1984: 3–8) suggests that researchers should show how their interpretations are bound up in the study of a culture by detailing descriptions of activities, verbatim accounts of talk, key illustrations of their interpretations and a chronology of research experience. In doing so, a reflexive account can consider in some ways the interplay between the researcher's subjectivity, experiences in the culture and the analyses that are made.

The in-depth qualitative richness of ethnography also creates some dilemmas.

- *Seeing what you want to see.* The hallmark of ethnography and grounded theory consists of the researcher deriving his or her analytic categories directly from the culture under investigation, not from preconceived concepts or hypotheses (Charmaz 1995: 32). Theories, models and typologies must be teased out of an immersion within a social grouping (Harré 1981; Bannister *et al.* 1994: 74). However, as Glaser and Strauss (1967) pointed out, qualitative methods are impressionistic and unsystematic. All descriptions are analyses. As method and analysis work from one another, in a hermeneutic-dialectical fashion (Erlandson *et al.* 1993), the researcher's own analytical ideas become tangled up in description and analysis. Consequently, researchers may only see what they want to see. For example,

Gerber (1990) appraised Edgerton's (1967) ethnographic study of people with learning difficulties in institutions (see also Edgerton 1976 and Edgerton and Bercovici 1976 for follow-up studies). While acknowledging Edgerton's compassionate appeals for reassessing how institutions stigmatized 'the retarded' [*sic*], Gerber (1990), along with Luckin (1986), suggests that Edgerton's naturalistic view of 'retardation' lurked behind the stories of those he presented. Consequently, the resilience of those who had been institutionalized was only partly highlighted because Edgerton's analytical framework failed to recognize the socially constructed nature of learning difficulties. During ethnography I saw things that I did not expect to see. However, as much as I tried not to place *a priori* concepts on to the data, my subjectivity directly affected the ethnographic findings. For example, Chapter 8 tries to make sense of advisors' support as interventions or actions which can be seen as reflecting discourses of disability. I had started to formulate this analytical framework during my involvement with groups. As much as I made conscious efforts not to, my observations were in part directed by this framework. Schatzman and Strauss (1973: 99–103) acknowledge that ethnographers will inevitably combine 'observational notes' (the who, what, when, where and how of human activity) with 'theoretical notes' (interpretations, inferences, hypotheses and conjectures) and 'methodological notes' (the timing, sequencing, stationing, stage setting and manoeuvring of research). Indeed, they go further and say that the 'model researcher starts analysing very early on in the research process' (p. 110).

- *Only seeing what groups want you to see.* Beresford (1992: 24) approached a self-advocacy group to ask if they would help him with a handbook on user involvement. One member was bothered: 'If we talk about how we do things, if that's written down, then services who want to will know how to block us.' Participants may 'act up' for observers so as not present themselves in a bad light (Orne 1962; Swain 1995). Such impression management is understandable if Barton's (1996) observation is a fair one – that most sociological appraisals tend to look for failings in the social world. Observations are further problematized when they are a researcher's biased observations of unnatural and contrived behaviour. Moreover, complicated events are often simplified when observations are written up as field notes (Walker 1981).

- *Ethnography changes contexts.* When social contexts become research contexts they are changed (Parker and Shotter 1990). Researchers become part of the cultures that they describe, and researcher and participants interact to produce the data (Charmaz 1995). One example of this in my ethnography was when I tried to take a 'back seat' in meetings but was seen by a number of self-advocates in one group as a 'helper'. While I continued to try to negotiate myself a position outside the context, I was actually part of the context. Ethnography's involvement with a social context changes it into a research context, making the representation of naturally occurring behaviour seem impossible.

Questions remain over whether or not ethnography can fully grasp the meanings and processes inside self-advocacy groups. While I accept the limitations, ethnographic study provides a vehicle for *my* appraisal of a number of groups, at specific times, in particular contexts, in an attempt to capture authentically some of the experiences of a few self-advocates and their supporters.

The four groups

The four groups at the centre of ethnographic study in this book reflect some of the different ways in which self-advocacy groups are organized. They are not, in the positivist sense of the word, 'representative' of the movement. Only so many groups could be studied in an in-depth, involved and qualitative manner over 14 months. Attempts were therefore made to capture some of the specificities of self-advocacy. Specificity acknowledges the mutable nature of social life (Hisada 1991; Bannister *et al.* 1994) and recognizes that research studies are of a particular time carried out in specific contexts. I aimed to build up rapport, familiarity and trust. Four groups appeared manageable. It was hoped that the four groups in this study would provide rich enough specific contexts to 'Analyse the specificity of mechanisms of power, to locate the connections and extensions in order to build, *little by little*, a strategic knowledge' (Foucault 1983: 197).

As Chapter 2 outlined, two main areas of self-advocacy have been used to distinguish between groups. First, group types have been identified that differentiate groups on the basis of their accountability to and relationship with other organizations. These include independent, divisional, coalition and service-based types (Crawley 1982, 1988, 1990, McKenna 1986, Simons 1992, Dowson and Whittaker 1993). Second, the status of advisors has been used to discriminate between groups. Advisors can be independent, service-based or have ties with divisional or coalition groups, and may offer their services voluntarily or as part of their jobs (Hanna 1978; Worrel 1987, 1988; Clare 1990; Sutcliffe 1990; Sutcliffe and Simons 1991; Simons 1992; Dowson and Whittaker 1993). Four groups were chosen from responses from a postal survey (see Goodley 1998c) because they reflected various group types, encompassed different advisor positions and were accessible in terms of distance:

- *The 'Centre Group'*. A day centre's working group that aims to represent all users' concerns. Ten members are voted in by centre 'users' and meet weekly for two hours in a room in the centre. Support comes from a paid staff advisor who supports the group as part of her job. A number of members also attend a local monthly advocacy development project meeting. Financial support comes from the centre. No major funding is required for transport or the hiring of rooms because meetings are centre-based.
- *The 'Social Group'*. Meeting at a local social club for two hours every three weeks. Advisors with independent and service affiliations voluntarily

support 15 members. Advisors include a key worker, a centre manager, a retired social services employee, an advocacy project development worker and an employee from the local train station. The group functions as an informal get-together, though a number of members also attend conferences, workshops and formal 'consultation' meetings with local authorities. The group is funded through small-scale fund-raising activities and 'handouts' from local businesses.

- *The 'Advocacy-supported Group'*. Meeting monthly in the premises of a youth club with support coming from a volunteer, independent of services, and two advocacy workers who support the group as part of their jobs. All 14 members recently lobbied the local council about the state of roads in their village. Members are also involved in a number of projects set up by the advocacy organization and pay 'subs' for the use of the room and carry out their own fund-raising.
- *The 'Independent Group'*. Boasting its own office. Funding comes from the county council, which offers the group as an alternative to local day centres. Three independent supporters are paid by the group out of funds to support between nine and 12 members. The group provides training programmes for a variety of organizations, which they get paid for. Separate management and executive committees meet up, though the office is open throughout the week as a 'drop-in' centre for people with learning difficulties in the locality. The group has links with organizations of disabled people.

These groups reflect some of the complexities behind the 'types'. For example, the Independent Group may on the surface be deemed an 'autonomous' type. However, the financial input of the county council and the way in which the group is offered as an alternative to day centres brings in 'service-based' affiliations. Generally, the four groups have apparently internal contradictions and overlaps of 'type' and 'advisor status'. It was decided that they would be useful collectives within which to examine the elaborate nature of self-advocacy in action.

May (1995) distinguishes between physical and social access. Physical access begins with initial contact and concludes with the beginnings of involvement. Groups were contacted (between September 1995 and April 1996), referring to telephone numbers obtained from a postal survey, and introductory meetings were arranged. All group contacts (three of which were advisors, one a self-advocate) consulted group members before agreeing to our first meetings. Social access involved prolonged and continuous negotiation of my involvement with groups. Three groups addressed my interests at the first meeting. Two found places for me on their agenda and another gave over the floor to a self-advocate who presented a 20-minute introductory account of the group. For the Social Group, it was not until the third meeting that I decided that I should formally and publicly introduce myself to all members, as opposed to a few individuals.

Groups were reminded of the postal survey they had responded to and told of my ambitions to 'sit in' on groups to see how self-advocacy groups work. The main reasons for my interest were disclosed (to understand self-advocacy and to publish my findings), as was my involvement as a volunteer to a self-advocacy group. I explained that I wanted to take a back seat and learn from them about self-advocacy in action. This back seat role was open to change and renegotiation. To facilitate access, members were presented with and taken through an introductory booklet that combined prose and pictures (Appendix 3). Members appreciated the use of pictures because it appealed to 'non-readers' and was similar to the format that they use in their minutes. Others picked out illustrations as we went through the booklet: 'Is that you Danny?' 'Is that you pointing to us, the group?' Some members asked me to go through the booklet with them individually at later meetings. In addition, attempts were made to use terms chosen by groups in the introductions. This is what Goode (1992: 208) terms 'emically informed language', like 'talking out' if the group used that instead of self-advocacy, or 'supporter' instead of advisor.

Members and advisors were instrumental in tackling the initial stages of social access. For example, after going through my introductory spiel, the chairperson of the Centre Group (a self-advocate) told me, 'Thank you Danny. You can go now. It was nice to meet you as a friend and a person.' I was then led out of the room so that the group could decide whether or not they wanted me to attend subsequent meetings. At another introductory meeting a chairperson asked everyone to introduce himself or herself. I left a quarter of an hour before the end so that the group could have a chat about my research.

The amount of contact time with groups depended on how often groups met up and what they deemed a fair amount of involvement. Two groups met for two hours every three weeks (Social and Advocacy), one got together weekly for two hours (Centre) and the other had one main designated drop-in day per week, along with monthly executive and management meetings (Independent). Travelling to groups was time-consuming – a six-hour round journey (including meeting time) was required for the Social Group. Groups were spread over three counties and four separate local authorities were represented in the services used by self-advocates in this study. Contact time was as follows:

- *Centre Group* (April 1996 to November 1996). Six meetings were attended and contact was had with group members outside of meetings in the centre. Contact time was around 24 hours.
- *Social Group* (November 1995 to January 1997). Nine group meetings, one 'user consultation meeting' called by the local authorities (attended with a number of group members) and time spent with members before and after meetings. New Year 1997 was celebrated at a local restaurant. Total time was around 27 hours.
- *Advocacy-supported Group* (May 1996 to November 1996). Six meetings were observed, time before and after meetings was used to chat with members

and the local advocacy project AGM was attended along with a number of the group members. Contact time was 18 hours approximately.

- *Independent Group* (November 1995 to September 1996). Eight trips to the group's office where various members dropped in. Time spent with members preparing agenda, discussing training and chatting about this and that. Trips out shopping, to the bank and helping the group to move into new office premises. One executive committee meeting was also sat in on and a meeting was held with representatives from the county council with members of the executive committee. Contact time was approximately 23 hours.

Observational field notes were made after all meetings (audiotaped and written up). These consisted of reflections, personal feelings, hunches, guesses and speculations, as well as observations and vignettes of actions and conversations (Schatzman and Strauss 1973: 99–103; Bannister *et al.* 1994: 23). Such qualitative description and analysis highlighted a number of concerns associated with my subjectivity. This emerged as a separate point of analysis (see Goodley 1999a, b). In addition, groups' own documents were gratefully received. These included outlines of group histories (all groups but Centre), group constitutions (Social and Independent), minutes (all groups), details of local advocacy forum (Centre), invitations to and details of outside meetings (Advocacy and Social), training documents and introductions (Independent).

Group discussions were carried out in order that members had their say and formally to close my involvement. Introductions to group discussions were made with reference to a booklet and a list of questions and prompts was brought along to sessions. Sessions varied in time from 15 minutes (Social Group) through to two hours (Centre Group). Three of the group discussions had advisors present, the Centre Group had only members. Written notes were taken and later written up, combining pictures and prose, as feedback reports for each group. These were read through by groups and advisors, and alterations were made, producing the reports presented.

Finally, groups had a number of requests. The Independent Group had been asked by their main funding body, the county council, to find an independent person who could evaluate its project. The group put my name forward. I attended a meeting along with representatives of the county council and the Independent Group's chair, vice-chair and a supporter. Later, I had another meeting on my own with one of county council representatives to talk about the evaluation report that I was to write for the group. The major source of the evaluation was members' comments gained at the group discussion. I was also asked by the county council to canvass the views of some organizations that have received training from the Independent Group. An evaluation report was written up and presented to the county council. The same report in a different format was sent to the group. Other requests included a rewrite of the constitution and introduction for the Social Group and, following discussions with the Advocacy-supported Group, a leaflet on voting was posted to all four groups.

Analysis of ethnography

Analysis is approached in three ways in order to make sense of the group processes in self-advocacy groups. Chapter 7 describes the dynamics of each group. Then, working from a grounded theory approach, ethnographic material obtained from each group is used to test out 12 points about 'self-advocacy groups in action' that emerge from previous literature and from the groups themselves. Chapter 8 delves more deeply and specifically into group processes by considering how self-advocates are supported in the context of the group by advisors and peers. With reference to the observational notes, the analysis becomes more theoretically driven as models of disability are employed to make sense of incidents of support observed in the ethnographic study. Finally, in order to address the subjective bent of these analyses, it was necessary to consider how the ethnographic exercise and my experiences as a supporter in a self-advocacy group informed subjectivity and analysis: 'If we are to understand the way that power operates within a particular context, we have to examine the detail of that context, and to interrogate our assumptions regarding the various power configurations' (Paechter 1996: 76).

Working from the presumption that one can have an *a priori* or *ad hoc* knowledge of another's culture is disputable. The 'knowing position' is complicated even further when, in contrast to informants, the researcher is not disabled (Barnes and Oliver 1997). One way of conceptualizing the position of the researcher refers to a gradual process of learning to know some things about informants; 'getting to know' if you like. This position is located in the ethnographic project of immersion within a culture and may be seen as anthropological by design. It is a process that with hindsight was a necessary part of my research. A major tool of anthropologists when they are attempting to understand another's culture is participant observation. As Malinowski (1922: 25) put it, the ethnographer attempts to grasp: 'The native's point of view, his relation to life, to realize *his* vision of *his* world' (Quoted in Edgerton 1984: 498). Immersion within the culture under investigation sensitizes the observer to the subtle rules, roles, social etiquette and tacit understandings that exist in that culture. Over time as one becomes more familiar with a given culture then one becomes more culturally aware. Yet the process of getting to know another is complicated and constantly ongoing. For Peberdy (1993: 50):

> Participant observation is the foundation of anthropological research, and yet is the least well-defined methodological component of our discipline. It involves establishing rapport in a community, learning to act so that people go about their business as usual when you show up . . . and to a certain extent participant observation may be learned in the field.

'Knowing' refers to an ongoing project of building a researcher subjectivity that learns from the experiences of people in the field under investigation. This project is one that resonates with my own research experiences. The 'field', for me, was constituted not only by the research contact with four research groups but also by my independent involvement as a volunteer to a self-advocacy group prior to, during and after the ethnography.

My experiences of self-advocacy played a part in how I interacted with research groups. These experiences also seeped into the stages of analysis and writing up. In the first year of my research I became involved as a volunteer to a self-advocacy group and this has continued to the time of writing (five years). The group has helped me to carve out some understandings of self-advocacy groups in practice and to appreciate the heterogeneous experiences of people with learning difficulties. My role as observer in the ethnographic study for this book was partly formulated through my experiences as a volunteer. Usher (1995: 50) notes that the very elusive nature of subjectivity makes it difficult for researchers to enter into a process of reflexivity. Identifying those aspects of subjectivity that shape research is a daunting exercise. Usher suggests that 'Because reflexivity is an integral and constitutive part of any research practice it need not be imposed in a direct and obvious way' (*ibid.*). While accepting that participant observation is often a messy, serendipitous and arbitrary process, a number of experiences as a volunteer affected how I saw, acted with and understood the four research groups. These experiences contributed to the building up of what I will term my 'researcher template'. It is to this template that I will now briefly turn.

Involvement as a volunteer was informative in the development of my observer role. After meetings I would make observational field notes (following Schatzman and Strauss 1973: 99–103) but backtrack and try to compare my notes with my experiences as a volunteer. My volunteer status may have meant that I was too close to the processes that I observed in the research groups – I lacked an 'objective' stance. Perhaps I was primed to see what I considered good and bad practice in ways that may have said more about my ideas of being a volunteer than my views of the research participants. My volunteer and observer roles combined in ways that were advantageous to the ethnographic project. A number of overlapping experiences come to mind, two of which are outlined below (see Goodley 1999a for a fuller account of this template, which outlines five points of analysis where my experiences as a volunteer and ethnographer combined to inform observation and analysis during the research with the four self-advocacy groups).

Recognizing individuals and stifling social structures

There are many different people in the self-advocacy group I am involved in:

> James is in his sixties now and walks with two walking sticks. He wanted to go to Tech and asked that the Centre lay on transport for him so he could go down and see his friends. Eventually his requests were granted and a taxi picks him up from the Centre to take him down to tech. Paul, like James, has spent a lot of his life inside group homes. He loves football and writes down the scores of each match every weekend. Witty and outspoken he encourages others to speak up for themselves.

He is waiting for a social worker to find him a house back in his home-town. Jean first came to a meeting last year but did not return for some months. The staff in her home would not let her walk to meetings on her own because they said she was not 'road-safe'. With the help of the group, following long-winded bureaucratic complaint procedures, she became a regular at meetings, getting in by taxi. Recently, however, she has not attended, apparently the staff are not waking her up in time. Over the last four months she has lost three stone in weight and has asked people not to tempt her with chocolate biscuits. Irene looks after her mother who is old and frail. She works part-time in the library and has done some reception work at the centre. She no longer comes to meetings because her mother gets upset when she leaves. Asif is the group's secretary and lives with his parents. He works at least six days a week, two of them on the market selling shoes. He is saving up for his holidays. Sophie is a lively and loud member of the group. She is cur-rently touring the county with her drama group presenting a show in which she is one of the dancers. This freedom of movement contrasts with her earlier experiences of life in an institution where she was made to wear weighted boots.

Like any social group the members described above have very different lives but also have some shared experiences. As I got to know more about them they allowed me to start 'getting to know' about disability on three levels:

- *Individuals*. I was reminded of the people that exist behind a label of 'learn-ing difficulties'. James, Jean, Irene, Asif and Sophie, people with learning difficulties, are far from constituting a homogeneous group (Whittemore *et al.* 1986). They are people first. Behind the social construction of disability individual lives exist.
- *Social structures*. I was sensitized to socio-political structures that stifle life opportunities by listening to the experiences of members shared at meet-ings. Their accounts allowed me to contextualize the theoretical and politi-cal explanations of disabling society offered in the literature of the social model (e.g. Oliver 1990). Their stories gave me a view of disablement in individual lives.
- *Resilience*. I soon came to recognize resilience in the face of adversity. People have rich experiences to reflect upon. Even when institutions, professional attitudes and societal discrimination threaten to prevent the emergence of lives – lives still go on. With this in mind I was reminded that labelled people are not passive recipients of oppression. They are active and resilient social members (Ferguson 1987; Skrtic 1995a, b, c).

The label of 'learning difficulties' would creep in and out of my way of seeing and continues to do so. Some stories were very similar to my own: watching the cup final, going out for a drink with friends, health worries, earning money to spend on holidays. Stories were told of getting jobs, becom-ing responsible, being creative, wanting to be heard and shouting up for rights. At the same time some stories were novel and alien to my own: people being put in a house with strangers, not being asked where they would like to live, prevented from going out because others think they are incapable and of archaic treatments in institutions. I was forced to see people having to shout up for their basic human rights, yet doing it none the less.

Disciplining cynicism

Schatzman and Strauss (1973: 110) assert that the 'model researcher starts analysing very early on in the research process.' Accordingly, I made a number of 'theoretical observational notes' from the early stages of involvement with research groups. Sometimes a rethink of my field notes revealed cynicism on my part. Take the following extract from my observations of a 'bad supporter': 'A supporter brought up the issue of service charges. Why they had to bring it up I am not sure because it didn't receive much attention. What about what members have to say?' (Social Group, second meeting).[4] A further look at field notes shows a rethink:

> Initially I was suspicious of the advisor introducing a discussion topic – what would the outside observer make of it? Dominant and intrusive, 'disempowering', but is this not a role of the supporter to bring along information?

A questioning narrative (me as volunteer) existed alongside the theoretical narrative (me as observer). I remembered bringing along some notes on the Disability Discrimination Act to 'my group'. I would hope that doing this for the group was not 'disempowering'. The interventions of the advisor in the Social Group were seen differently when I re-examined analyses with my volunteer hat on. Another extract shows a time when I thought I had identified a 'bad group': 'The group really functions just in terms of a social activity. People seem to just come along for a drink and a chat with friends. The Bill Worrels of the world would have a problem with this' (Social Group, first meeting). It makes me cringe to read these comments – '*Just* in terms of a social activity' indeed – as similar analysis could be made about 'my group': There is Carl who says nothing at meetings but still comes and Pam who likes to meet her friends and then go into town afterwards shopping. This critique of the group was re-assessed soon afterwards: 'But surely aren't members making friends? Integrating themselves? They are close. They go off and chat with each other, just like you would down the pub. Aren't these important parts of self-determination?' (Social Group, first meeting continued).

It would appear that the building up of a researcher template enhanced access and subsequent interactions with groups. My personal experiences allowed me to pick up on some of the subtleties and complexities of group dynamics. While ethnography demands learning from the culture under investigation it would be foolish to assert that researchers do not bring aspects of themselves to the research context. Indeed, the very doing of disability research that is aligned with a social model of disability requires researchers to take a stance – most obviously to be on the side of disabled people and so to document their perspectives, experiences and challenges to disabling conditions (Barnes 1997; Barnes and Mercer 1997; Moore and Goodley 1999). Perhaps as a product of these allegiances, I felt tensions in being part of members' lives and then leaving when the research ended:

> I reminded the group that the next meeting was my last. People said they would miss me. Sarb asked if we could go on holiday together. I said I couldn't afford it and suggested he talk to Chris about it. Karen asked when I'd be coming again. There was talk of the Xmas meal and I told her I'd love to come down. There's something really shitty about all of this. Just another temporary figure in people's lives. But let's not forget – do I mean that much? No!
>
> (Social Group, penultimate meeting)

> I feel sad. I come in for a few months, get involved, people open up, then I go. It doesn't feel right.
>
> (Advocacy-supported Group, last meeting)

Groups were told that their involvement was central to my attempts to try to understand self-advocacy and of my hopes that other self-advocacy groups would get something out of reading about them. In addition, group discussions were used to tackle the process of disengagement. In these sessions members were asked, 'So what do you get out of self-advocacy?' Afterwards, written and pictorially presented feedback reports of what members said were given back. Other reports, evaluations and group constitutions that I had been asked to complete were also finished and handed to groups. These steps allowed me to leave groups in a clear way. My involvement has had an impact on groups although I am sure not to the detriment of those involved. I hope that participants share the sentiments expressed in the comment by Rudi, the vice-treasurer of the Advocacy-supported Group: 'We've learnt a lot from you Danny and we hope you've learnt a lot from us' (extract from group discussion).

Conclusion

This chapter has introduced the methodologies, methods and analyses employed in this book to appraise different elements of self-advocacy. While not flawless, the life stories and ethnography are considered to be useful tools for examining the contemporary self-advocacy movement, the impacts of self-advocacy group membership on life experiences and the process in self-advocacy groups. The next part of the book turns to narratives of self-advocacy.

Notes

1 For some useful discussions see *Disability, Handicap and Society* (1992, Special Issue, 7(2)), Barnes and Mercer (1997) and Moore *et al.* (1998).

2 Recent studies that have utilized resources such as photographs and personal documents to help to elicit storytelling include Taylor and Bogdan (1984: 91), March (1992) and Minkes *et al.* (1994).

3 Following Barnes (1994), Simons (1994) and Walmsley (1995), the booklet introduced the research(er), and explained how informants were contributing to the writing of a book and what would happen to participants' disclosures (life stories in book and published papers). Also explored was what both parties would get out of research publication, copies of life stories for informants and hopes for publication.

4 Unless otherwise stated, quotes are taken from observational field notes recorded after each session with the four groups.

 PART **II**

LIVING SELF-ADVOCACY

 **5**

Five life stories of 'top self-advocates'

This chapter presents the life stories of five top self-advocates. Four of the stories are collaborative efforts between me and their narrators. Joyce Kershaw wrote her own story, which is presented in this chapter, while our collaborative effort is presented in Appendix 2. I hope the fluency of the stories comes through, reflecting a joint effort between myself and the narrators. All narrators agreed that these narratives authentically captured a selection of their experiences that others may read.

Jackie Downer: 'Ask self-advocates'

Jackie is in her early thirties but already an experienced and well known self-advocate. She has worked as a self-advocacy development worker since 1990 and is involved with many organizations, workshops, research projects and service users' forums. She is a central figure in the Black People First movement. At the time of being interviewed she lived with her mother near to her office but was looking around for her own place. Jackie sees self-advocacy as a diverse phenomenon and encourages others to value the differences among people. Self-advocacy can mean different things to different people. For her it is linked to her experiences as a black woman. This is Jackie's story.

From school to the library

I was in special schools up to the age of 16. Funny buildings, you were *labelled* as soon as you got there. You should have a choice, you should be able to go to normal schools with support. I didn't then. No motivation, no exams, put you down, embarrassed, no positive things about it. Afterwards I went to college and was there for five years. That made you grow up, a 'slap in the face', no one tells you about the stresses you have when you leave school. You feel isolated and you get depressed but at least you're not going mad watching TV 24 hours a day. God bless college. I changed colleges because I couldn't get a job, not even basic stuff like shop assistants, rejection upon rejection. It starts to make you feel small. I stayed at home and was depressed for a year. I wanted a job. I thought about myself as a black woman with learning difficulties. People look at your disability and not you as a person – that's a common experience. I didn't like the term mental handicap and still don't. A lot of people still use the term but I don't like it. It's like the word 'nigger', it puts up a barrier against you. The term mental handicap is still used in a lot of policy and lots of professionals still use it. People want to keep it in policy because it gets them money. It says these people are poor. Like MENCAP they used to use 'mental handicap' – we used to call them 'MENCRAP'. I'm not mental, I've got a disability – that's more dignified. We've all got some kind of handicap and we all need some support especially when we get old. I prefer learning difficulties and learning disabilities. I'd choose both, they're as positive as one another. It's up to the person, it's up to the individual. Some people might not like to be called or labelled anything – I'm just me. You should ask the person.

Mum was strong. She was very protective because I wasn't like my brothers and sisters. She wanted to protect me more and it was hard for her to let go. Parents are very scared to let go of their children. Some parents *want to* but don't know how to – always looking at disability. Parents say, 'I want my child to die before I die'. They still have a hold on to you even in adolescence. My Mum found relationships hard. Parents think they don't know about sex – they find it hard to talk about things. It's harder even now because I'm grown up and I need a life. I sat down and talked with my Mum. I told her 'there's things I've got to do, I'm one of the lucky ones, others have more severe learning difficulties.' 'I'm 30', I told her. She's gotta let me go and she found it hard. Some parents won't want their kids to do things and they need to have their own support group.

Eventually I got a job in a library – It gave me confidence. Right place, right time. I was involved in a training programme, different organizations provided different jobs. I chose the library because it was an easy option – I couldn't handle working with kids, or parks in the winter. I was there for six years, bored after three.

Becoming involved in self-advocacy

I had no real involvement with self-advocacy. I used to help support other people with learning difficulties in evening classes as a volunteer. In 1990 I heard about the job I have now – 'self-advocacy development worker'. Advertised all over the place, it said that a person with learning difficulties was wanted rather than a professional. It said that the person would be looking at services for people with learning difficulties and supporting their choices and say in the services. I was desperate for the job. A teacher helped me fill in the application forms and I handed them in personally! I thought, 'I won't get the job.' The interview was two weeks later, I got there one hour early. When it was my turn I went in and five people were waiting. I was scared, some of the questions they asked I didn't know, and I told them 'I'm nervous'. They got back in touch with me two days later and told me I got the job. It brought tears to my eyes, it meant so much to get that job I was over the moon. Mum wasn't bothered, just pleased for me. People show love in different ways. She never cuddled me. She said, 'That's fine'.

Since then I've learnt a lot from so many people and done things I'd never dreamed of doing. I went to the 1993 International People First conference in Canada. It's beautiful and clean. It was a celebration for people with learning difficulties to get together. A really nice experience, people uniting from all different countries in the world. In July 1994 I went to Jamaica *and* India. The India conference, involving MENCAP and others, looked at services for people with learning difficulties over there. There are very little and the ones they have are inadequate. I worked with the Norah Fry Research Centre looking at services for black and ethnic minorities. We had a conference and a book came out but other people are getting the credit for it. I speak to professionals and some professionals are . . . professionals. Others are ace – they know where users are coming from. Some service managers are good, some bad. Some listen, some don't. We usually target ones that listen and want to change things. Some speak jargon, don't know how to speak to people with learning disability because they're doing paper work. We only see them when there's problems.

In my job I talk with people with learning difficulties about many things. Things they like about themselves, how they feel about each other and about coming to the group. Campaigning, training, conferences about themselves. We have workshops on leaving college, getting a job, being independent, relationships, parents, when to say yes and no. We set up parties, events, we go to pubs together and the church. And we produce a newsletter. People have changed so much. I would have done the job in my own time. It's great to work with people you know. You know where they're coming from. They give me strength to do that. You might get it wrong but you can try.

What self-advocacy means

People with learning difficulties sometimes don't know what self-advocacy means. Broken down it means 'speaking for yourself', 'communicating in other ways', but it's *personal*. For me it means that I can speak for myself. It means I've got a voice and even without a voice I can communicate in other ways. It means yes and no – most important – 'No, I don't want tea, I want coffee, I didn't want sugar' – all the things we take for granted. It means people must listen to me, I can take a risk, I can have a relationship, that can be hard. I can think for myself, I can go to the shop with support and if I need help, people can help me. I can cry if I want to cry. Take responsibility and make myself responsible. It means other things to other people. Linking it to myself as a woman, as a black person. Sometimes that can be hard if you've always been down, had negative vibes, that's important. My mother gave me strength to cope with life. My mum is a single black woman – she gives me strength. The Lord as well gave me strength. I believe in the Lord. Faith has helped – I'd be crazy by now, I can believe in myself only so much. Lord gives me strength. And friends are important to me as well. When you leave college you get cut off from friends, then what happens? Coping with bereavement, when you talk to someone about your feelings – that's part of self-advocacy.

Self-advocacy is a network of people supporting one another. You need a support network – am I doing my job in the right way? I need help. Everybody, even if you haven't got disabilities, needs support. What would I say to others who want to get into self-advocacy? I would say – this group is going. How do you feel? As people with learning difficulties, we're campaigning and this is great just for you to relax and say what you wanna say. We're not forcing you to come, but you can come if you want – talk about things from heavy to light things. You don't need to go over the top organizing pictures, theatres, parties, meeting with other groups or self-help groups. Basic stuff first and campaigning later *but* you don't have to. You can just chat – you don't get the chance in the centre or at home. People First is both self-help and politics at the end of the day – it's up to the person to decide. If I make a mistake, then support me. No wrongs or rights.

How to support self-advocacy groups

As a worker I know I have power to tell people with learning difficulties what to do. I can use it and abuse it. How I see my power as advisor, I need to look at. Workers can spoil members by being too caring. That's dangerous, they relax. Be careful about caring. Paid workers create problems. I've got more power, I know that, and I've got to be careful. I'm their own worst enemy sometimes, pushing too much and people need to go at their own pace. Advisors need to explain to groups – break it down and ask. The ideal advisor is someone who supports the group, keeps their mouth shut, encourages the group to do what they want to do, be independent. They're there to support, write down for people who can't, advise a little bit, sometimes don't advise. Try to work together to give help when self-advocates need help. I would prefer outside advocacy supporters because they have no involvement with services. The more independent you are the more free you are, but it really depends on the advisor. There are good supporters, good advisors but it needs to get better.

On the self-advocacy movement

Self-advocacy is the in thing now. If you're not speaking to users you're having problems. The movement is going from strength to strength and things are gradually happening but taking time. It's happening more in some places than others. The picture is good. Users are challenging, with support. Years ago policy-makers, managers did it, now they're scared. Users are getting more and more involved in different kinds of ways but cuts in education and support for groups will affect people with learning disability. People with mental health problems, children, people with physical disability get more support. People with learning disability get some support but not the same.

Everyone from the health minister to professionals goes to certain groups but they need to network with other People First organizations. Certain groups get mega bucks but they need to delegate to others. It's unfair if other groups want to have, say, a mini-conference and the chance to talk about things. With some groups everything is me, me, me – they think they can do everything. They need to network, need to share work. One or two groups can't do everything, if you think this you are treading on dangerous ground. What do I think of England People First? Who's England People First? Who are they? Who's in control? At the start I didn't know but now they're trying to get people with learning difficulties in control. Supposed to be people with learning disability. People with learning difficulties are in control when they delegate work among themselves. If one group does it, they're not uniting together, no network. There's always one People First group, one organization, taking the power – we need to share things out. Black People First? If you see one you tell me – no such thing. It was gonna exist but it doesn't. People need space and choice – black, gay men and women, children. I set up a black friendly group and it was stressful. People were saying 'Why can't we have mixed groups, what's wrong with us?' You can segregate yourself, people need to unite and segregating doesn't help the movement.

Postscript: words of advice

At the end of the day you've got to be yourself in the so-called movement. This is my experience. Every experience is totally different. And you need to go back and ask other self-advocates. I like others to tell me if what I'm saying is okay. You can't just go by my experiences, I've not got all the answers. Instead of reading about it, ask other self-advocates.

Lloyd Page: 'Go for it'

Lloyd was 36 years old at the time of being interviewed and a long-time member of the self-advocacy organization People First. He has been involved in projects for university courses, consultation with various committees and the production of many reports. His involvement with People First began in 1984 and he hasn't looked back since. Lloyd argues that self-advocates are 'adaptable', as shown by his People First group, where many opportunities are available to learn new skills. I first met Lloyd at his group's office. He was photocopying a report that he had co-written, evaluating local hospitals. He was keen to explain the many projects that he and his colleagues were doing and made me feel very much at ease. This is Lloyd's story.

From the centre to People First

I was in day centres for 17 years. In those places I didn't do a single thing. Everybody kept sitting around doing nothing, just sat on their backsides – *doing nothing* – like I was doing. We used to get 75 pence for a day's work in the centre – that's a pittance. You could say that things changed for the better about ten years ago, when I heard about People First from a couple of social workers at my centre. In 1984 I went to the first international People First conference which was held at St Mary's College in Twickenham. When I went to the conference it was hellish! I gave a speech to over 300 people – it was nerve-wracking. In the early days, self-advocacy and People First grew mostly in America, starting off in Washington DC and in '84 self-advocates came to England from different parts of America. At the conference the England people said that they wanted to start up a People First group, so we all said, 'Why not'.

I came back from the conference and helped set up a group. At the time our group was called People First and now there is another group which is a spin-off. There were over twenty people in the group at the start and I was link person there. I was also secretary for quite a while. At the start we'd meet in people's houses but now the group meets in a community hall that's let out once a fortnight – it's a regular thing. We would talk about transport, day centres, holidays and because we were losing our four pounds pocket money – the *pittance* that we used to get from the centre. Right from the start people were very chatty because they'd been given the chance to speak.

Around that time I also got information back from Twickenham. I had letters from all the other groups so I wrote to them. They told me that the next international conference was going to be in Canada. To get me over to Canada my mother and about four of her friends fund-raised for four years. They got £4,300 and that meant we could send four self-advocates and one supporter to Canada. When you're at these conferences you go and visit places and you go and have chats. I gave a speech and I also remember singing on the karaoke over there – this was videotaped by somebody but I haven't heard from them yet. I met lots of people, quite a load, some who I have kept in touch with. One person I met was Pat Worth – it was great because you listen to his life story and it's brilliant. I got involved with my present group ten years ago. I went down to their offices and I asked if there was any work and they said, 'Yeah, there's plenty of work for you to do'.

Why self-advocacy?

Why did I want to get into self-advocacy? Because it's a good thing to do – speaking up for yourself. Being in a group helps you to speak out. By speaking to people in the group it gives you the confidence to speak to other people. Sharing ideas you can get more out. Self-advocacy means that people with learning difficulties have a right to speak up for themselves. To see how they can express themselves in ways that people, members of the general public, can understand. Then you can start to think about what you're going to do and what you're going to say. At first it's difficult, it took me a long time but you need to gain confidence for yourself. You also need to believe in yourself, what you're saying and what you need to do. I didn't get the chance to do it before I joined People First – not a chance because I was stopped from speaking out. There wasn't anybody to listen to you and when I did speak out I was shouted down. Other reasons why I wasn't give a chance to speak out? Lack of community I think – lack of community, like neighbours. I'm quite lucky – I've got lovely neighbours, I feel that I've been more accepted into the community now more than I would ever be. That's not just because of the way I am. Right from the beginning Mum said that I had a place in this world and I have got a place. My mum and I, we went for it, we said that people outside had to learn about people like me. That I wasn't daft, I wasn't a danger, I am a human being – I'm just a normal person like all of them and I have a right to live in this community. Being in my church has also helped – the church accepted me. There was a bit of a debate going on if we wanted women priests or not – we voted against. I said, 'No women priests for us mate.' No way boy – no way hoosay!

Why learning difficulties?

I prefer the term learning difficulties – it's a better term. Why is it better? Because it's much nicer – we want to learn and *I like it*. I got the council to change the name. I told them that we weren't mentally handicapped, we were just ordinary people with learning difficulties, like members of the ordinary public. I also wrote to our Labour councillor and I gave them some strong words – phwoar! The councillor said, 'All right Lloyd, I'll put it to the council and I'll let you know in the next couple of days.' Well, he spoke to the council and he wrote back to me and I got the name changed. They didn't use mental handicap in centres after that. The same thing happened with MENCAP. They didn't want the label of mental handicap changed because they thought it would interfere with their fund-raising. Now MENCAP have called themselves learning disability – I don't like that term. Some people still use the old terms as well but that happened more in the old days when institutions were beginning to close down. If you ask people who have the label of learning difficulties they prefer it – and that's what it's all about – this is what it's all about and here we are.

Lloyd the self-advocate

People First has been brilliant for me. Get up, get washed, dressed, listen to some music in the morning, go to work as normal – do what you gotta do and that's it. In our office jobs are shared out. Typical normal day? Phone rings, phone rings *again*, chat to people, look at what jobs need to be done, photocopying, write letters, send things out – I'm sort of one of the administrators. I get loads of phone calls from universities and people enquiring about information. Once one project is finished another one arises. I take it in my stride.

I've worked with so many groups. Like the Central Council for Education Training and Social Work and I'm on the Equal Opportunities Committee. I'm working with the special investigations team up at MENCAP. They've asked me on board to do articles for their new magazine *Viewpoint*. Also I've worked with the Open University on the *Equal People* course. Let me tell you about it. This is from a leaflet about this course – 'It is for everybody, people with learning difficulties and carers. If you are interested in finding out more about learning difficulties then this is the course for you. You can work on your own, with a partner or in a group. It is written clearly and uses pictures, it uses videos and audio tapes – you don't have to read or write well to do the course.' Here's another bit about it, 'It shows people with learning difficulties as equal people' – we are equal people – 'It shows family and carers as people with needs, wants and lives outside their family. It shows the needs of paid staff and others who work with people with learning difficulties. It shows ways of working which give people with learning difficulties, staff and carers a better quality of life. It shows how people with learning difficulties, carers and staff are prevented from doing things and how they can change this. It shows how everybody can have more control and power over their lives. It shows how everybody can work together to plan and change things that affect their lives.' I'm going to do a five-minute stint about this course at a conference soon. I was on the course team and we put forward ideas – we just didn't want to be on the sidelines – another way of not being involved. I gave a presentation to the senior management team at MENCAP. MENCAP should use it – they need to know a bit more about us as well – now they have accepted us as people with learning difficulties.

I'm also involved with a day centre for people with learning difficulties to get them to speak up for themselves – the users. I'm working on a hospital project and I've taken some photographs of all the hospitals that I visited. I give talks at universities to doctors, nurses, professionals. I think that's important because professionals necd to learn about us, they need to understand us. I must admit that I've got a bit of a negative view of doctors, nurses and professionals. You see, they don't listen to us. But they're beginning to listen – what do we need? I talk to students and do lots of workshops on self-advocacy.

I've also been to the Houses of Parliament when I fought for people with learning difficulties' civil rights. That was around the time when Nicholas Scott was Minister for the Disabled – stupid man. I work for the Suzy Lamplugh Trust at the Home Office, see, I'm also a government official as well you know! No wonder my bedroom is full up with papers! If that's not enough, I've also appeared on the television a couple of times. I did a video for the police and it was shown on TV. I was made out to be a psychopathic murderer called 'David Mackensie'. There was the detective there – he was quite a nice person actually. Anyway I had to pretend to be picked up on the street, taken into a police station and put in a cell. They filmed me through the cell – it was excellent. There was a serious side though to the film as it showed people with learning difficulties being charged with something that they hadn't done. And it explained that now, if people with a learning difficulty are taken in by the police, they must now have an appropriate adult with them. Also I have done a video for London Transport (another Channel 4 production). They came up to see me at the day centre and they took me on the tube. They were filming how I'd react to tubes and to see how London Transport was helping people with learning difficulties. I also helped with a thing on London Transport for a magazine on accessible transport – that's how you can portray people with learning difficulties as they really are.

I've had an exciting life – I've enjoyed People First more than I did at the day centre because you do things all the time. I've done lots of things – I suppose there's not many self-advocates who could say they've been on the television twice. How do people react? I should say, 'Aye, aye jealousy will get you nowhere'! No it sounds like I get a lot of flak – it's only good fun. I think other self-advocates look at me and say, 'Blimey, he's done well for himself'. Do I think they see me as some kind of role model? Sometimes, yeah, sometimes. If anybody asked me any questions about a project they'll go, 'Oh, I think Lloyd knows' – they come to me. Now my Auntie Joan she calls me a 'gopher' – 'go for this, go for that'! No, seriously, my friends and family think me working for People First is really good. They say, 'Blimey, where's he off to this time?' It's been really quite fruitful. My mum has never stopped me at all – it's great – she's encouraged me right from the very start, she's backed me 100 per cent and I'm really grateful for that. I've got wonderful friends and a lovely family. Has it given me a purpose? Freedom of life – it's great. You know I have made so many friends and I've seen them come and go. The best friends I ever got were the friends at the office. I've got to know so many people and I've got to know a lot more things than I would've known.

On the movement

I've seen People First grow in ten years that I've been there and I'm one of the original ones that started it. It's grown in good ways and I think it's grown for the better. I think self-advocates have got the power to do what they want to do. I don't think there's anything that can stop that power. Self-advocacy is looking good – more stronger. Now with England People First I don't know what to think about it. A good or bad thing? You've got to weigh up the balance between England People First and the other groups as well. There's a question of money and if it runs out it's a difficult question to answer. I would like to see England People First getting in contact with groups – getting groups together. Our group is a much better set-up in all the groups really and it's much more central than others as well. We have got five paid supporters and ten voluntary workers. The self-advocates don't get paid but are given their expenses back. I cannot be paid because I'm on benefits. We need supporters for everywhere we want to go and the money we charge for supporting groups and carrying out workshops goes to the office. This all helps us to keep going. At first I did think we should be paid but this is not possible. I am really pleased to be part of all this so don't mind for not getting paid. In ten years time I'd like to go on to much bigger things, do some more work for universities and stuff like that.

Postscript: Words of advice

What would I say to other people with learning difficulties if they wanted to get involved with People First? One word for that, 'Go for it.' I'd say, 'Hey you, get out there and do your piece and I'm not gonna stop you.'

Joyce Kershaw: 'Raise your voice and not be frightened'

Joyce Kershaw is now a pensioner and founder member of her People First group. Her long-term involvement within the self-advocacy movement has led to her being widely recognized as something of an expert in the field. She was co-researcher and author of a groundbreaking study of services for people with learning difficulties by people with learning difficulties (Whittaker *et al.* 1993) and remains active within the movement. Outspoken and to the point, Joyce comes 'straight out' with her opinions. She asked me to write the following statement down:

> Danny wrote two stories. Joyce couldn't read the first and she didn't like the second one. Joyce kept pulling Danny up, so she wrote her own. You will see that I have been going over the things Danny missed. If there's anything that I have missed that I told Danny before he wrote his story, about the centre and other things, well I'm 65 and I just kept forgetting bits. As you read my story you will see that I keep going back over the old days, when I kept remembering little things. So I would like you to read both stories (Danny's and mine) but I think you'll think mine is better.
>
> (Joyce Kershaw, November 1996)

'My story' is presented in Appendix 2; Joyce's story is presented below.

Joyce's story

As far as I can remember, is when we came back to live on Northgate. I remember we used to have a grocery shop. I had to stop off school because of my fits. When the war came my brother Harry and my brother Dan were called up like a lot of both men and women. When there was an air raid we used to go in my Grandma Marsden's cellar, till it was all over. I also had to stop having piano lessons. When I was 13 or 12, my mother got a telegram to say my brother Harry had been taken prisoner of war. A week before we got the news, a gypsy asked my Mam if she wanted to buy something from her and my Mam said, 'I'm sorry but I haven't got any money.' The gypsy said, 'That's not true, you have some small pence, but you need it.' Then she said,

'But you're worried about something but don't worry you're going to hear some good news.' That's when we heard about my brother. Soon after that a lady came to our house. She said I had to go to this school near Liverpool. I didn't want to go but they said I had to go for my education. When I got there it seemed strange being away from home. There were two nurses and a matron. When morning came around, the night nurse woke us up at 5.00. Then at 5.30 we had to get up, get a wash and get dressed. Then make our beds, then we had to go into the little dormitory and make one of the girls' beds, all before matron came downstairs at 6 o'clock. When we'd done that we had to dummy the dormitories, they were heavy too, then we had breakfast. The first week I was there, I didn't like the porridge, it was like sludge. Also I never used to like the marmalade but I soon got to like both of them when they wouldn't give you anything else. I soon got hungry and began to eat anything they gave me. We used to play Monopoly, cards and pool, except for Wednesdays when we helped to bath the little ones. Then on Friday we used to sit round the fire and darn our stockings and if there was anything else to mend we mended them too. On Sunday we went to church. I used to be in the choir. At 14 I was confirmed.

I didn't have many visitors like the other girls had. Once every year we went home for two weeks then we had to go back. When I was 16 I left school and I came home for good. My first job was at Woolworths. My Dad went with me and he explained to the manager that I had fits and he told her I hadn't had one for two years. The manager was a lady and she said, 'Yes, you have a job, I don't mind helping people with learning difficulties.' That's where I met my husband. He was a cook in the army. He was walking around Woolworths and he asked me if I would go to the pictures with him because he didn't know his way around. He was from Oldham. We went to the pictures that night and he asked me if he could see me again. I said yes. When he went back off leave I wrote him a letter every night. I also got a lot of letters. When he came out of the army, he got a job baking. Every weekend we used to go off on the tandem. When I was 18 I was married. My husband was 20. We had a little house up the Paddock. I had a little job in a fish and chips shop. My husband got a job as a bus conductor. Then he got a job as a driver. We were married for seven years. Then he went off with my best friend. We had been friends since we were little.

When my husband left me, my mother and sister came up to see me and I went back home with them. I lived with my mother for a while. Then both my mother and myself went to live with my brother. We used to look after both my sister's two boys, the youngest was two the eldest was ten. We also looked after my brother's two boys, youngest four, eldest ten. My sister died when she was 34. I stayed with my sister for two nights before she died, so my brother-in-law could get some sleep, so he could go to work. Both me and my mother used to keep the house clean. I used to help her with the washing. We used to wash my brother-in-law's shirts and his two boys, and my brother's things and his two boys. We didn't have a washing machine then. We used to do all the washing in a tub, scrubbing board, scrubbing brush and wringing machine. My mother used to love baking and cooking. When she wasn't doing that she used to knit things for the boys. When she had done that she knitted me a bed jacket. She couldn't follow a pattern. She just made her own patterns up as she went along. I remember my Auntie saying to me, 'Your Mam was such a good cook, we used to go up when we knew she was making buns or cakes and ask if we could have some.' When it was Christmas my mother made some smashing cakes. We used to like scraping the dish afterwards. I used to love hearing my Mam talk about the old days when she was young. I could listen to them over and over again.

I went to hospital to have a cyst removed. When I came out my Mam was very poorly. My brother brought my Mam a bed downstairs. She wouldn't go in hospital. So three nurses used to come every day, but she wouldn't let them touch her. She used to say, 'I can do it for myself.' But after they had gone, I had to do it for her and make her bed. I used to sleep on a two-seated couch and I was up six or seven times a night. The nurses told me if I didn't stop and get some sleep I'd be gone before me mother. I used to weigh ten stones and I went right down to seven stones. After my Mam died I could hear her shouting at me for a long time, because while I was looking after her she used to always be shouting 'Joyce'. Even if I went into the kitchen or away, she'd shout my name over and over again. But before she died, she saw my eldest brother's boy get married and my brother Harry's two boys and my sister's boys.

My Dad came and took me to my aunt's because I wouldn't go out and I used to wear navy blue for a long time. My auntie used to take me out with her. We went shopping for some new clothes. Also I had my hair cut and permed for the first time. I used to go a lot to my auntie's. She lived in Batley. My brother used to take me and bring me back. I used to stay either two weeks or sometimes a month. I went on holiday with my aunties and uncles to Blackpool.

My Dad used to come over to see me every two weeks. Once when he was going back home, his legs let him down and he was in hospital for a long time. The doctors said he couldn't go back to living on his own. So my brother said, 'He won't have to, he can come home with me and I'll look after him.' So when he came out of hospital my Dad lived with us. My brother put him in bed in the other sitting room and he slept downstairs. My Dad had arthritis in his legs and in his hands. I had to put a cigarette in a holder that he had, then I would put it between his little finger and the other fingers. Gradually his hands got a lot better because he used to try and pick things up until his fingers straightened out a bit further.

Then I went to the SEC. The first day I got there I met Stuart. He lived with his Mam and Dad in Sheepbridge. He asked me if he could come to our house, so I asked my Dad. He said, 'Yes, if he wants to.' The next day I told him he could come. He got on with my Dad and brother. He used to come down every night then, except for Saturday and Sunday. Then I went up to his house for my tea. All his brothers were there with their wives and children. His mother used to go out helping an old lady because she wouldn't have anybody else.

That was after she had retired. I often thought about my Mam telling me about how her mother used to take in washing to help with the house keeping and when she went to school everyone had to stand in line while the teachers inspected their nails and their shoes. If they hadn't cleaned them they sent them back home to do so. Also she said children these days don't know when they're lucky. When there was a wedding or a party my mother used to give me sixpence and I went to see if there was any food left over. I used to come back with a big bag full of food. She also told me whenever she went out when she was a young lady she put on her best costume. When she came back home she went straight upstairs and changed into an old dress and put her pinafore on.

Stuart started going on holiday with my aunties and myself. Then one day my auntie said, 'Next year why don't you go on holiday with Stuart's mother, I bet she'd like that.' So when we got back home, we told Stuart's Mam what my auntie had said. The first holiday we went on was to Belgium. Then Spain, we went there twice. Then we went to Germany and to Amsterdam. The last place we went to was Italy. Stuart's father was poorly. He went in hospital and had one of his legs amputated. They wanted to amputate both but they said it would kill him. So that meant if they removed his second leg he'd die and if they didn't he'd die. Sometimes you just don't know what to do for the best. So after that he died. Two years later we went on holiday. Then the last time Stuart's Mam asked me, 'Where do you want to go this year?' I said I wasn't bothered and told her to pick somewhere. She said, 'I'd like to go to Italy.' I said, 'Well, that's all right with me.' But before she could make reservations to go she died and I haven't been on holiday since.

I remember when Stuart came to see me after he had been to town. He used to bring me two or three packets of cigarettes and a bag of fruit or chocolates. His mother used to give him £10 or £20. She spoilt him. I told her she'd be sorry some day. When Stuart was fostered he didn't get £10 or £20 a day, he gets either £8 or £10 to last him all week. He couldn't understand it at first. It took a while for him to realize that he couldn't have what his mother used to give him. Now, when he comes down to see me, I give him some cigarettes. His foster parents told me I hadn't to give him any. But I remember the days when I hadn't got a lot of money and he gave me cigarettes and other things. I don't forget things like that. My Dad used to pay for all my holidays that I went on with Stuart and his mother. One year, near Christmas time, my Dad was very poorly and everyday when I went to the centre I used to call the doctor. All he gave me was a prescription. Then on the 20th December we broke up for two weeks. Then the next day on the 21st December, my brother came and woke me up at 3 o'clock in the morning. He said, 'Your Dad wants you.' So I got up and went downstairs. He was sat in his chair, he asked me to rub his legs, so I did, then he said, 'Help me up, I want to have a little walk.' I helped him. The second time he wanted to try and walk he had a stroke. I had to put him on the floor and lean him up against my armchair. Then I went upstairs to fetch my brother. He came down and we both helped him into his chair. We hadn't got a telephone then. So I went out in my nightie to the next door neighbours. When I couldn't wake them I went a bit further down and they were up, so I asked them if they could phone for a doctor because my Dad had a stroke. Then I went back. My brother had to go to work. When the doctor came at nine o'clock he said to me, 'Your Dad's a very poorly man.' I said, 'I've been telling you that all week.'

Then he got on his phone and called an ambulance. I went with him. I had to sign some papers. Then they called my brother to come and pick me up to take me home. When I got home, I asked my neighbour if I could phone the centre. I remember they were painting and Mr Jones, the centre manager, was there. I told him about my Dad and he came straight up and sat with me. He made me a cup of tea and had one himself. When we had finished our tea, he told me to stop crying, to wash my face, and try and get some sleep. He said, 'You don't want your Dad to see you like that, it might upset him.' So I cried myself to sleep. Then at three in the afternoon my next door neighbour came and woke me up. He said the hospital was on the phone. When I answered it the nurse told me my Dad had just died. When my brother came home, I told him what had happened. So we both went to the hospital to see my Dad. They said he died of a heart attack. I kissed him. He always told us, whenever he died, he didn't want anybody crying over him. But when you've had a Dad as good as mine, I couldn't help it. I still miss my Mam and Dad after all these years. My Dad was all for People First. He believed that we had as much rights as anyone else. I used to go all over making speeches.

How People First got started. Mr Jones gave me a small pamphlet and I asked him what it was about and he said, 'Speaking up for yourself and being independent.' So I asked him if there was a People First around near us. He said, 'I don't think so.' So I said, 'Well, there soon will be.' I asked students if they would like to join. At first there was five, then there was fifteen, now we have over twenty.

When we first started out, one of the staff said, 'I'll give you a year' and we've been going now for ten years. I work in the café at the SEC. In the old days I was the only one in the café so they named it 'Joyce's Café'. Since we opened it to the public, they call it 'Swallow Café'. After Christmas they are going to expand it. When I was 60 years old they asked me to stop on and run the café. But Lesley, who used to be my key worker, she gets all the new ideas for the café. Lesley has always been good to me, like Mr Jones in the old days. When I was depressed Lesley would say to me, 'Have you got any money?' I'd say, yes, and then she'd say, 'I'll take you shopping after dinner.' I remember she always used to say, 'I love spending other people's money.' I used to feel a lot better afterwards. When Lesley was my key worker, if I was 15 minutes late she would phone to see if I was all right. Now she's not with us all the time, nobody cares like Lesley used to. But when she had a break for a drink of tea with her group in the café, she asked where I was. Then she went to the office to phone me up. But I was on my way. That's what Lesley's like. It's not just me, but everyone in her group. If they're late, she'll phone to see if they're all right. If Lesley had something to say she would say it, then we would be friends again. I like her because she says what she has to say to you.

She doesn't talk behind your back like some do. I'd rather tell people what I think, then forget it.

My brother and I now live in a two-bedroom flat. It's nearer work. I went to ask if I could go to the hospital for an X-ray, on my feet and back. When the results came back, he told me that I had arthritis. Now I have to have a stick. My brother used to like underwater diving. But now he goes playing golf three times a week – sometimes more. He goes all over playing golf.

We look forward to the future in People First. I could have said a lot more things about when I was a little girl. Such as you don't see children playing hopscotch and skipping and rounders. There were lots of games we used to play when we were kids. Now the kids these days, only think of going dancing, pictures and sex – if you give them 5 or 10 pounds these days they look at you daft. I used to go on to Molly Meals for halfpenny carrot. If we had sixpence we thought we was well off. All you hear about these days, someone has been raped or murdered, not just by men and women. Children commit murder as well. You can't leave your door open these days like you could when I was a young girl. When people go to jail, instead of hard work they have pool tables and television, instead of working. They'd rather live off the dole. Most don't know what work is. I blame the government.

I started to tell you about People First, then, by accident, I went on talking about something else. In the old days we used to call the staff by their last names. Also two staff would stand and say which row could go for dinner. But they used to eat their dinner in a little room. So I asked the boss if I could have a word with him. He said, 'Yes, what's the matter?' So I said, 'Aren't we good enough to eat with?' and he said, 'Yes why?' I said, 'Well, it doesn't seem so – the staff eat in a little room of their own.' So he said he'd see what they'd say at the meeting. Then I asked him, 'Can we call the staff by the first name?' He said, 'Why don't you ask them?' So I did. Some said yes and some said no. Those who said no I said, 'Well call me Mrs Kershaw.' Well, after all, Mr Jones said People First was about sticking up for yourself and helping others stick up for themselves.

When I used to be talking to staff, one of the other staff would come and butt in. We just used to walk away. But if they were talking and you butted in, they'd say to us, 'It's bad manners to butt in when people's talking.' So one day I was talking to the staff, when one of the men staff started talking, and they both started talking, so I said to him that interrupted, 'I was talking to him, it's ignorant to interrupt.' I said, 'At least that's what you told me.'

People First started in 1986. I also made sure that they didn't pick on those who were too frightened to talk back. Also in People First we share one another's troubles. People look up to us now and listen to us, where before they used to make us look small, and they never listened to what we had to say. Also we are people with learning difficulties, not what people used to call us. I won't say the word because we got rid of it in some places, but there's still some that use that name. Never mind – we'll win some day. Even if we aren't there, we're thinking about the future for those children who haven't been born yet. That's what we do, think of the future, more than these that build houses and shops. They don't think about those in wheelchairs, who would like to do their own shopping. I helped to start a lot of People First groups up. One of the groups has their meetings in a centre. We have a room outside the centre. Also they have the staff for their advisor and we don't. Some of the staff tell them what to do, practically run it for them. We've never done that, we don't let anybody join, only people with learning difficulties. It's our group and nobody tells us what to do and that's how it should be.

Some parents still treat their grown up sons and daughters as children. That's not right. My Mam and Dad never treated me like that and I'm a lot better for it. I loved to buy my brother grapes, oranges or plums. I like to buy him something for his birthday and Christmas. When I ask him what he would like he always says, 'I don't want anything save your money', but I always buy him something. The thing is I'm running out of things to buy him because he has everything. When I say, 'Do you want this or that?' he always says, 'I've got it.' It's easier to buy for a woman than it is for a man. I feel good when I'm helping people. It's not just my relatives. I like helping everybody.

I've just remembered something else about the centre in the old days. The staff used to put a show on for us at Christmas. They used to throw custard pies at one another. One Christmas, Mr Jones and two other men staff took 'The Three Degrees' off. They got dressed up in long dresses and wigs. Then Lesley pretended to have an operation behind a screen. Then they carried her off in a coffin. Some of the students went home and told their Mams and Dads, or whomever they lived with, that Lesley had died. They wrote in to say how sorry they were about losing Lesley. They'd only just got to know she had died. The staff had a good laugh over it, and so did the parents when they got to know it was just a show. Then three of the men staff dressed up in ballet clothes and while they were dancing, Mr Gaunt's skirt fell down. Every time he picked it up and put it back on, it just kept falling off again, so he gave it up as a bad job. On my way home I couldn't stop laughing on the bus. I haven't thought about that up until now. But the Christmas my Dad died, we put on a show for the staff, just for a change. They called the play 'The witch that nicked Christmas'. We played in on the day we broke up. That was the 20th December. Then on the 21st December my Dad died and I was the witch in the play. So that was Christmas. I never thought about it until I was writing my life story.

Every Friday we used to play games, not just any game. They used to play the games that were on television. Such as *Play Your Cards Right, Mr and Mrs* and a lot of other games. Every time there was a new game on the TV we used to try out on Fridays. They used to be good at *Name That Tune*. I won some medals for swimming. That last medal I won for 40 lengths non-stop. I also got a gold medal for shot put, discus, archery and javelin. The only thing I didn't get was one for shooting. I'd love to go abroad again. I've got my wish after all these years. I always wanted a till for my café but they used to say they were too much money.

I don't know. These days if you break into a £10 note, or a £20 note, it goes in no time. You sit down at the end of the day and wonder where it's all gone to. It used to go a lot further in the old days.

When I lived up Nethroyd Hill, every night when I came home, I used to help all the old ladies off the bus and across the road. I used to call them 'my little women'. Some of them were bigger than me. I remember once, I had both my arms in plaster and one of the little ladies came and brought me a lovely big bunch of flowers and a card. When I read the card it said, 'Get well soon, we all miss you.' I sat down and cried. Because I broke my arms, a nurse used to come in the morning and dress me. Then at night she used to come and get me ready for bed. Since then I've had someone to come and help me get in the bath. There's Margaret, Brenda and Moira. Peggy doesn't come any more. They are all nice. They think of other people first. I like them all, I wouldn't change them for anyone else. When I was asked if I wanted someone new I told them, 'No, I'll do without a bath first.' There was an old lady that used to live on Northgate. She used to sit on her front steps and smoke a clay pipe. Her name was Mrs Riley. She was a nice lady.

I know I keep going back to when I was a girl, and the old days, but things keep coming back to me. Like before the war my Mam and Dad bought me a big doll and pram for Christmas. When I was at the school near Liverpool, my Mam wrote and asked if she could give my dolls and my pram away to someone who couldn't afford to buy their little girl anything for Christmas. So I wrote back and said, 'Yes, I'm too old for them now anyway.' When I came home from the centre one day, my brother-in-law was just driving his car in my brother's garage, when he turned round and said, 'I've forgotten to give Harry this and he's working over.' So I said, 'I'll give it to him when he comes home.' Then, instead of turning left, I turned right and fell off a high wall. I don't remember hitting the ground. When I came round I was in hospital. I kept asking the nurses and doctors, as they walked past, if I could have my clothes. They kept on saying 'in a minute'. Then when my brother came up at teatime, I said, 'They won't give me my clothes' and he said, 'You banged your head and you hurt your fingers. They might want to keep you in overnight.' I asked him where my clothes were. So I got dressed and went home. When I got home my Dad said, 'You're not going to work for two weeks.' But the next day I got up and went to the centre. My Dad said, 'You must have a head made of iron.'

We opened the café to people outside. I look after the money. After Christmas there is going to be a change. It's going to be made bigger with a bigger counter. It's going to be really nice. It'll cost a lot of money. Me and my friends go into the bus station café for a drink. We pay in turns. The café students and staff are going out for our Christmas dinner. I'll have to have my hair permed before I go. I should have gone to the hospital but I forgot. My brother Harry is taking me up in the car, then he'll be playing golf. He's the best brother anyone could ask for.

Well I can't see into the future so I'll finish now. I will say one thing more, and that is, I don't go to church now, but that doesn't mean to say I don't believe in God, because I do. I can't go to sleep at night if I haven't said my prayers. That's one thing I never forget. I pray for everyone in the world, not just for people I know. I know there will be a lot more to say as time goes by.

I might write again soon, I'll keep a diary, then I won't forget next time. I'll end on the 14th November 1996.

Anya Souza: 'It's not Down's syndrome, it's up syndrome'

Anya used to work for a self-advocacy group. A couple of incidents led to her leaving and she now spends much of her time designing and making stained glass ornaments, mirrors and frames. She also supports and promotes respite care, and has spoken widely about the rights of people with Down's syndrome. She was 34 when we met in her spacious and artistically decorated flat. Anya sees self-advocacy as an individual as well as collective concern. Although she herself now has little to do with self-advocacy groups, she still encourages others with learning difficulties to check out what they can get from being involved. This is Anya's story.

The early days

I was born in Hampstead in 1962 and in those days it was Mongol. When my mum had me she was 44, which is quite old actually to have a baby. When the doctors had me in their hands to hand me over to my mother, she asked them, 'Is my daughter okay?' The Doctor said, 'No, she's not okay, she'll be mentally and physically handicapped for the rest of her life', basically. My mother couldn't make head nor tail of that initially. She was shocked. Then a nurse came up to my mother and said 'Mrs Souza your daughter will be fine, you'll get pleasure out of her.' So I did, I gave her pleasure. A few years later, around '87–'88, we were on television with Esther Ranzen, and my mother told her what the doctor had said. I felt like saying, 'Can I speak now? You should see what I've got – I've got two arms and two legs, I'm not physically handicapped actually.' I could have said that but they didn't give me a space to speak. I felt a bit angry inside myself. People were talking in the audience and all that and it came back to my mother again. When Esther said, 'Don't ever give up', I thought that's a bit silly, because you've got to give yourself a chance to move in life – not give up. A bit silly I think.

We're half-Indian from my father. He's Indian Catholic. My mother was Jewish, she came from Prague. She came here when she was 16 and couldn't speak a word of English. She married twice, before she met my Dad and had us. She came in March 1939 and the war started in September of that year. She was Jewish but she wasn't practising. The same with my Dad. His family are Catholic but he doesn't practise. My Dad is a well known Indian artist. My sisters, Francesca and Karen, they were born before me, I was the last one. I had support from them when I was young.

I was at nursery school and after that I went to a special school just for one term. I didn't like it there anyway basically, neither did my mother. I was only about five and at one point this teacher made a stuffed fish out of paper and two brown rabbits. *She* made these things not *me*. She made them as decorations for the school. Now you weren't allowed to bring them home but I sneaked them in my bag and came home with them. I showed them to my mother and said, 'Well, I didn't do this mum, so why am I at school? I should be the one learning.' I mean why are schools here on earth? You've got to learn it for yourself, not the teacher – they know already! We don't. So after that my mother said, 'Right, well that's it – you're not going there any more.' So I left that special school and went to a mainstream school for eight years. Normally you go for seven years but I stayed on for another year because of my disability. How did I find it? Well you catch up on all sorts of things and I can remember around that time that I was wearing plastic glasses. It got frustrating for me because I couldn't see the blackboard. So in the end I needed proper glasses. I made lots of friends there and I still know them now.

From primary I went on to a mainstream comprehensive school and made some more friends. I came out with three CSEs – I did French, drama and housecraft. I did grade 3, 4 and 5 in all of them. I also did an exam in typing so I know how to type, and I also had piano lessons. I learnt the piano for about ten years and after that I played the guitar too. My mum paid for the lessons, which was good for me. I was there for five years instead of six years. I made some good friends, but then I get this thing after five years from the headmistress saying to my mother behind my back, 'Why is this Mongol person in my school?' I felt really angry, very angry. Well, the moment my mother heard that, bloody hell, she went to the high court of justice and *we* won, the headmistress lost – because you don't say those kind of words really. I think we sued her, because my mother didn't want that saying about me really. The headmistress's attitude was that I shouldn't be there, but what was I doing there for five years? Going off to France because I was learning French, you know and all that, and I get that at the end of it.

After that I went to another special school. I went from a mainstream to a special. Silly isn't it really. I was 18. That's how I met another friend Jennifer, who I still know now. She was at a mainstream school although she also has learning difficulties. She doesn't class herself as being one, but I know she is. She has learning difficulties, it's the way she speaks, the way she does things, which is slow, you know. Anyway the trouble was she was bunking off school all the time because her mother was dying. That happened when she was about 12, and because she was doing it all the time she didn't really do her work in school. So when these two social workers saw her, they said, 'Okay we'll do it.' So what they did was to take her by the arms and put her in a special school, where I was, in the same class. And that's where I met my friend Jennifer. I met this other friend as well but she was a bit stroppy actually!

I didn't like it at all and only went for a year. The mainstream school was a lot better. Although I had one or two mishaps there, one boy pushed me in the playground crushing all my fingers. Someone else spat at me down my back. In my special school everyone picked on me all the time – non-stop – either because I had Down's syndrome or I was the odd one out. I am too bright to be in a school like that because my Mum brought me up in her natural way. To be as normal as possible. So these other teenagers were totally backward basically. I remember this other girl, Brenda, I remember her well. She was really naughty and it was very bad what she did to me. One day she poured boiling custard right down me. It was total craziness to do that. She thought it was very funny, it wasn't funny. I was crying and she thought it was funny. Stupid twit. So in the end I left. I couldn't stand it. It was a huge mistake of my Mum putting me in that school. There was one time when the teachers and the headmistress were talking. Middle class 5 were throwing plastic cups at me. I stormed up and I said to the teacher, 'Can you tell them not to do that.' She never did, she still kept yacking away to the headteacher, totally ignoring me. I thought, well, this is lovely isn't it? I thought, well, this is it and I've had enough – goodbye. So I was there a year and I left straight away.

Then I went on to a mainstream college and I did a pre-vocational course in office skills. When I was still at that college, I had an interview for another college. First they suggested a course on 'community care' and I thought, well, that's not what I want to do. I thought that's a bit silly. I looked down the list and it said 'food'. So that was it, 'Yes', I said, 'I'll go for that one!' So I did a food industry course in catering in the end with both colleges. One of them is very famous for catering and I did that for about two years as well as a general course at the other. I became a chef, a waitress, I did a project on continental foods, Swiss recipes, German recipes, French recipes, Italian recipes and they were totally thrilled with my work. I laid on a tea for my mother. She came in and it wasn't like a cup of tea, there was more to it than that, it was sandwiches and cakes – 'high tea'. She loved it. I showed her my work, she enjoyed that too, she was very impressed with my work. I also went into hotels, Claridges, the Dorchester, big hotels, and after that I started working in '84.

Starting work

I started working with the Down's Children's Association. I was 21 and I met my first boyfriend there, Paul, who I'm now back with. When I first started in '84 it was the Down's Children's Association, children only, but now it's spreading out. It's called the Down's Syndrome Association. I was there for ten years. I was very popular. I was on the TV and radio. I was there when my mother was dying. I took a week off. Also when I was there I had my accident in '86–'87. I was run over by a motor bike. I had a broken shoulder, collapsed lung, broken ribs, you name it, not in a pretty state at all. My mum heard and she was in total shock. I was rushed into hospital. There's also another bit I should come to. When I was lying on the ground waiting for the ambulance for 20 minutes, I was conscious throughout. I felt a blanket coming over me and after that a lady walked up to me and I remember her asking, 'Why is this Down's syndrome person walking on her own?' It's inconsiderate to say such things. I mean I have to do things on my own. Who would do it for me? No one. Because my mother's not here, I have to do it for myself. Paul won't do it for me. Soon afterwards I was back at work and they wanted me to do lots of things like hoovering and taking heavy parcels to the post office. I told them, 'I can't do that, I've only just got out of hospital, for god's sake, I can't carry heavy things with this arm.' They were actually using me as a dogsbody, they weren't using my skills.

If you have a Down's syndrome baby, you have to know the right things to do, keep it warm, keep it clean, give it love and care. The problem with that lot was that they'd never had a Down's syndrome baby. 'Normal people' were in the association, I was the only one with Down's syndrome working in that office for ten years. Non-stop. There was also at one point going to be a fund-raising event, a ball, and I had my mind fixed on a nice dress and lovely shoes. Then I get the office manager saying, 'Anya can't go because she ate at the wrong table', because I was eating my lunch at the wrong desk. I think that was so stupid. Here I am because I've got Down's syndrome, I will give publicity to other people like Marti Webb and those mega-people who were there at the ball, and they don't let me go. I could have given them publicity about Down's syndrome because I have done and I know. I can, because I have Down's syndrome, others don't, they don't know what it's like to have it. Who has 47 cells? I have. They haven't, they've only got 46!

I stayed there for ten years and I left of my own accord. When my Mum was dying, they wanted to help me. They saw me sitting there doing nothing, so I said, 'Right, I'll do something about it' and left. I moved on to another job at this Society for the Mentally Handicapped – which is learning difficulties. It was an office job, but again they didn't use me for my skills. I used the typewriter, but not much, so I asked to use the phone. I use the phone at home – it's easy. So I started taking phone messages, photocopying, everything, I really got into it. I was there for a while and I thought they were pushing me out, but they weren't, they were moving me up. So they promoted me higher to work with a self-advocacy group. I had to apply for the job and it said on the application form, 'Why do you want this job?' I thought, 'Go for it, you can speak up for yourself', so I went for it. At the interview it was like a kangaroo court, beginning to end. There were all these workers and supporters and they were all looking at me. One of them, Peter, his eyes were sparkling at the time, because when I got the job, I became his girlfriend.

Speaking out: in a group and on your own

I started in 1993, the day after my sister's birthday. I was the 'Young Development Officer'. Going everywhere to places that I'd never been to before. I was giving sessions up and down the country, talking about safe sex to kids with learning difficulties. Everyone had a support worker and a co-worker to work with them. Like, Julie was in a wheelchair and she had her support worker. There were, like, workers, self-advocates and non-workers who are normal people, like James, Carol and Luke. The supporters help you to physically do things. They shouldn't bite your head off all the time, but everyone was doing that to me.

They did help though. If I went to conference they'd do all the writing and I'd do all the speaking. We did a video about first time sex education. It's about this couple, Julie, and her boyfriend Chris, and she wants to know about having sex and a relationship. I mentioned that in my own film, *First Sex*, which was shown on Channel 4. I mean Down's syndrome people don't know what it's about sometimes, to have a boyfriend and all that. I mean, here I am living alone in my own flat and I do stained glass, which I sell. Sometimes people don't know about being independent. I don't think many Down's syndrome people know how to do stained glass. They don't have my skills in other words.

I've done conferences on Down's syndrome. I came up with the history first before I started. Originally the guy himself, Dr Landon Down, started it off. He was based at Richmond in the Norman Field hospital. I remember seeing a sculpture of his head. A very amazing man who actually invented the word Down's syndrome. It was him who got the word going. From that I got all the history, some from the Down's Association and some from the Open University. It came out very well at the conferences. I brought in other things like plastic surgery and sex. Sometimes people with Down's syndrome don't know about their sex lives, they don't know what it's about, having Down's syndrome, or what it's like, because people get floppy armed, double jointed in their hips and other things. I hate the words 'plastic surgery', totally, because we all have different faces. Why do you want to destroy it? I mean look at Michael Jackson, it's disgusting. I really hate that, I really do.

I went to a conference in Barcelona to talk about testing on Down's syndrome. It was a massive conference, with doctors, researchers, you name it. It was terrible, really bad. They didn't have a meaning of why we are human beings, and they should know the meaning of a human being. We're not animals, are we? When I was on that stage I really gave my mouth to them, I really did. Everyone had these earphones to listen to their interpreters and I actually said to them, 'We are not guinea pigs we are human beings.' They were looking at Down's syndrome babies from the age of two, and they were testing on them, it was preposterous. I mean, how dare they do that to us? Treating us like guinea pigs. This year I'm off to Helsinki, which is about technology and Down's syndrome, and I'll be speaking up then. I mean, in my day it never happened. If you had Down's syndrome you couldn't do anything about it.

The term 'Down's syndrome', is okay, but it's like my Dad said to me, 'You're not Down's syndrome, you're "up syndrome"!' I remember when Speaking Up groups went to Canada in '93, I had to do a poster on different labels and names – 'retarded', 'handicapped' and so on, until there were no labels at all – just your name at the end. I mean, it's silly using a label all the time. You can't say you're 'just handicapped', because you're labelling somebody and that's not the way to speak to someone. Like on TV sometimes you get people saying that all the time – 'You're handicapped, you're handicapped', when you're not. It's like sometime back, I've got an article on it, in a *Touch of Frost*, there was a young man who had Down's syndrome. He was getting married to his girlfriend who also had Down's syndrome and they went upstairs to a bedroom. Even the man in *Touch of Frost*, David Jason, and the other bunch of people were saying, 'Why is this handicapped person doing this?' It was a murder case and they thought it was him doing it, but it wasn't, yet they frame him, the person with Down's syndrome. Same in *Brookside*. They don't show Max and Patricia's baby because she has a Down's syndrome baby. They how it negatively because they're not showing the baby much, are they? We see the people but we don't see the baby – where is the baby? Its the same in *Neighbours*, Cheryl's got a Down's syndrome baby too, even though the baby doesn't look like it has.

The label learning difficulties. Do I think it's a good term? It is actually, yes. That's the new version, it's the same as using Down's syndrome instead of the old term. It's good to use so that everyone can recognize the term. This lady who had a Down's syndrome baby, he died when he was two, and she wrote a book about it. It's a true story and she's been on TV twice and I know her very well. She's a lovely lady, amazing, and she was totally thrilled when she met me because I have Down's syndrome. She really wanted to see someone with it. Would I say I have difficulties learning? No, I learnt well enough. I picked up things very quickly.

Leaving and looking back on the group

When I was in the self-advocacy group I was being the star and they hated it. I was going on TV, I was on the radio, in the papers, even with my conference I did on Down's syndrome I was in *The Guardian*. You name it and they were jealous of me. I remember going off to do *UK Living* or something. They were jealous of me, because I'm bright, I can do all these fantastic things, I'm too clever for them. I know what's good for me and when I left, they lost a good person, they let me down.

I left for a number of reasons. It's difficult for me to tell you. I can't give the details, I said something I shouldn't have. I meant to say one thing but another thing came out of my mouth. That was my mistake. I did that, but we all make mistakes. I was only worried for the members of the group. Other people overreacted. My second mum, June, said they used me as a scapegoat and gave me abuse. They did. Nasty piece of work. Then there was all this stuff with another member of the group. They accused me of doing something that I didn't do. It wasn't fair the way they treated me. You need discipline and your independence, I mean I had those from my mother. When I was young, I went to my friend's house and came back at 11 at night. I rang my mum to say I was coming home. When I came through the door I got disciplined sternly from my mother because she had been so worried. I learnt my independence and my discipline together. I don't need discipline from that 'speaking out' group. That's what I don't need.

Being in the group was worthwhile because I was actually doing things. Using my skills. It was good and bad. A bit of both really. Having the job and using my skills, going out and meeting people all the time. We did one session about using drama to speak up. People who were there really enjoyed themselves, it was brilliant. It was okay until that happened at the end. No job to go to, what was I going to do? Sacked, totally sacked. It's a good organization but they should have helped one another out more. They haven't really spoken to me since. It's very strange really. I was sent this folder about 'services' and on the bottom is 'speaking out group' and I thought, 'Oh this is lovely', they send me this stuff and I was there when they were writing it. I'm in the folder myself. There's a word that the group doesn't like – 'respite care'. Now they don't like that word and there I was trying to promote it. It's good to have 'respite care' for young people, to get away from their parents, it's respite for both. I mean I still have respite myself, though I haven't had it for a long time, and it does me the world of good to go away for a little while and come back into it again. It did my mother the world of good. For young people to have it is the best thing really. It's for both the parents to have their break but also for the young people to have their break, to do what they want to do. But the group didn't like it you see. I was meant to be on a management committee for 'respite care' but they didn't want me to do it. 'Do it in your own spare time', they told me. We were at this conference, and I said to them all, 'You're always thinking of yourselves, me, me, me, what about other people?' I really put them in their place. They were all complaining at me, and I thought, 'Yeah, I can put my person into it now. You listen to me now, I've got my say now.'

There's another word they didn't like – 'bereavement'. But you have to go through it. My mother died, right, I had to see a counsellor, I needed that. When a great friend of mine died, she was like a third mother, I was in a total state of shock. I couldn't go into work. They were telling me to come into work. They must be physically mad when I was in a state of shock. I couldn't go in. I didn't want to anyway, crying my eyes out, and they said come into work on the same day. They even phoned up to see where I was. They didn't even pay for me.

Family and the future

There's this woman I know with learning difficulties. She got her independence by passing her driving test, and she has her own car and a telephone inside it. Lovely girl, long blonde hair, very skinny, quite shy, lovely parents. We went to see her, me, and my second Mum. June said, 'Right, Anya you'll have to drive too.' But I thought, 'No, you can't say that June, you've got a car, I haven't.' You've got to learn the skills to drive, have your car parked outside, there's lots of difficulties and it's lots of money. I mean there's buses here and I have a free pass. Mind you, I've been waiting for my pass for a month now and still haven't got it, it's ridiculous, it really is. I mean I'm forking out £2.60 for a return to my drama class.

It's like getting married. My neighbours keep saying, 'Come on, you've a lovely flat, how about getting married.' They even said to Paul, 'You've now turned 43, you can get married.' I thought who are you? It takes time to get married, it's a big step to go through in life. Things can wait. I'm young, I'm 34 and I'm single. I have my independence. It might affect my benefits. I mean that all comes into it. For me, there's still lots of things to happen. It might take a little time to get married because it takes a long time to get organized before that. I want to get new things in, new clothes, a new ironing board. They come in before all that stuff.

My Dad said before he left to go back to America, 'I will do it for you Anya, if you want to get married, I'll do it for you.' And let him do it. I won't do it. I haven't enough money. I'm unemployed. So's Paul, he's unemployed, even though he's got a little job he hasn't got much money because he's only doing it voluntarily. So if we do want to get married eventually it will take time, but my father will have to pay for me. He's loaded – he's an artist. He lives in New York. I went over once to see him when I was 17 with my mother. It was okay, but I would never live out there, it's better here. I had a phone call one morning from my Dad's girlfriend, saying your Dad's here in England. I thought that's funny what's he doing here? Strange he didn't ring me. He just came round to my house and he was having an argument with his girlfriend. I said, 'If you're going to have your argument then have it outside, I'm not having it in here.' I hadn't seen him for six years. I told him, 'My mother's dead, you didn't come to the funeral, no flowers, so what are you doing here? You didn't care about me then, did you?' He didn't say anything about that. Been on the alcohol again, after all these years, after my mother got him high and dry, back on the booze. I got away for a little while to see my second mother, June, and when I got back on the Monday morning the whole place was in a mess. So I say to my Dad's girlfriend, 'Okay, get out there and get a pint of milk.' She was bossing my Dad about and I said, 'Look I'm the boss not you, because I'm the boss of this flat.'

I've known Paul for ten years. I met him through country dancing, which is a really nice thing to do. It was on a country green outside Oxford. My mum knew what was going on! She knew Paul. We split up for a time. When my mother died, he didn't make it to the funeral. Then, some time after my sister bumped into him and invited him back for a coffee. There I was, just about to go to bed in my nightdress, and he came in. He told me, 'I should have been there at your mother's funeral.' I asked him, 'Where were you? Because you should have been there, because you knew my mother', I told him. But his grandmother wouldn't let him go. She said all sorts of things about me. She was against me. Later she apologized. It got well out of hand with Paul at the start, but I was in love with Paul, I was pushing him to stay over with me. So he said he'd ring his grandmother. I was pulling him one way and she was pulling him the other. I said, 'You should show your grandmother what you can do for yourself, show her you have your independence.' She died in 92 but now he's got his independence. She always had him under her wings. Little baby boy in the school cap and all that stuff. It took her a long time to see him as a grown up man. He was 33 when he first knew me. Silly, because his parents had split up, his father lives in Monte Carlo in the south of France and his mother lives in San Diego. She actually sent us some presents last

Christmas, really nice of her to do that. We also sent the video of me and Paul – the *First Sex* one. She's shown it to all her friends.

The time when we got back together. That night I went to see one of my friends. We had a Chinese meal together, and on the way home, on the train, there was Paul on the platform talking to his friends. So I got off at the platform and thought, 'Hello, what are you doing here?' And the one thing that I said to him, those magic words I used, 'Come back for a cup of tea.' It was more than a cup of tea! That night we got back together on the 24th April and we've been together ever since.

Children are something I'd consider in the future, not now, very much in the future. I mean I've got three nephews, one niece and one god-niece and that's enough. I mean one, she is four, and she is a little monster and very bright! She wants everything, she wants the lot, like in the Argos catalogue. She can want it but she can't have it! I'm on the management committee of an organization for children, five or under, with learning difficulties. I've said to them that they have to use accessible language, with words and pictures.

Postscript: words of advice

My advice to people with learning difficulties about self-advocacy? Try and speak up, get what you want in life, get your voice across. I think self-advocacy groups can help you do that. Even now, when I bring things up about self-advocacy, I tell them about my old group, but I do tell them not to mention my name.

Patrick Burke: 'It is true. I know it is'

Patrick was institutionalized in the mid-1960s and subjected to physical, mental and sexual abuse. He wanted his story to be read by others. People First 'set him free', as he put it, and he has enjoyed being the group treasurer. He has made quite a name for himself as an advocate for others with learning difficulties. He contributes to his group's newsletter, has represented the group at numerous conferences and recently spoke with members of his local council about the unnecessary use of jargon in leaflets about services. Self-advocacy changed Patrick's life by equipping him with the confidence and words to speak out about things close to his heart. At the time of being interviewed, Patrick was a key complainant in a case being brought against the staff who abused him and many others. He collected the names of his fellow 'patients' who said they had been abused and presented the long list to a service manager. Many of the victims were unwilling to go to court; others were deemed as too weak a witness by the police. Patrick was the main figure in the trial, which was eventually successful in prosecuting a number of staff. He now shares a flat with his dog and a friend who is a fellow ex-resident of an institution. This is Patrick's story.

Institutions to homes

I haven't had an awful lot of opportunities for work but I have done work in the past. Clearing up, dusting, and all that business. I've done household work, gardening and farm work. There used to be a farm where I lived which they're pulling down now. They're using the land for houses. It was run by a charity. They had an awful lot of farmland there and we used to look after it. There was me, Tommy, Peter, Arthur, about five or six of us. I was there for 30 years. They ran it how they wanted to run it. They didn't let you have a say about how it should be run. It was for people with learning difficulties and some of them were really bad with learning. The staff really took over – 'You can't have this, you can't have that.'

It was for men like ourselves with hospital staff looking after us. The hospital staff, they could be a bit on the 'bent side' – if you know what I mean. That was a problem. They took it out on the lads who were there. That's why the majority of men don't like the hospital staff. We took them to court over a few things as well. They got fined for what they were doing. They're not running here any more. They've gone abroad, but they'll be doing exactly the same over there. I moved there in 1966. Living there was hard. I got knocked left, right and bloody centre. That's why I was afraid to speak up. It was very hard for me to say anything I wanted to say because if you're not big enough to fight, then you'll get a hammering. And if you're big enough to have a fight, you're all right. If you can stick up for yourself, you're okay, if you can't, then watch out.

Sometimes I couldn't stick up for myself at all. Every day I was getting beaten. There was not a day missed out without me getting a good hiding. Then I would be getting raped and all that business. People don't realize it. It is true. I know it is. The people out there experiencing it, they'll tell you that it's true. Others will say it isn't. But these days you've got to look at it. People who have been in homes all their lives will tell you it is true. The outside people have never been in – they won't. Now I know they're the ones who are in the wrong, not us. We paid their wages, but once they got money in their hands they could do anything with you. They were in charge of you. They could have you walking round the home all day with no clothes on. They used to say, 'We're over you.' As long as they're over you, you've got to do as you're told.

Same with bath nights. There was only two baths in the place. The whole lot of us would get bathed in them on one night. So every man's waiting and they've all got no clothes on and they're all waiting in this big line outside. Bathing in the same water. Some of them had bad skins. Bathing in the same water every time. Now since I've come out of there down to People First, I've come out an awful lot. I've told people since. There's been compensation but it is awful what they've done. If that wasn't bad enough, I ended up being in another place that was even worse. This other place was even worse because the staff would do things what the hospital staff would do. You'd get raped left, right and centre in that place. Until I started going to an advocacy group, which set me free, I couldn't put my views across, tell people what I thought of them, tell the DHSS, tell anyone. I couldn't tell the staff where they were going wrong.

I'm living in a flat now. There's only two of us there. When I moved my stuff in, I moved some of it into my house and some of it into a spare room. There's a spare bedroom, you see. The bloke I share the house with, he was in that home as well, where the hospital staff were. He got taken from his family and put into a home from the early sixties. He'd not seen his family for 20 years and now he's only just started to meet them again. He's about 53 and he'd never met his family at all. I've got family, but they're living abroad. I've got aunties in New Zealand, one aunt in Essex – that's about all. So all my family are nowhere in England apart from the one. Last year we had a flood in the flat and we had to move out and go to another house and we had to wait six months until it had dried out. They had to re-decorate it, put it back, but its not even better – they haven't even got the beds, you know. I've got the dog to keep me company. It's a different thing now. It's no longer, 'You've got to be in at 9 o'clock', coming back as soon as you've gone out. Now I can please myself, though I've got to be careful what I'm drinking, medication-wise. I look after bills and all that. I'd never seen a bill in my life. I wouldn't have known how to pay it. I'd never paid one in my life. I'd never been taught how to pay a bill.

With the flat I'm in now, I was moved from pillar to post and I had no say in it. They moved me from house to house. They wanted me to move out of these houses because I was telling them what to do. Back then – I wasn't given a say. People are being given a say now but, then again, people were not being given a say in them days. With it, people didn't know which way to turn. They only had a certain way to go. People always asking, 'What are you doing?' 'Where are you going?' It's wrong. And now, people have the right to say, 'I want this and that.' If they have the money they'll get it. I think it's good for them. It's good for them to see us and see how it is working.

People First

I started People First about four years ago. The place where I lived, I'd been there since the early sixties, started up an advocacy group. So I went along. I just wanted to see what it was all about. It was all right. Then Jackie and Guy from my present group came down, one evening when we were having a meeting. I didn't know them. They were starting up an advocacy group and they wanted me to help out. I thought, 'Fair enough', and I've been in this advocacy group ever since. When I started off with People First I found it awful hard because I didn't know what to say, how to say it and who to say it to. I was afraid of people. Now, I could tell you about the past, the future in 15 years' time, how I'm going to cope, will I cope. I didn't have any idea how to speak out until I met People First. Other members helped me. Guy was chair for about eight years and now we've got a chair and a vice. He helped out. Others gave me confidence. Guy says, 'Look, do you want to say anything? If so, shout it out. If people tell you to shut up say, "No, I won't. I'll speak like I want to speak not how you want me to speak".' I've got a loud voice and if you don't like it you can lump it.

People First is good. You can get your views across. It's still happening all over the place. And it will happen all the time. You get a young kid, a young girl or boy, they'll go to that kid and have sexual intercourse with them and nothing's been done about it. What you've got to look at is the kid's point of view. They've got to have their point as well. They've got to have their rights as well. I would give the rights to the kids. What you've got to look out for is they can have too many rights and all of a sudden they blow up on it. Kids are very vulnerable. People First has helped me out an awful lot. I think the set-up's good. It's helped to bring me out of things that I wanted to be brought out of. Wendy's helped us out, Rachel has, Guy has. People like that have given me a push. Like they say, 'You're not doing that right, I'll show you how to do it.' I think going to different places, like conferences and workshops, has brought me out an awful lot. It's helped me to speak up, what to say and how to say what you want to say. How people with learning difficulties should be involved in it, not just staff. I'm the treasurer. Looking after the money, signing cheques, how much has got to be taken out or put back in. Where and how is it going to be sent. They want to know where all this money is going. I enjoy it. I've been treasurer for a while – I'm getting there. It helps getting food, buying a pair of trousers, why not get socks instead of trousers. I was voted in by the group. If I'm not doing the job properly, they tell us and I want them to tell me.

We've been campaigning, going to trade union centres, going to the town hall, trying to get money off them. Then we go to other advocacy groups, and disability groups to get money for Wendy our supporter. We're going to get more money if we can for the office. See if we can keep our organization going and to see if it will work out. We find it hard, it's difficult, but it gets us out. I think it gets the men and women out. They've done a lot of good. They're learning how to say no. Now if you said something to me and I didn't agree with it, I'd say, 'Hang on a minute, I'm certainly not doing it. You're wrong on that. Let me tell you the other way, see how it works out on that.' And we'd try my way. That's how we do it. Instead of keeping their mouths shut, they've got to learn how to say no all the time and yes when they want. That's what the group is about, the supporters can't do nothing about it, we're paying them after all.

How do I find the advisors? Some of them can be a bit pushy and some of them can be a bit bossy. But they do say, 'Well, you're paying my wage so you've got to tell me what to do.' These are the advisors and we're telling them what to do. It's good. Now some of the members don't do that yet but they're getting there slowly.

The advisor comes in and writes down the minutes. We don't get the advisor to say anything – she'll type it up in the office. If there's a mistake, we get them to write it again then send it out to the members. I think the supporter should be an outsider. People should say, 'Hold on, we don't want a member of staff as advisor because we can't say what we want to and we can't say a lot. We want an outsider to come into the group.' I would go along with saying get an outsider, not a friend but someone off the street. I don't want the staff to do it. I'd tell them, 'I don't want you to tell the staff what we've said.' They'll get funny ideas. But then again we tell the bosses what we think of them, what they're doing wrong. When they're supposed to be working towards something and they're not doing it, why are they doing something else and not the other? You get paid to do one job not two jobs. We've got every right to tell the support worker what we think. That's the best way. We're the ones paying the staff and if the staff cannot handle it, well, they know where the gate is. That's why they wanted me out of the house, because I started telling the staff what to do. I didn't do it before – I learnt it off People First. I took my ideas from the group up to the house where I lived and said, 'Hold on, we pay you. If you don't like it you know where the door is.' They used to say, 'Oh god, here comes Paddy!' I've still got friends up there and they tell me what's not being done. I'll take notice of the service users before I take notice of the staff – that's me. Because I know they tell the truth. I know they are. I'll find out if they're telling a lie. Then I'll go back and say, 'They tell me you're not doing this job properly, why aren't you doing it properly? You get paid to do this job properly.' The majority of staff don't like me for saying it. But if they don't like it, that's their business. Why don't they do the job properly in the first place? There's a lot of unemployed people who would do their job as good as them. We pay them. If they can't do it then that's it. There'll always be aggro with the staff because they don't like to be shoved around. They can shove us around but we can tell them where to go – us service users.

Changing services

We went to a conference last week and we said there should be more for people with learning difficulties, not just for members of staff, that way it would be a lot better. And it would be easier as well, both sides getting the picture and with that they can see how it can be worked out with staff and with people with learning difficulties. We should be involved with the services and when we are they'll realize. It will be a lot better because we'll be learning off each other. The majority of staff can't see it in that way. The majority of staff will say okay, but when it comes to the crunch they won't do it at all. All talk – no action. With that they are not learning nothing at all and they should be learning an awful lot.

We went to the Town Hall for the launch of a guide written by the local council. We said they should have people with learning difficulties on the committee for planning services. I think they'll learn an awful lot from people with learning difficulties because they've got a lot more experience than those people in the Town Hall. It's all right them saying they've got loads of ideas. They sit on their arses and say that but are they getting their ideas from people with learning difficulties? Are they paying them? How are they gonna get someone in the office, to see how they work, put their ideas together? They'll learn an awful lot, not big bosses sat around a table saying, 'We'll do this and we'll do that.' If you look, it's people with learning difficulties' lives. What you've got to look at is getting two people with learning difficulties on that council saying how it's working, not talking jargon, but asking questions. I tell you something you'd be a lot better off. Everywhere you go they're using jargon and there should be a leaflet out saying no jargon should be used at all. If you can't not use it then don't talk at all. What we've been doing is writing letters to people and saying, 'We don't want no jargon in letters, talk. If it's a lot of jargon, it's a lot of crap.' Often people don't know how to speak, they haven't the faintest idea how to. If you can't speak – shut up. I would tell the council. I think I could put them in their place. I'd say, 'Shut it.'

Mental impairment? Now what the hell's that? Never heard of it. I've heard of learning disability. I think mental handicap is still being used but they shouldn't. We've been going through our MP, we've been writing to say that those hospital staff still use mental handicap. Why are they using what they used to 20 years ago? When they're getting the money they can call us what they want, which I think is all wrong. I think for ourselves, we are men and women, and we should be treated as such. You are a man or woman, then why not call us men and women? I think its only fair. Just because we have learning difficulties, but then again we can get there in different ways. Maybe we're slow but we'll still get there. I think we should drop all labels because all labels have gone by the book. They're still flagging us down as learning difficulties, but we are men and women with a learning difficulty. They are still keeping that name, mental handicap, so they get money off the government.

People on the outside

You've got to keep reminding people – especially people on the outside. You know, like mothers, families, you've got to remind them all the time that we are different to what you are. Which, fair enough, we are different. We've all got our own ways of living. Education is important, especially with young people. My experience of young people – they've got to be trained. If a person has got a difficulty with reading and writing, or they have to have medication, they need to be helped by the other person. They've got to. Then he or she will grow up and have friends, but she won't have friends who are on the opposite side, like I had. If he or she has friends in the school then they can give them a push. Like say, 'Come on, let's see if you can do this.' As I see it, it's young people's lives, they're the future, and they've got to do the best with it. If they want to make it good, they'll make it good. They've got to keep building on it. Make sure they've got a foundation on it. We didn't get told how to build a foundation. We just got thrown into a home and they said, 'Right, that's it, you're in there for the rest of your life.'

When I went to my first home, I thought I was going to be in there for good. I didn't know how things worked in those days. They said, 'Oh, 30 years is a hell of a long time, you'll not get out.' But I told them I wanted to get out. So

I went to psychologists and doctors. Headcases, bloody headcases they are. They sit around and tell you what to do, you're stuck in a chair, you've got staff beside you, you've got students all across – 'What's the do with this person, why's he like this? How is he like this? Put it on a flip-chart.' They're only students – what do they know? These psychologists – what do they know? When it comes to the push, they know nothing. They can read it, that's good, but doing it in the mind, they're different things. Summing up my experience of psychologists – nowt. Now doctors, well, some are all right, some are up for themselves. Doctors are able to keep you functioning but they seem to be going for money these days. Doctors have got to give people with learning difficulties a chance to talk. Say you got a doctor, what he says might go over my head. I'd say, 'Right, hold on a minute, why go over our heads. Why not say it to our face? If there's something wrong I want to know, no need to go over my head. I want you to say what's wrong with me and tell me.' The same thing has happened with psychologists. They talk over your head – which I don't think they should do. They should talk to you and if they can't talk in front of you there's something wrong with them. I've had bad words with psychologists, they always talk over your head. They think they know everything. They don't know nothing. They think they're better than us. They come to see us and they'll talk to the staff but they won't talk to us. But if they come to see us, why don't they come to see us, instead of talking to the staff?

Choosing what you want

Now social workers, I've even had experience of them. They'll push you round from pillar to post. Some are getting better, some are not. They'll just push you into a home where you're not wanted. With the house I'm in now, I wasn't asked if I wanted to move there. They just said, 'You're going into a home', and they got us into the house. I went to London that week and they said you're going to so-and-so house when you get back. I didn't even know where it was. If they're going to move anyone around they should ask the person. They should ask the person where they want to live, who they want to live with, and what staff they want in it. I think they should ask the person, 'Do you want to be moved, yes or no?' They should give them that choice. If they say no, then they should say, 'All right then, I won't move you, I'll leave you where you are.' If you say yes, they should ask, 'Who would you like to be moved in the house with? A man or a woman?' They should have that choice as well. They should have the choice of staff, male staff or a female staff. Would you like to have a pet? A dog or anything like that. Would it be okay to have our friends sleeping over? Just like a normal person.

That's the way they should be looked at. They should be looked at as people with learning difficulties. As long as they have close friends, as long as they can go out in the evenings, as long as they're able to say, 'Right, I'm going to the pub', 'I'm going to meet a lady friend of mine', that's the way I look at it. Like, I didn't have any close friends. I'm only just starting to have a few close friends now. Before I had no close friends at all because I'd been locked up all my life. And when you've been locked up all your life, you can't have no close friends. With that it's hard to make friends. Very hard. Now I'm starting to make friends and with that I'm starting to go out in the evenings, and go to the pubs and clubs and make friends that way.

Some of our men and women go into work and get paid, but what they get is little or nothing. If they get a tremendous amount of money, they get some of their benefits stopped. Same with me. I've had no real opportunities for work but I have worked. I had an experience in an office, I had a job the year before last, part-time like, and it was really good. I was pleased to get it. I've done gardening work, done farm work, done office work. That's the only kind of work I've done up to now but I can do other type of work as well.

Words for others and the future

If people with learning difficulties wanted to get involved like ourselves I'd say, 'Hang on a minute, right, you want to get involved, we'll put it to the vote with our self-advocacy group first, that you want to join.' If they all say yes, we'll invite that person in, then we ask her what she wants to say, get every-one to shut up because she might be timid and shy. Let her break the ice. I think it's good – that's how I started. I was awful quiet and they all shut up and listened. My first time, it broke the ice, how I thought about it, and how I thought it would work out. They asked everyone to shut up and I started to break the ice. My advice, don't get too worried, don't get too shy, you'll get confidence when you're speaking. If you want to speak put your hand up and we'll put it down on a piece of paper.

In the future I would like more money in our pockets, a bit more education and more ideas to keep the office working and the supporters. I would like to see this office to go for another 10–15 years for our future. I'd like someone to say, 'Here's 20 grand to keep us going.' If we're still there then we're all right. What do we think of this generation? How is this next generation going to go? Will they tag along with us? I want to see their ideas. It's just a ques-tion of whether we'll last. If it does I hope so. I think it will.

 **6**

Learning from life stories

From life story to narrative analysis, we now move to an examination of what the stories tell us about the impact of self-advocacy. It was initially proposed that if self-advocacy has a history, then this history and the effects of group membership would be read in the stories of people who had been involved in the movement and groups for many years. In fact, narrators introduced a number of themes that went beyond this original broad research question. Analysis falls into four sections. The first traces narrators' lives from childhood to adulthood prior to joining self-advocacy groups. The second examines the impact of groups on the continuing development of narrators' self-advocacy. The third draws together narrators' opinions on the workings of groups and the movement. The fourth and final section considers a number of general lessons that are gleaned about life as a self-advocate. The life stories illuminate the struggles of narrators throughout their life courses and highlight how self-advocacy groups enhance self-determination.

Pre self-advocacy group days: the making of a self-advocate

The life stories highlight a number of childhood and adulthood experiences prior to joining groups that appeared to be informative in developing narrators' self-advocacy. These experiences can be slotted into three main themes: family ties, inside institutions and outside institutions.

Growing up and family ties

> I know I keep going back to when I was a girl, and the old days, but things keep coming back to me.
>
> (Joyce Kershaw, her story)[1]

The life stories draw attention to the influence of family life on the development of narrators' self-determination. Three of the five narrators were brought up by single parents, three spent most of their early childhood in their family homes and three shared their home life with siblings. Two narrators were still living in their family homes at the time of being interviewed. A recurring theme for those who spoke about their family life was the determination of parents. Lloyd Page's mother had told him that there was a place for him in the world. He and his mum 'went for it'. Jackie Downer's mum was strong and a great source of strength. Joyce Kershaw's dad was all for People First (her story, Appendix 2). Anya Souza's mother pushed for Anya to attend mainstream schools:

> In my special school everyone picked on me all the time – non-stop – either because I had Down's syndrome or I was the odd one out. I am too bright to be in a school like that because my Mum brought me up in her natural way. To be as normal as possible.

Defiant parental figures emerge in the narratives. Systems were challenged and struggles were shared with children. However, parents' fears can lead to tensions when children reach adulthood (see Flynn and Saleem 1986; P. Mitchell 1997, 1998). Jackie Downer and Anya Souza felt the ambivalence of being encouraged but protected by their mothers, though all narrators, if they mentioned parents and family, looked back at their influence with admiration and understanding of difficulties faced. These difficulties emerge as the transition to adulthood is often hampered by dominant disabling images of 'adult with learning difficulties as child' that enter familial relationships (Koegel 1986), along with the contrasting opinions about independence held by parents and children (Zetlin and Turner 1985):

> Sometimes people with Down's syndrome don't know about their sex lives, they don't know what it's about.
>
> (Anya Souza)

> Parents are very scared to let go of their children. Some parents want to do but don't know how to – always looking at the disability.
>
> (Jackie Downer)

Both Anya and Jackie spoke with their mothers about their desires for independence. After separating from her husband, Joyce Kershaw cooked and cleaned for members of her family and cared for both her parents when they were ill. Notions of readiness for independence appeared to have been worked through in the context of the family. Suggestions of class and cultural identities are also picked up in the accounts of family ties. Dates of birth range from the 1930s through to the 1970s. One narrator is black, one Irish and one mixed race. Anya Souza's mother came from Prague, her father from India. Jackie Downer's cultural heritage is something she is proud of, as she thinks more and more about herself as a black woman. Joyce Kershaw reflects on the 'old days', post-war, when things were cheaper, with trips down to the local grocer past an old woman who used to sit on the steps of her home smoking a clay pipe (Joyce's story). The life stories pitch life as a disabled child in the web of familial identities. Disability was one of a number of identity and experiential positions held by narrators that appeared to have informed their understandings of self and others (see Stuart 1993 for discussions about race and Morris 1991, 1993a, 1996 on women):

> I had a little job in a fish and chips shop. My husband got a job as a bus conductor. Then he got a job as driver. We were married for seven years. Then he went off with my best friend. We had been friends since we were little.
>
> (Joyce Kershaw, her story)

Accounts recognize that narrators' identities were not framed solely in terms of disability in familial relationships. By contrast, Patrick Burke mentions little about his family or background. From childhood to adulthood his home life was an institution:

> I moved there in 1966. Living there was hard. I got knocked left, right and bloody centre. That's why I was afraid to speak up.
>
> (Patrick Burke)

This lack of family life may partly explain why he lacked conviction in speaking up for himself prior to joining People First: 'It really doesn't help a person's character the way the system treats you. One thing that's hard is that once you're in it, you can't convince them how smart you are . . . you're so weak you can't really fight back' (Ed Murphy in Bogdan and Taylor 1982: 218). While families and heritage were important in developing the independence and identity of some narrators, a number of other similar experiences came to play a part in narrators' childhood and adulthood, as indicated in the next section.

Inside institutions, outside society: resilience in adversity

> A lady came to our house. She said I had to go to this school near Liverpool.
>
> (Joyce Kershaw, her story)

All narrators experienced institutionalization. Lloyd Page was in day centres for 17 years. Jackie Downer was in special schools up to the age of 16. Joyce Kershaw spent her teens in a boarding school. Anya Souza spent a year in a special school against the wishes of her mother. In the hospital Patrick Burke had few close friends – 'because I'd been locked up all my life'. Stories of institutions describe a continuum of exclusion. At one end institutions are boring and devaluing places, 'just sat on your backside, doing nothing' (Lloyd Page). At the other end segregation creates power inequalities which can foster sexual and physical abuse, attacking identity through psychological terrorism (Swain and French 1998):

> They were in charge of you. They could have you walking round the home all day with no clothes on.
>
> (Patrick Burke)

These anecdotes have parallels with accounts documented in previous studies of long-stay hospitals, centres and special schools (Goffman 1961; Edgerton 1967; Braginsky and Braginsky 1971; Zetlin and Turner 1985; Potts and Fido 1991). In some way the stories contribute to the insider literature on the history of institutionalization: 'The telling of their experiences by people who lived for years in the large, segregated institutions has been one of the most powerful arguments for deinstitutionalisation during the past 20 years' (Ferguson *et al.* 1992c: 300). Institutions endanger the development of inmates' independence. Consequently, institutional practices and community care policies threaten to erase or reduce family ties (see Banton *et al.* 1985; Potter and Collie 1989; Morris 1993b; Swain and French 1998). It is common for many disabled people and their families to live in a kind of cultural prison of constant poverty and social control (Ferguson *et al.* 1992b: 13). Stories contrast good and bad experiences of family and institutional life. Narrators also reveal the politics of diagnosis and incarceration (contributing to other critiques, such as Bogdan and Taylor 1976; Ryan and Thomas 1987; Oliver 1990):

> My mother asked, 'Is my daughter okay?' The doctor said, 'No, she's not okay, she'll be mentally and physically handicapped for the rest of her life'.
>
> (Anya Souza)

> I didn't want to go but they said I had to go for my education. When I got there it seemed strange being away from home.
>
> (Joyce Kershaw, her story)

In special schools, 'You were labelled as soon as you got there' (Jackie Downer). The impacts upon family life of social policies of yesteryear are picked up on in these personal accounts. For example, Joyce Kershaw's experiences hark back to times when: 'Institutions were organised for the reception of the imbecile and idiot class of defectives who in many cases suffer from *epilepsy* and physical infirmity' (Potts and Fido 1991: 11; italics added).

Previous literature has documented the effects of institutionalization, such as low self-esteem and loss of identity (Goffman 1961, 1963; Edgerton 1967; Craft 1987; Jahoda *et al.* 1988; Barnes 1990):

> Far from being alleviated, people's handicaps were increased by restrictions that stifled personal development and autonomy . . . At its most benign, the system viewed patients as perpetual children and treated them accordingly.
>
> (Potts and Fido 1991: 44)

> I was stopped from speaking out. There wasn't anybody to listen to you and when I did speak out. I was shouted down.
>
> (Lloyd Page)

However, despite these effects of institutionalization, the life stories lend support to the idea that constraints have the paradoxical effect of promoting resistance (Foucault 1975; Fairclough 1989):

There is, in short, a space within any oppressive social structure where human beings can operate from their own will. That autonomy may be born out of pain, or misery, out of the very forces that seek to extinguish it; but its resilience suggests the existence of a human individual separate and independent from the culture in which he operates.

(Sullivan 1996: 4–5)

Swain and French (1998) argue that because the voices of disabled people have been informed by their experiences of segregated settings, there are many lessons to be learnt from their accounts. For example, narrators' scepticism of authority may be seen as a consequence of their struggles inside the system:

Psychologists and doctors, headcases, bloody headcases they are.

(Patrick Burke)

The headmistress asked, 'Why is this Mongol person in my school?' I felt really angry, very angry.

(Anya Souza)

I've got a bit of a negative view of doctors, nurses and professionals. You see, they don't listen to us.

(Lloyd Page)

Moreover, sceptics publicly criticize. Joyce Kershaw told the staff to call her by her surname. For all his anxieties around people, Patrick Burke remembers how he sometimes felt able to stick up for himself against the staff who abused him. Now staff are anxious when Patrick walks in the centre: 'Watch it, Paddy's here'. Anya Souza reprimanded a teacher for not acting when she was being bullied. Experiences of exclusion appear to equip people with a sense of injustice and ideas about good and bad practice:

There's a lot of unemployed people who would do their job as good as them. We pay them. If they can't do it then that's it.

(Patrick Burke)

Those professionals that had narrators' interests at heart are remembered:

Some professionals are . . . *professionals*, others are ace – they know where the users are coming from.

(Jackie Downer)

A nurse said to my mother, 'Your daughter will be fine, she'll give you pleasure.' So I did.

(Anya Souza)

Joyce Kershaw was encouraged to speak up by the nurses in her boarding school, Lesley the key worker and the centre manager Mr Jones. In Patrick Burke's later days in hospitals he attended an advocacy group. Staff members were not all bad. These accounts substantiate Duncan Mitchell's (1997) biographical evidence that patients and workers inside long-stay hospitals suffer what may be termed a 'shared stigma', which in turn may promote resistant professional practice: 'Staff too are seeking new and better ways of meeting needs as we leave behind the uncertainties of the past' (Lawson 1991: 71).

Finally, the life stories highlight the friendships that were made in spite of the segregatory effects of institutions. Jackie Downer remembers feeling cut off from her friends when she left college. Anya still knows a lot of her peers from school. Joyce Kershaw used to play Monopoly, cards and pool with her friends in the boarding school (her story). Now she meets with her mates for a cup of tea, in the coffee bar of the local bus station. Lloyd Page feels quite lucky having lovely neighbours. As Edgerton (1984b) illustrated, while institutional cultures stress productivity, hidden and often ignored 'client subcultures' (friendship groups) emphasize sociability and harmony and maintain self-esteem.

Outside institutions, inside society: resilience continues

> I'm living in a flat now. There's only two of us there. When I moved my stuff in, I moved some of it into my house and some of it into a spare room. There's a spare bedroom, you see.
>
> (Patrick Burke)

The life stories stress how narrators' resilience continued outside of institutions. All narrators now live in the community. Two live with a parent, one with a friend, one with a brother and another with her partner. Three no longer attend centres and spend their daytimes working with self-advocacy groups instead. Institutions threaten to deculturize inmates but the community offers more opportunities for meaningful lives to be led (Wetherell 1996: 305). Moreover, an increase in the self-confidence of leavers of institutions has been demonstrated, suggesting that institutionalized stigmatisation is reversible (Edgerton and Bercovici 1976). Community living can aid the development of stability and independence (Cobb 1972; Edgerton and Bercovici 1976) and is favourable to becoming drawn in and taken over – leading a life primarily in a service world rather than in the world shared by others in the community (Humphreys *et al.* 1987: 119). However, narrators recall those times when communities exclude:

> When I was lying on the ground, this person asked, 'Why is this Down's syndrome person walking on her own?'
>
> (Anya Souza)

> Another reason why I wasn't given a chance to speak out? Lack of community I think.
>
> (Lloyd Page)

> Children in the bus station shouting, 'Where's your yellow minibus?' I told people to ignore them.
>
> (Joyce Kershaw, her story)

Surveillance continued in some professional–client interactions:

> They sit around and tell you what to do, you're stuck in a chair, you've got staff beside you, you've got students all across – 'What's the do with this person, why's he like this? How is he like this? Put it on a flip-chart.' What do they know?
>
> (Patrick Burke)

When given a chance to make it outside, perfection is demanded and assessment is deemed necessary (Booth 1990, 1991): 'In the bungalow training, he is given marks out of ten for a tidy room, well-made bed, clean floors, etc. How many so-called normal people would be disqualified from a normal existence on this scale?' (Ryan and Thomas 1987: 82).

Despite these knock-backs by the community and interference by 'experts', narrators actively sought a place in the community outside of service settings. Growing up was hard for Jackie Downer – 'a slap in the face' – but getting a job in a library gave her confidence. Joyce Kershaw states she had always stuck up for herself even before People First. Anya Souza enjoyed getting an office job that gave her more responsibilities. This desire of people with learning difficulties for a more normal life as part of society is insufficiently listened to, but none the less there to be heard (Ryan and Thomas 1987: 160). Narrators do not describe communities as places of care but in terms of the various opportunities that are (or are not) offered such as work, independence and friendship:

> As long as they have close friends, as long as they can go out in the evenings, as long as they're able to say, 'Right, I'm going to the pub', 'I'm going to meet a lady friend of mine', that's the way I look at it.
>
> (Patrick Burke)

> When Stuart comes to see me I give him cigarettes. His foster parents say I shouldn't but I remember the days when I didn't have any money and he gave me cigarettes and other things.
>
> (Joyce Kershaw, her story)

The narrators recall some of the bad times that all community members go through, from losing a job or a relationship breaking up to parents dying. In addition, their narratives document exclusion in communities alongside their attempts to be included.

Reflections on pre-group days

The life stories indicate that the lived experience of self-advocacy occurs despite parental fears and practices of the individual model of disability: diagnosis, surveillance and institutionalization. The determination of others, particularly parents, staff and friends, were informative in narrators' developing self-determination. When reflecting on the stories of 'fit people who were removed' from social life into institutions, Potts and Fido (1991: 139) concluded:

That side by side with a painful awareness of lost lives, we have also become sensitive to their humour, resilience and determination. Far from accepting their lot in life, they recognise its injustices and have eagerly grasped the opportunity to give their view of The Park [a long-stay institution] and its history.

Similar conclusions can be drawn from the five life stories presented in this book. Despite disabling barriers, narrators' early experiences indicate that resilience occurs before joining self-advocacy groups – in friendships (Taylor and Bogdan 1989; Goode 1992) and family (Simons 1992), throughout childhood and into adulthood (Daniels 1982; P. Mitchell 1997).

Being in self-advocacy groups: coming out as a self-advocate

Some of the seeds of narrators' self-advocacy were sown before self-advocacy groups were joined. In addition, narrators were asked for their experiences of self-advocacy groups. Four themes emerge with respect to the self-advocacy group: the origins of the movement, as a context for defining resilience, as a context for support and friendship and a place that offers practical gains.

Joining groups: origins of the self-advocacy movement

In the early days, self-advocacy and People First grew mostly in America, starting off in Washington DC and in 84 self-advocates came to England from different parts of America.

(Lloyd Page)

Narrators recollect the beginnings of the self-advocacy movement. Their accounts add to previous literature that has been written by people without learning difficulties (presented in Chapter 2). The stories provide other insights: 'It's no use asking some authority for what he thinks, well, let's not say it's no use, but it's not as important as asking the people of the streets, in the streets, people that actually live in West Belfast' (Parker 1994, on finding out about life in the North of Ireland).

Three narrators spent their daytime in centres or homes prior to joining self-advocacy groups. Jackie Downer joined a group in her twenties, Lloyd Page and Anya Souza in their thirties, Patrick Burke in his forties and Joyce Kershaw when she was 55. Groups were joined in different ways. Anya Souza and Jackie Downer got jobs as self-advocacy workers. The arrival in the UK of American self-advocates inspired Lloyd Page to set up a group. He later left to join a group that he was working for voluntarily at the time of being interviewed. Joyce Kershaw obtained some information from the centre manager and helped to set up a People First group in 1986 (her and my stories). She meets with her group in her spare time. Patrick Burke had been involved in an advocacy group that met in the hospital where he resided. Then Jackie and Guy from his present self-advocacy group came down and told him of their aims to set up a People First group: 'I thought, "Fair enough", and I've been in this advocacy group ever since.'

Groups started up in houses, centres and hospitals, providing the impetus for a larger movement to grow. Narrators remembered enthusiastic staff and parents who had an input in the movement's early days (as documented by Crawley 1982; Worrel 1987: 31; Dybwad and Bersani 1996). Self-advocates also encouraged peers to join groups. The beginnings that narrators remember have parallels with the origins of the UK disability movement (see, for example, Oliver and Zarb 1989; Shakespeare 1993b; Campbell and Oliver 1996).

Early days in self-advocacy groups: Groups as a context for defining resilience

> Until I started going to an advocacy group, which set me free, I couldn't put my views across, tell people what I thought of them, tell the DHSS, tell anyone. I couldn't tell the staff where they were going wrong.
>
> (Patrick Burke)

Life stories depict groups helping narrators to recognize, understand, clarify and develop their resilience. Patrick Burke found People First 'awful hard' at first because he 'didn't know what to say, how to say it or who to say it to'. He was still living in the hospital at the time and was afraid of people. Similarly, life got better for Lloyd Page when he heard of People First. Initially, groups provide members with opportunities to recognize their voices formally and publicly. This is an important factor for oppressed people who are often unaware of their rights or their voices. As the Canadian self-advocate Pat Worth puts it, 'Before People First I had no reason to live. Now I have a reason for getting up in the morning' (Yarmol 1987).

Groups can exist as forums in which members speak out to others who listen. As the earlier experiences of narrators indicate, self-advocacy may be nothing new but listening often is (Worrel 1987). As Joyce Kershaw puts it, 'In People First, we share our problems' (her story). At first, this can be quite threatening: 'What you've got to look out for is they can have too much rights and all of a sudden they blow up on you' (Patrick Burke). Jackie Downer advises new members 'To start with basic stuff first and campaigning later but you don't have to. You can just chat.' Patrick Burke prescribes a softly-softly approach at first: 'Don't get worried, don't get shy, you'll get confidence when you're speaking.' Attending a place where speaking out is supported and emphasized, and has importance attached, may be a novel experience for some. This may explain why Patrick Burke initially found People First hard, because he had had few opportunities to speak out and to be listened to before. In other ways groups built upon narrators' previous experiences of resistance. Narrators began formally to recognize and articulate their experiences:

> You don't need to go over the top organising pictures, theatres, parties, meeting with other groups or self-help groups. Basic stuff first and

campaigning later *but* you don't have to. You can just chat, you don't get the chance in the centre or at home.

(Jackie Downer)

Groups provide a material outlet for self-advocacy. The confidence gained with group membership can aid the transition of self-advocacy skills into other contexts, such as individual programme plans, home and workplaces, and at formal set-ups such as user participation meetings (Barnes and Wistow 1992a): 'People have changed so much' (Jackie Downer).

Groups as a context for support and friendship (and tensions)

Guy was chair for about eight years and now we've got a chair and a vice. He helped out. Others gave me confidence. Guy says, 'Look, do you want to say anything? If so, shout it out. If people tell you to shut up say, "No, I won't. I'll speak like I want to speak not how you want me to speak".' I've got a loud voice and if you don't like it you can lump it.

(Patrick Burke)

In Todis's (1992) study of Wilbur and Grace, a married couple with learning difficulties, Todis suggests that what each found supportive about their relationship was that the other was thoroughly familiar with the life circumstances that result from having 'development disabilities'. Similarly, life stories in this book highlight the affiliations that can develop among people in the context of a self-advocacy group. A supplementary source of support was offered. The best friends Lloyd Page has ever made were the friends in the office. For Patrick Burke, 'When you've been locked up all your life, you can't have no friends. Now I'm starting to make friends.' These support networks gave narrators valued roles and relationships in which to work together on various issues ranging from, for example, when parents became over-protective to service abuse:

I can take a risk, I can have a relationship . . . I can cry if I want to cry.

(Jackie Downer)

People First has helped me out an awful lot. I think the set-up's good. It's helped to bring me out of things that I wanted to be brought out of.

(Patrick Burke)

In contemplating the prevention of sexual abuse of people with learning difficulties, Brown and Craft (1989: 9) observe that many people with learning difficulties have to do what they are told in care settings: 'So that obeying someone comes to be equated with being good. A great deal of corrective work is needed to help students see themselves as valued individuals who, like anyone else, have personal preferences and rights.'

Self-advocacy groups may provide contexts for self-correction. Nevertheless, as with all collectives, groups should not be romanticized. In-group tensions and politics affected narrators. Jackie Downer has reservations with groups that threaten to exclude others. Anya Souza is happy no longer to be part of a group. Groups have parallels with other friendship or work groups. Tensions are tied up with support. Furthermore, self-advocacy groups are not necessarily the central focus of narrators' lives. Patrick Burke enjoys the freedom of having his own flat, sharing it with his dog, coming back from the pub when he feels like it. Joyce Kershaw thrives on working in the coffee bar at the centre. They call it 'Joyce's Café'. Jackie Downer has her religious faith: 'I can only believe in myself so much.' At the very least, groups provide contexts for critical friendships to be formed.

Practical gains offered by self-advocacy groups

> I enjoy People First more than I did in the Day Centre because you do things all the time.
>
> (Lloyd Page)

According to Wolfensberger (1972b), community living serves both practical and emotional needs of people with learning difficulties, by promoting a 'valued role' (hence the more recent term of 'social role valorization'; Brown and Smith 1992a, b). Regardless of normalization procedures, self-advocacy groups provide emotional (expressive) gains (as cited in the above section) and serve a number of practical (instrumental) needs of narrators. The life stories highlight narrators proactively taking up valued positions within and outside of groups. Here they have used the opportunities offered by groups and developed their own self-advocacy (see Brooks 1991). As Lloyd Page says, People First gave him a sense of purpose: 'Get up, get washed, dressed, listen to some music in the morning, go to work as normal – do what you gotta do and that's it.' Later, the group offered Lloyd grander opportunities, like working with the Open University, meeting the Minister for the Disabled ('stupid man'!) and going to Canada. These opportunities may build on family ties:

> To get me over to Canada my mother and about four of her friends fundraised for four years. They got £4,300 and that meant we could send four self-advocates and one supporter to Canada.
>
> (Lloyd Page)

Anya Souza appeared in a documentary on the TV. Joyce Kershaw was contacted through the self-advocacy network to take part in some research (my story). Jackie Downer has 'learnt a lot from so many people and done things that I'd never dreamed about'. Patrick Burke rather modestly proclaims he is 'coming on'. Four narrators have worked for self-advocacy groups on a regular voluntary basis.

After institutionalization the acquisition of a job or other valued role can restore adaptability, self-respect and independence (Edgerton 1967; Edgerton and Bercovici 1976; Abraham 1989). Following Brandon and Towe (1989: 20), Bhavnani (1990) and Sparkes (1994), self-advocacy may allow another way of conceptualizing empowerment that is less paternalistic in nature:

By speaking to other people in the group it gives you the confidence to speak to other people . . . self-advocacy means that people with learning difficulties have a right to speak up for themselves. To see how they can express themselves in ways that people, members of the general public, can understand.

(Lloyd Page)

Narrators conceptualized 'self-advocacy' in ways that contrast with literature that considers self-advocacy as something that people with learning difficulties are trained to do (for example, Sievert *et al.* 1988). Anecdotes are offered of self-empowerment rather than normalization (see Mesibov 1976).

Self-advocacy groups as a context for self-definition

Can I speak now? You should see what I've got – I've got two arms and two legs, I'm not physically handicapped actually.

(Anya Souza)

The life stories pick up on the self-defining aspect of group membership. Vincent (1998) uncovered similar opportunities for self-definition, or what she calls the making of alternative frameworks of sense, in African Caribbean parents' groups. Definitions have been a key component of the self-organization of disabled people, like the UPIAS (1976) document that separated definitions of impairment and disability: 'Transforming personal and social consciousness is one of the key factors that separates new social movements from the old, more traditional social movements' (Campbell and Oliver 1996: 105).

Groups provide a context for re-evaluating old terms and coming up with new ones. This may be useful in view of the anxieties that parents face in explaining the label of learning disability to their children (Todd and Shearn 1997). Narrators prefer the term 'learning difficulties', reflecting the People First organization's chosen terminology:

We are people with learning difficulties, not what people used to call us, I won't say the word.

(Joyce Kershaw, her story)

Learning difficulties is more dignified.

(Jackie Downer)

Mental impairment? Now what the hell's that? Never heard of it. I've heard of learning disability. I think mental handicap is still being used but they shouldn't.

(Patrick Burke)

The term 'learning difficulties' implies that people want to learn and recognizes that all people have some learning difficulty one way or another:

A man couldn't do woman's work . . . I said, 'You want to come and see some of them working in the centre and I bet they'd have to teach you how to do it.' Come and try and do our work and you'll soon find out if you've got a learning difficulty or not.

(Joyce Kershaw, my story)

In this statement Joyce questions the embodied nature of learning difficulties that is assumed to exist solely for people diagnosed with such naturalized notions of impairment. Instead, Joyce broadens out understandings of (in)capacity, demanding that we rethink. Such demands parallel Booth and Booth's (1994) idea of 'distributed competence', succinctly defined by Martin Levine, a Canadian self-advocate:

> I may need help in some things, but I'm not retarded. I can take care of myself . . . Everyone needs help. Some people need more. Even the ones in the outside – the normal people, have marriage counsellors and other people to help them.

(Quoted in Friedman-Lambert 1987: 15)

As narratives paint phenomenological landscapes we are invited to place ourselves in the picture. In turn we may start to unpick the specific visions of what constitutes the subject matter of learning difficulties. Soon we notice that this still life called 'learning difficulties' is open to an abundance of interpretations beyond the unemotional socio-biological take. Interestingly, having knowledge about the label of learning difficulties provides people with self-understandings that can be applied in everyday life (Roffman *et al.* 1994): 'Who has 47 cells? I have. They haven't, they've only got 46' (Anya Souza).

Narrators recognize how labels prescribe 'difference' through the values that are attached to them. However, having 'learning difficulties' does not mean that it has to be associated with 'handicap': 'It's good to use so that everyone can recognize the term' (Anya Souza). In line with other disabled commentators (Hevey 1992; Barnes 1993), media representations of people with learning difficulties are pinpointed and challenged, including characters in popular television series, soap operas, documentaries and newspapers:

> This woman had put in the local paper, 'Mentally handicapped are simple and happy people.' I read it and thought the cheeky so-and-so.

(Joyce Kershaw, my story)

Likewise, charities that play on people's pity as they fund-raise for 'the handicapped' are criticized – like 'MENCRAP', as Jackie Downer puts it. Opinions expressed in the stories highlight the various ways in which labels are internalized. Jackie Downer separates herself from 'less able' people with learning difficulties – 'I'm lucky I'm not like people with severe learning difficulties' – a case of using dominant disabling images of self-hood? Anya Souza dismisses the label: 'Would I say I have difficulties learning? No, I learnt well enough. I picked up things very quickly.' Joyce Kershaw contrasts having learning difficulties with physical impairment:

> Learning disabilities – I don't like that, disability makes you believe that we are in wheelchairs and we can't do anything for ourselves, when we can. We've got jobs now, we've got paid jobs.

(My story)

Joyce's comments have parallels with those of a self-advocate cited in Sutcliffe and Simons (1993: 24): 'If you go for a job and you've got the label "disabled" they won't give you a chance.'

The suggestion that people with learning difficulties are not 'as handicapped' as physically impaired people is controversial. Nevertheless, it provides an interesting mirror image of prejudice expressed by some in the wider disability movement: 'I have to keep proving I'm not mentally disabled' (Elsa, in Campling 1981: 85). To reiterate a point made by Simone Aspis:

> People with learning difficulties face discrimination in the disability movement. People without learning difficulties use the medical model when dealing with us. We are always asked to talk about advocacy and our impairments as though our barriers aren't disabling in the same way as disabled people without learning difficulties. We want concentration on our access needs in the mainstream disability movement.
>
> (Quoted in Campbell and Oliver 1996: 97)

Some readers could suggest that narrators are hiding or minimizing their impairments (Barnes 1996b). Another interpretation is that self-advocacy groups remind members of what they can do as opposed to what they can't do – what Booth and Booth (1994) call taking the 'capacity perspective' over the 'deficiency perspective':

> It could be argued that whilst the disability movement has fought the colonisers of disability (e.g. the medical and allied professions) for the right to define disability on their own terms, the fight against the colonisers of learning difficulty is of a different order; it is a fight against the denial of humanity itself; hence, this group's insistence on being perceived as *people first*.
>
> (Gillman *et al.* 1997: 690)

Perhaps labels are unnecessary shorthand:

> You can't say you're 'just handicapped' because you're labelling someone and that's not the way to talk to someone.
>
> (Anya Souza)

In the long run dropping labels altogether may be better: 'I'm just me' (Jackie Downer), 'We're men and women' (Patrick Burke). The personal and political aspects of self-advocacy are highlighted in the ways in which narrators have considered the labels they were given.

Reflections on the early self-advocacy days

> That's why they wanted me out of the house, because I started telling the staff what to do. I didn't do it before – I learnt it off People First. I took my ideas from here up to the house where I lived and said, 'Hold on, we pay you. If you don't like it you know where the door is.'
>
> (Patrick Burke)

Narrators came to groups often late in life from a variety of contexts. Past experiences affected how narrators experienced early days with groups. It is easy to understand the significance of People First for Patrick Burke in view of his time in hospitals. However, Patrick, like other narrators, has other arenas of life that are just as important as the group. As with all friendship and work groups, tensions exist that may become too much, as they did for Anya Souza. Life stories point to the potential of groups at least to build upon past experiences of resistance, provide additional outlets for self-advocacy and add to the richness of lives. Taken for granted ideas like choice, independence, debate and having a voice are given a material base and context for enactment.

Learning from experience: expert advice on self-advocacy

Accounts are interspersed with narrators' opinions about the doing of self-advocacy. Chapter 2 of this book represented a number of debates about the organization of the (inter)national self-advocacy movement and the tensions associated with the workings of groups. The involvement of self-advocates in these debates remains questionable. Therefore, this section revisits some of the arguments as considered by the narrators: how to support groups, the state of the movement, the self-help and political nature of self-advocacy, and the future.

Supporting self-advocacy groups

Narrators have lived through the 'learning difficulties experience' of diagnosis, assessment, classification, surveillance, institutionalization and training. Such experiences may breed awareness of good and bad practice. Add to that the vast experience narrators have had of self-advocacy groups and some informed understandings of support are articulated. To consider support, narrators were asked for their views on the role of advisors in self-advocacy groups. Narrators said they preferred independent advisors who work only for members, thus supporting previous literature on the 'independent advisor'.[2]

> The group is for people with learning difficulties, not the advisors.
>
> (Joyce Kershaw, my story)

> People should say 'hold on we don't want a member of staff as advisor because we can't say what we want to and we can't say a lot. We want an outsider to come in to the group.' I would go along with saying get an outsider, not a friend but someone off the street.
>
> (Patrick Burke)

Furthermore, paying independent advisors may be fruitful, for then:

> We've got every right to tell the support worker what we think. That's the best way. We're the ones paying the staff and if the staff cannot handle it, well they know where the gate is.
>
> (Patrick Burke)

Other narrators are not so sure: 'Paid workers create problems' (Jackie Downer). Narrators have little time for staff advisors, backing up previous negative appraisals of the staff advisor (see, for example, Hanna 1978; Worrel 1987, 1988; Clare 1990):

> I think there's a problem with advisors who are staff because you see them every day . . . She was always watching you.
>
> (Joyce Kershaw, my story)

Yet life stories cite episodes of conflict between narrators and all types of advisor – taking understandings of support beyond the independent–staff dichotomy. An overarching theme was the power that any advisor can hold (Worrel 1988: 35):

> Some can be a bit pushy and some can be a bit bossy . . . we're telling them what to do. Now some of the members don't do that yet but they're getting there.
>
> (Patrick Burke)

> Workers can spoil members by being too caring. Be careful about caring.
>
> (Jackie Downer)

Joyce Kershaw, for example, felt that she was fighting a lonely battle against an advisor:

> I told the advisor, 'You've frightened them all into putting their hands up. You frighten them into it instead of explaining, you just take it all on your own. The group isn't for you, this is for people with learning difficulties . . . it's for what we can do.'
>
> (My story)

Life stories highlight the complexities of support offered by advisors. Jackie Downer has worked as an advisor herself and has felt the tensions in pushing people a bit too far: 'I've got more power, I've got to be careful, I'm their own worst enemy sometimes.' Narrators' experiences suggest that the power of advisors may be located within a number of roles and interactions rather than simply being a reflection of independent or staff status:

> The more independent you are the more free you are but it really depends on the advisor.
>
> (Jackie Downer)

The label of 'staff advisor' may hide the various roles and positions taken by the advisor in the group. Moreover, to assume that such a label is synonymous with limiting support forgets narrators' reflections on 'good staff'. As Jackie Downer puts it, 'Some professionals are . . . *professionals*. Others are ace – they know where users are coming from.' While advisors are important – 'We need them for everywhere we go' (Lloyd Page) – life stories emphasize the self-empowerment of narrators in addition to the support that is offered by others.

Views on the self-advocacy movement

> The problem with that lot was that they'd never had a Down's syndrome baby. 'Normal people' were in the association, I was the only one with Down's syndrome working in that office for ten years.
>
> (Anya Souza)

Narrators were asked for their views about the self-advocacy movement. They were outspoken in their analysis of recent and current developments. However, the interviews and the subsequent life stories tended to focus on each narrator's achievements and setbacks rather than wider issues such as disability movements. This personalized bent to the interviews and narratives may explain why the movement is not held up as a significant factor in the lives of self-advocates; as Jackie Downer puts it, you have to be yourself in the so-called movement anyway. Nevertheless, while questions still remain about the relative significance of the movement to groups and individuals, a number of opinions were expressed.

First, narrators assert that people with learning difficulties should lead the movement, for then 'They'd get more people helping them' (Joyce Kershaw, my story). Second, dangers were perceived in the movement becoming advisor-led. Self-advocacy is the in thing now and open to abuse (Jackie Downer). For example, both Joyce Kershaw and Jackie Downer worry that advisors are taking over the setting up and running of England People First.[3] An article by Lloyd Page and Simone Aspis (1997) takes up this point. They suggest that self-advocacy in the UK has become a professional industry for staff, service providers and researchers, rather than a political collective for people with learning difficulties. Third, the movement's lack of financial support and the implications of these lacking resources were identified. Jackie notes the discrepancy in some groups getting 'mega bucks' and others getting little. This point also concerns Lloyd Page, who suggests that there is a need to weigh up the balance between England People First and other groups. Fourth, a number of anecdotes support seeing the People First movement as a social movement: 'It's a network of people supporting one another' (Jackie Downer); 'I've seen People First grow in ten years, It's grown for the better' (Lloyd Page).

Some of the experiences of resistance recalled by narrators have resonances with Marx and McAdam's (1994: 3) definition of social movements as: 'Organised efforts to promote or resist change in society that rely, at least in part, on non-institutionalised forms of political action.' Jackie suggests that unity is important – a point often made by physically impaired activists in the disability movement (Stuart 1993; Morris 1996; Shakespeare and Watson 1997). The similarity of experiences expressed in the five life stories in this book highlight shared ground that can be used as a starting point for unity in self-advocacy groups: collective identity as a base for self-empowerment and organization (Oliver 1996).

The self-help and political nature of self-advocacy

> I thought who are you? It takes time to get married, it's a big step to go through in life. Things can wait. I'm young, I'm 34 and I'm single. I have my independence. It might affect my benefits.
>
> (Anya Souza)

In descriptions of self-advocacy inside groups, stories are told of travelling the world, speaking at conferences, having words published and carrying out research. There are anecdotes of appearances on TV and radio, the lobbying of MPs, involvement at user consultation meetings and the starting up of self-advocacy groups. These achievements appear even more remarkable along-side tales of cries for help in various institutions, sexual and physical abuse and separation from family members. Many of these experiences may be alien to readers but they will also identify similarities; like the anxieties of going to school, leaving and getting a job, the importance and difficulties of relation-ships, and hopes for the future. Self-advocacy is described in personal and political terms: 'It's both these things . . . It's personal, there's no wrongs or rights' (Jackie Downer); 'We're just ordinary people with learning difficulties' (Lloyd Page). Self-advocacy is presented in terms of personal gains:

> With that I'm starting to go out in the evenings, and go to the pubs and clubs and make friends that way.
>
> (Patrick Burke)

> Me and my friends go into the bus station café for a drink. We pay in turns.
>
> (Joyce Kershaw, her story)

These qualities come with tensions. Anya Souza left People First because of various squabbles ('I was being the star and they hated it'), and Lloyd Page has noted others' envy, ('Aye, aye, that'll get you nowhere'). Narrators do not rely solely on groups for personal and political benefits. While groups may provide a safe context for taking a few safe steps towards independence, nar-rators recognize that life goes on outside: 'I have to do things on my own because my mother's not there' (Anya Souza).

The political aspects of self-advocacy permeate the narratives from informal incidents like asking for tea not coffee (see Jackie Downer), through to formal user consultation meetings, where people 'should learn to talk properly' (as argued by Joyce Kershaw, both stories, and Patrick Burke; along with Sutcliffe 1990: 28; Wertheimer 1990). Self-advocacy emerges as something materially and actively understood in the anecdotes told by narrators. Groups appear to provide a context in which the personal and political are voiced and acted out.

Reflections on doing self-advocacy: and so to the future

> I could tell you about the past, the future in 15 years time, how I'm going to cope, will I cope?
>
> (Patrick Burke)

In reflecting on the past, narrators see a bright future. Joyce Kershaw hopes that her efforts will be of use to young people with learning difficulties (both stories). Lloyd Page thinks that self-advocates have got the power to do what they want: 'Self-advocacy is looking good – more stronger.' Jackie Downer reckons the movement is going from strength to strength: 'The picture is good, but it's happening more in some places than others.' Consequently, there is still a lot of work ahead for self-advocates and groups – to build a foundation for younger members for the future (Patrick Burke). This includes publicizing the concerns of self-advocates (see Walmsley 1992) and hopes for a 'New World' (see also Finkelstein and Stuart 1996):

> You've got to keep reminding people – especially on the outside, you've got to remind them all the time that we are different to what they are, which, fair enough, we are. We've all got our own ways of living.
>
> (Patrick Burke)

Narrators recognize the complexities of support, self-advocacy as a movement and the personal, political characters of being a self-advocate.

Reflections: life stories, the self-advocacy group and resilience

The analysis thus far has examined the emergence of narrators' resilience in and outside the self-advocacy group and presented a number of pointers about doing self-advocacy. This final section draws together more general conclusions. Two themes are presented: the storied nature of self-advocacy and relevance of the accounts to other self-advocates.

The storied nature of self-advocacy

> One person I met was Pat Worth – it was great because you listen to his life story and it's brilliant.
>
> (Lloyd Page)

Cohler (1991) asserts that life stories are a useful medium for documenting responses to adversity. Story tellers often present stories in ways that accent resilience over adversity, so as to maintain a sense of coherence and personal integrity across the period of life that is being told. Consequently, narrators may recount past experiences in ways that emphasize their activity, intention and direction. This may be the case particularly for narrators who readily agree to tell their accounts and so have stories that they want to publicize. However, these incidents of bias may not be a bad thing when the narrators are from a marginalized group. Too often people with learning difficulties are submerged under the system, the therapeutic technique or the goals of the sponsored programme (Heckel 1968). By contrast, their life stories can high-light the other sides to life that are often ignored by dominant institutions and practices (Gillman *et al.* 1997).

The five life stories in this book can be seen as examples of a different narrative type from the 'problem saturated' descriptions offered by case histories and other formal documents (Gillman *et al.* 1997: 689). Their accounts introduce the idea that narrators do have influence over and become active in their own lives. In this sense they are counter or alternative documents that contribute to a revision of official learning difficulties documentation:

> People with learning difficulties might form a 'resistance movement' – perhaps through the already well established self-advocacy movement – in which the subjugated voices of people with learning difficulties can be heard in the telling and 're-authoring' of their own stories.
>
> (p. 689)

These stories present another side of self-advocacy than previous literature that has been concerned with generalizations, organizational typologies and the role of advisors. The five narratives highlight the everyday nature of resilience despite the oppressive conditions outside groups and present tales that give meaning to the term 'self-advocacy'. Formal and informal, low and high-level, individual and group, private and public aspects of self-advocacy are articulated. People with learning difficulties can lead busy and varied lives. Moreover, the life stories challenge accounts of people with learning difficulties that view behaviour in terms of an oversimplified linear relationship between some ill-defined (and ever-changing) state of 'retardation' as cause and 'retarded behaviour' as effect (Levine and Langness 1986: 192). Narratives remind us that people with learning difficulties are not helpless, involuntary victims of genetic adversity, or the degenerated shells of individuals who 'might have been' (Whittemore *et al.* 1986: 5).

Self-advocacy as resilience, an inclusive social model of disability and the relevance of the stories to other self-advocates

> I was awful quiet and they all shut up and listened.
>
> (Patrick Burke)

Resilience is a recurring theme throughout the life stories. Perhaps self-advocacy can be defined as the public recognition of people with learning difficulties' resilience. For Bogdan and Taylor (1982: 52) a strength of life stories is that they force readers to think of narrators as people so that categories of all kind become less relevant. In this sense, resilience is typical to any life account, particularly for those who have survived 'the learning difficulties experience'. As Atkinson (1993a: iv) observed about the people involved in her oral history project: 'They do not emerge in their accounts as victims, but as people who survived, and often defied, the worst aspects of the system.'

To pinpoint when narrators were involved in self-advocacy illuminates their larger narratives. Their stories show that 'self-advocacy' is not necessarily given to or learnt by people with learning difficulties in self-advocacy groups, but exists in a variety of contexts. However, the experiences that are documented are those of high-fliers in the movement:

> This is my experience. Every experience is totally different and you need to go back and ask self-advocates.
>
> (Jackie Downer)

Perhaps narrators' past experiences of adversity and opportunity have made them into the strong characters that they are today. Nevertheless, their stories have wider links with people with learning difficulties generally. In terms of supporting self-advocates, these stories have highlighted that self-advocacy already exists prior to joining a group. Supporters could bear this prior self-advocacy in mind. Stories also illustrate how structures impact adversely on lives, though resistance does occur and self-advocacy groups can enhance resistance. These accounts are historical documents of a past epoch of exclusion. However, their contemporary relevance remains, in the light of recent policy changes in Britain and elsewhere that reinforce segregation and recategorize an individual model of disability (Potts 1998). Finally, these life stories highlight the relevance of a social model of disability to people with learning difficulties – that self-determination flows within people who have suffered the indignities of discrimination.

Conclusion

This chapter has considered the relationship between self-advocacy, self-advocacy groups and some of the life experiences of narrators. Against a background of structures that threaten to deny communication, the human drive of people with learning difficulties to communicate is presented. The will to move on and achieve independence is articulated, while barriers that create dependence are recognized. Moreover, the capacity to rebuild shattered lives and the power of self-advocacy, with others' support, are illustrated. In this chapter I have drawn upon these life stories in order to examine the lived impact of self-advocacy. Part III takes up the advice of top self-advocates to examine self-advocacy in action from the inside.

Notes

1 Note that the story in Chapter 5 – Joyce's story – was penned by Joyce herself, though she also agreed that my story constructed from our discussions – Danny's story, Appendix 2 – should be referred to in this book.
2 See, for example, Hannad (1978), Williams (1982), Williams and Shoultz (1982), McKenna (1986), Worrel (1987, 1988), Crawley (1990), Flynn and Ward (1991), Simons (1992), Downer and Ferns (1993), Dowson and Whittaker (1993), Sutcliffe and Simons (1993), Hampson (1994) and Shoultz (1997a, b, c).
3 At the time of speaking to narrators, a number of self-advocacy groups had met to discuss the setting up of a National Committee entitled England People First with various representatives from groups in England. At the time of writing no group has yet been set up.

 PART **III**

SELF-ADVOCACY IN ACTION

 **7**

Inside self-advocacy groups:
typologies and dynamics

This chapter examines self-advocacy in action. Four groups are described and ethnographic involvement is used to appraise 12 points that emerge from previous literature about the organization, workings and processes of self-advocacy groups. These points span four analytical themes that are further illuminated by my involvement with four distinctly organized self-advocacy groups. First, the relationships between the self-advocacy of people with learning difficulties and service providers are examined through my involvement with the *Centre-based Group*. This section contemplates the adequacy of service-supported self-advocacy initiatives, reflecting on whether or not they can transcend tokenistic offerings. Accordingly, the nature of support exercised by professionals (employees of services) who work as advisors to self-advocacy groups is probed. Second, the self-advocacy group type that appears to flirt with seemingly trivial leisure and social activities is considered in relation to the *Social Group*. Here the organizational 'independence' of this type of group is examined alongside the involvement of volunteer advisors who may bring with them other external and institutional modes of support that mould the group in particular ways. Moreover, the notion of triviality is reassessed. Third, the impact of advocacy initiatives on self-advocacy will be explored in the *Advocacy-supported Group*. In what ways does the politics of advocacy impact upon the self-determination of self-advocates? We will look at how advocates (who are advisors) balance 'working for' and 'working with' (advocates as comrades or dictators), while delving further into the bureaucratic involvement of people with learning difficulties in an advocacy organization of the voluntary sector (initiatives as inclusive or exclusionary). Finally, the 'idealized form' of organized self-advocacy, as it is consistently conceptualized in previous literature, is critiqued with reference to the *Independent Group*. Here a group resembling an organization of people with learning difficulties (and thus situating itself most readily in the wider context of the British disability movement) is investigated in relation to the involvement of paid independent workers (a new form of paternalism?), the committee hierarchy of the 'ideal type' (organization as stifling or enabling) and the desirability of 'professional self-advocacy'.

Introducing the appraisal

To describe, never mind appraise, what was observed over a period of 14 months is a daunting prospect. While the collation of ethnographic field notes is concerned with the accumulation of material, description and appraisal require simplicity and economy (Walker 1981). As a result, this chapter only picks at the richness of group dynamics. However, a more significant analytical tension emerges. Barnes (1994: 2) asserts that there is 'a moral onus on researchers at least not to add to any feelings of disempowerment or distress'. This chapter does *not* attempt to undermine the actions of self-advocates or advisors of the four groups represented but tries to shed light on some group dynamics of self-advocacy in action. First, the effort of supporters or advisors should be kept in mind throughout the critical commentary. This chapter and the next do not try to undo their acts but use them to critique the role of the supporter in self-advocacy groups. Many gave up their free time, picking people up before meetings and advocating for them at formal case conferences. They often bought the drinks at the bar, put the odd £20 into the kitty when needed and drove members to and from meetings. They did what so many others would not. Second, in aiming to provide a contemporary picture of what is happening in some self-advocacy groups in England, considerations of bureaucracy, dynamics and structure may, at times, take attention away from the members of the groups. A general finding was that people with learning difficulties were using the group contexts for a variety of reasons that appeared to contribute to their own aims and ambitions. This personal and political nature of group membership should be kept in mind throughout the appraisal.

On a material note, reference is made throughout this part of the book to observational field notes taken after each meeting with the groups (following Schatzman and Strauss 1973). Other sources include the views of members collected in the group discussions (written up for the groups as feedback forms), the group's own documents (including original group constitutions, information leaflets, training details) and documents that I constructed on the requests of the groups (evaluation report for the county council, collation of feedback from organizations that paid groups to offer training workshops).

Models of self-advocacy

Worrel (1987, 1988) provides a starting point for the description and appraisal of the workings of groups. Worrel illustrates through the use of sociograms intra-group relationships between advisors and self-advocates. He presents two forms around which groups may be organized (Figures 7.1 and 7.2).

Following Barb Goode, a Canadian self-advocate, groups that approximate Figure 7.1 are not People First groups but 'Advisors First' groups (quoted in Worrel 1988: 31). Worrel argues that potentially this structure imposes a number of limitations upon group meetings and other subsequent activities. First, lines of communication are directed through the advisor and not between members. This may promote a paternalistic culture where 'advisors know best' (Khan 1985). Second, members are encouraged to depend on the advisor and not on one another – advocacy rather than self-advocacy (Tyne 1994). There is a risk that an autocratic, advisor-led environment is bred. Third, there is no model of membership control (Worrel 1988: 49). For Crawley (1982, 1988, 1990), McKenna (1986), Simons (1992) and Dowson and Whittaker (1993), advisor-oriented groups are most likely to be found in service-based types and in some coalition and divisional organizations. While these intra-group relationships may be useful in the initial stages of setting up a group, groups that keep this structure are inevitably limited thereafter (see Crawley 1988; Barnes and Wistow 1992c). Worrel (1988) proposes an alternative way of organizing groups that holds greater potential for self-advocate leadership and the self-empowerment of members. Worrel argues that advisors should promote a group dynamic that follows Figure 7.2.

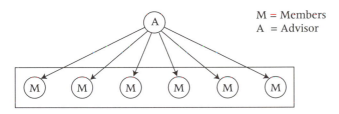

Figure 7.1 Advisor-oriented group structure (based on Worrel 1988: 48)

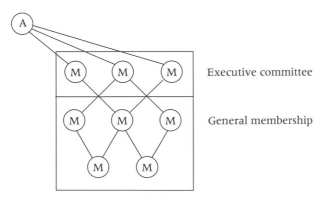

Figure 7.2 Member-oriented group structure (based on Worrell 1998: 49)

This hierarchy reflects the intra-group relationships of a number of high-profile North American and UK People First groups (Worrel 1988; Simons 1992; Dowson and Whittaker 1993). Worrel proposes that this structure is preferable to that presented in Figure 7.1 for a number of reasons. First, advisors' main port of call is the executive committee, which is comprised of a small number of self-advocates who have been voted on to the committee to represent the views of all members (Speak for Ourselves of Newcastle 1993). Second, a consequence of this committee is that members depend on the executive and one another rather than just the advisors for support. Communication occurs throughout the members as devalued persons are placed in valued roles (Worrel 1988: 50). Third, an interdependent, interactive, cooperative culture is bred that helps to promote solidarity between members (*ibid.*) – a key component of the self-organization of disabled people (Oliver and Zarb 1989, Oliver 1990, 1996). A number of observers have suggested that this group structure is readily found in the 'autonomous group' and 'coalition' types (Worrel 1988; Simons 1992; Dowson and Whittaker 1993). Independence and non-accountability to service or divisional organizations provides the group with the potential for self-determination and self-organization.

Worrel (1988: 50) recognizes that the structure of groups does not unequivocally lead to different types of self-advocacy in action. A number of questions remain. First, is there a link between group 'type' and ways of organizing? Second, do the group structures proposed by Worrel exist in practice? Third, what group processes occur within these structures? Fourth, are these processes the consequence of group structure or of other deeper group dynamics? The remainder of this chapter examines the processes and dynamics that occur in different groups. To make sense of these processes and dynamics, a number of points that emerge from the literature associated with self-advocacy in action are considered in the light of my observations of specific examples of self-advocacy in action.

The Centre Group: service-based self-advocacy

The Centre Group meets in an adult training centre situated on the woody outskirts of a city in the north of England. The nearest place is Quarry Village,[1] about a mile away. Surrounded by trees and close to a small industrial park, the centre is marked out by a sign reading 'Centre for Mentally Handicapped Adults'. It is separated from built-up residential areas, and a high wooden fence surrounds the perimeter of its grounds. Some 40 years old, the centre resembles a primary school at first sight. There is only one level, ensuring wheelchair accessibility, and brightly coloured posters and artwork adorn many notice boards. Through the doors of the main entrance, visitors are faced with the reception desk where they have to sign in. Loud requests to staff and 'users' come over the tannoy system. The atmosphere is claustrophobic, what with the grating sound of the tannoy and the compact layout of the corridors and rooms. During my visits the canteen was always full of people but there was never any evidence of early morning coffee or tea.

> I met an elderly man, in his sixties, with walking stick in hand. He spoke of the dangers of crossing the roads round his way. 'They drive like bliddy maniacs.' Other greetings were offered when I entered the common room. An elderly woman with smiling eyes walked up to me. Gestures, Makaton, handshakes . . . A teenage lad wrapped up in a winter coat took my hand but said nothing. The man with the walking stick re-appeared, 'Oh this bliddy catheter's killing me – do you have that problem?' The staff members often sit together. My 'hellos' were always ignored.
>
> (First meeting)[2]

Some exchange eventually occurred between the staff and me:

> Over lunch, three female staff chatted about the weekend. Pubs and clubs were mentioned and jokes were exchanged. 'I like the gardens', I interjected, looking out of the window. 'Yes', replied the taller one. 'We have to patrol that area in the summer – that's where all the snoggers go.' In contrast, members of the Centre Group and their advisor Louise are like a breath of fresh air. The meeting is like a sanctuary, refuge. Little wonder that many uninvited users who join the group beforehand and during meetings are shooed away by the members.
>
> (Second meeting)

I wasn't to venture out into the centre much after the first couple of meetings. Taylor and Bogdan's (1984: 85) description of 'total institutions' fits my own perceptions of the centre, where 'for residents daily life is routinized and regimented'. Moreover, Potts and Fido's (1991: 11) reference to official documents written in the 1920s about long-stay hospitals has little resonances with my own mental picture of this centre: 'colonies, homely and simple in character and free from unnecessary repressive and restraining methods.' The Centre Group's meetings continued in this wider institutional culture.

The Centre Group fits descriptions of the service-system type identified in the literature, particularly the 'user committee' or 'working group' that attempts to represent the concerns of centre users (see Crawley 1982, 1988; McKenna 1986; Brooks 1991). Between eight and ten members meet every week for two hours in a room in the centre. This fills a morning of their week that would otherwise be taken by activities orchestrated as part of the centre's curriculum. The group had been meeting for about three years when I started attending. The centre manager set it up as part of an initiative to promote empowerment. Users vote members on to the committee in an annual ballot box vote. Photos and pictures are provided on the voting slips to aid non-readers.

Meetings start with the writing of an agenda by Lesley, the chairperson, and other members ('I'm a non-reader', she told me). Topics of discussion tend to converge around centre issues like fund-raising, food in the canteen and staff–user relationships. Often centre matters have been written down on the agenda beforehand by the advisor. However, personal issues come to the fore just as frequently. Lesley covers each point on the agenda:

> 'Don't forget the group rules', Lesley commands. She is quite a figure and members do conform, but she also has a sensitive side. Jane was upset by Lesley's bossiness and ran off to cry in the loo. Lesley followed behind, the pair returning arm in arm some moments later.
>
> (Fourth meeting)

Members of the group voted Lesley as chairperson and Denise as secretary. The group has no treasurer or funds. Louise, a member of the centre staff, supports the group. She took over from a previous advisor – 'an independent volunteer' (extract from group discussion). Louise supports the group as part of her job:

> As members sorted the chairs and tables and set about organising the agenda, Louise was in and out of the room, getting the kettle, cups, teabags, coffee and biscuits for 'elevenses'.
>
> (First meeting)

In addition to weekly meetings, members take turns to attend meetings of a local advocacy development project. A number of guests have been invited along to the Centre Group, including a speech therapist and the centre manager. Following Worrel's (1988) attempts, the Centre Group can be represented as a sociogram (Figure 7.3).[3] This sociogram is similar to Worrel's 'advisor-orientated' group (see Figure 7.1). Louise was a central figure in the group. Members often addressed her when they spoke in meetings and approached her when they had personal concerns. I found the group to have a friendly atmosphere, contrasting with the wider centre culture: 'I like going to this group. That is – when I'm in the meeting and not in the centre' (third meeting). While Louise was obviously important to members, additional lines of communication existed among the membership. Perhaps characteristic of any meeting, self-advocates tended to chat together in small friendship groups. These membership ties and Louise's member-oriented role problematize Worrel's 'advisor-oriented' model.

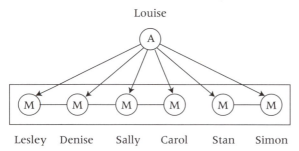

Figure 7.3 The Centre Group's structure

The Centre Group and previous literature

Claim 1: The staff advisor's role is an impossible one
Previous literature has highlighted the dilemmas faced by staff advisors like Louise (Worrel 1987, Dowson and Whittaker 1993; Curtis 1995). Hanna (1978) sees the staff advisor as a contradiction, an impossible role, stifled by conflict of interests. Louise was central to the group working well, as members themselves pointed out in the group discussion. However, Figure 7.3 might create the impression that Louise's position promoted an advisor-oriented group (Worrel 1988: 48). Members were critical of centre staff in the group discussion and during the meetings I observed. These views contrasted sharply with what they had to say about Louise: 'I'm buying his bike off him . . . She listens to us a lot more than other staff do . . . she makes the coffee . . . she's all right – she's coping!' (extract from group discussion). Members saw Louise's staff role as beneficial. They spoke favourably about the support offered by Louise, differentiating this from the inadequate support offered by a previous independent supporter and other centre staff. Moreover, Louise encouraged group acceptance. She appeared able to manoeuvre herself out of a professional identity, to use spaces within her working week, to build relationships with self-advocates and to gain access to their 'structures of feeling' (Vincent and Warren 1997: 158):

> Lesley helps to support the 'special needs clients'. She had fallen out with one of the staff in the unit over her comments to another 'client'. She was very angry and upset about this and brought it to the group. Louise told Lesley that she should complain: 'You can either see the Centre manager, I can see her for you, or we can go together.' Lesley appreciated the advisor's support but said she would go on her own.
>
> (Third meeting)

Louise had asked the group to be given a six weeks trial. She admitted that the group was already well organized and running smoothly prior to her coming in:

> In one of our few exchanges [Louise tended to speak to me only when members of the group were present] she told me that she was uncertain of the balance of the group, and wondered if it would be better if a more 'open meeting' was adopted, 'So users could have the chance to bring up things they want to talk about.'
>
> (Fourth meeting)

Louise expressed an aim to get the group running without her being there, to let go and fade into the background – something identified as a prerogative of independent, non-staff advisors (Dowson and Whittaker 1993). Throughout my involvement with the Centre Group, Louise's actions challenged my preoccupations and previous appraisals that have assumed the worst about staff advisors. Indeed, Shoultz (1997a) found that some staff advisors welcomed the opportunity to support a self-advocacy group because they could break free from the shackles of professionalism. As one put it, 'I can be myself, as opposed to acting like a professional':

> Denise spoke for a long time to the group about two of the users who are having problems with their relationship. 'What should we do?' she asked. At no time did Louise shout her down. Instead she suggested that perhaps they should be left to sort it out for themselves: 'Sometimes it's better not to advise just listen.'
>
> (First meeting)

On the other hand, volunteer supporters may feel that they should at least do something, constructing and playing out (pseudo)professionalized ideas of support (Oliver 1990; Dowson and Whittaker 1993).

Claim 2: Service-systems constrain the development of 'real' self-advocacy
Worrel (1987), Clare (1990) and Simons (1992) have expressed concerns with what could be called 'reformist' self-advocacy groups that concentrate on a centre rather than 'real' self-advocacy issues. As Lukes (1974, 1986) observes, power is often exercised by limiting the scope of decision making. The framing of institutionalized identities has historically threatened to deny people with learning difficulties a sense of self and autonomy (Goffman 1961; Potts and Fido 1991). Likewise, for Crawley (1988), when service-based self-advocacy groups focus on centre affairs, attention is taken away from wider self-advocacy issues associated with choice and independence. Centre issues were a central focus of meetings of the Centre Group:

> Denise was unhappy about going on holiday and leaving her boyfriend Simon. She was worried that a woman in the centre would 'start to bother him'. Louise, although allowing Denise to talk, reminded her that the working group was 'A place to talk about things in the centre, we can talk about that later together.'
>
> (Third meeting)

> The centre has received a £2000 donation, which means that they have £3500 towards the £5000 they need for the coffee bar. After announcing these details, Louise mentioned, 'We will have to start fund-raising for the new lounge area.'
>
> (Third meeting)

These incidents appear to highlight how service-based groups emphasize members' identities as centre-users. There is something paradoxical about caring for the centre in a context that, according to Worrel (1987), should be concerned with challenging the general inadequacy of services. Nevertheless, it should be remembered that day centres are one of a number of professionalized contexts inhabited by people with learning difficulties, so questions associated with them are obviously and rightly important to them:

> Members proudly told me of their involvement with a number of projects. These included canvassing the views of peers (leaflets were sent out to all the key worker groups so they could decide what they wanted to

eat at the Christmas meal) and fund-raising events that they had organized (like sponsored walking, car wash).

(Third meeting)

Beresford (1992), Beresford and Harding (1993) and Downer and Ferns (1993) identify the workings of centres as significant concerns of self-advocates. Perhaps problems occur when centre-based groups promote a culture in which the identities of members are framed only in institutionalized ways. Members of the Centre Group were asked in the group discussion what they got out of the group. All said the group gave them the chance to be with friends, to practise skills that had been denied to them before and to open up and speak out together. Rather than talking about their group membership in ways demarcated by the centre, their explanations reflect hitherto general understandings of self-advocacy (see Crawley 1982; Williams and Shoultz 1982; Cooper and Hersov 1986; Amans and Derbyshire 1989; Simons 1992; Sutcliffe and Simons 1993; People First Liverpool 1996; Huddersfield People First n.d.; Kennedy 1997), particularly collective identity (Dybwad and Bersani 1996; Oliver 1996). Wider self-advocacy issues were also put forward for consideration by the advisor:

> Louise played the 'Plain Facts' tape, which talked about relationships. Many of the members nodded their agreement to the point being made about people with learning difficulties having the right to have relationships. Denise said that she would like to get married and live with Simon.

(Fifth meeting)

The Centre Group may appear limited on the outside and reformist in character because it works within the system (Vincent and Warren 1997). However, members framed what they got out of the group in ways that suggest that an 'alternative framework of sense' was being promoted (Vincent 1998). Nevertheless, there appears to be some authenticity in the negative appraisals of service-based groups in previous literature. There were times when being service-based appeared to impact negatively upon group members. From my observations, these impacts appeared to be less to do with processes in the group and more to do with the larger centre context and the standing of the group in the centre's weekly curriculum. First, the fact that the group ran in the day sometimes caused problems:

> Sally has rehearsals for a new play and will miss the next meeting. Dorothy has just got a college place after years of trying. Unfortunately the classes are on Wednesdays and she will miss the group.

(Second meeting)

Second, members were at times possessive of the group as a safe haven apart from the centre in which it was located:

> At meetings, Stan pushes non-members out of the group. Other users that wander in are told to 'get out' by other members.

(Fourth meeting)

The group could be seen as promoting a division, an us (members of the Centre Group) and them (other centre users) atmosphere: 'I used to walk past the room and see the group' (Stan on his thoughts on the group prior to joining, group discussion). This possessiveness was understandable. When meetings ended, self-advocates stepped out of the room back into the centre. With that they were back to being 'users':

> After the meeting I followed Louise into the dinner-hall. A long queue had formed leading to the serving hatch. I was led to the front of the queue, the advisor had to get off early to take some 'clients' to a local college. No one asked if it was okay to push in. The advisor and I joined three other staff members in the queue. Two dinner ladies were telling off three users. Earlier in the meeting of the working group Lesley had been unhappy with the attitude of the dinner ladies. I could see why. One of the staff, Maggie, reassured the dinner ladies, 'I'll sort them three out later.' Maggie was some time before she joined the staff and me at the table. 'I sorted them out', she announced. 'Thank god we finish at four o'clock today.'

> (Second meeting)

While each member of the working group returned to this climate of exclusion, the collective identity of the group elevated members and the advisor and together they challenged the conflicts of 'us and them' present in the oppositions of working group members versus other users, and staff versus users:

> Lesley is worried about one client who is being left on his own in a room with staff. 'He shouldn't be in with the staff he should be with us.'

> Louise told the group, 'You know how we have a staff meeting every month, well we decided that from now on if staff are away this will be registered in a book by reception.'

> (Second meeting)

Claim 3: Service-based groups are tokenistic with little practical outcomes for members
There has been suspicion expressed in previous literature about service-system sponsorship of self-advocacy (Crawley 1982, 1988, 1990; People First of Washington 1984; Simons 1992; Dowson and Whittaker 1993; Tyne 1994). Centre groups may be nothing more than token gestures in the name of user empowerment, contexts in which to extend existing training activities, stifling potentially radical outcomes of self-advocacy as service initiatives take precedence (Sutcliffe and Simons 1993: 80). My ethnography highlights a point picked up on in Chapter 6 – that people with learning difficulties use group contexts for their own and others' ends. As users of the centre, members of the Centre Group were interested not only in finding out about centre matters but also in how they could get involved:

Denise told the group that when staff are in a meeting, early in the day at the centre, she has noticed that other centre-users who are not 'road-ready' or those who have fits are being left on their own without support. This was worrying because she had ended up supporting them herself and felt uneasy about it. Louise said that she would send a message over the tannoy to tell people where she would be if anyone needed her.

(Fifth meeting)

The council are now going to charge 75 pence a day for transport to and from college, the centre and other places. Members were furious. They suggested that other users should be consulted about the charges. That afternoon, two members represented the group at a meeting of the county advocacy project. Denise brought up the group's concerns about the transport charges.

(Second meeting)

These incidents highlight the centrality of centre matters in users' lives and their desire for change. To suggest that service-based groups have no or little practical impact upon members assumes that such groups and various services have no worth at all in the lives of people with learning difficulties (McKenna 1986; Barnes *et al.* 1990). Members made links between themselves and other users and centre bureaucracy:

Other trainees get something out of the group . . . We can help others – find out what is wrong and how we can help them . . . We can help other users with special needs, security and special diets.

(Group discussion)

I am struck by the strength of self-advocates to consider issues important to them and to support one another in speaking out. Often these issues are linked to the centre but why shouldn't these be important?

(Sixth and last meeting)

A 'suggestion box' is positioned in the common room so that users can anonymously make suggestions and or complaints. Members of the Centre Group empty the box weekly and bring along the comments to meetings.

(First meeting)

These vignettes describe Centre Group members taking up the concerns of other centre users. Their actions may be indicative of what Lukes (1974) terms the constantly shifting nature of power relationships that take place within institutions. A consequence of this shifting power was indicated in those times when actions by the group were taken out of the institution into other settings:

The group sends two representatives, usually Lesley and someone else, to meetings of a local advocacy development project. Consequently, the group has built up a number of useful contacts, one with a speech

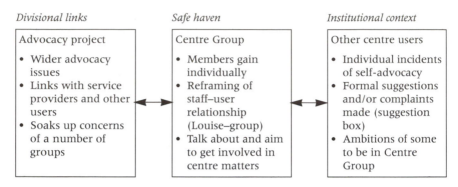

Divisional links	*Safe haven*	*Institutional context*
Advocacy project • Wider advocacy issues • Links with service providers and other users • Soaks up concerns of a number of groups	**Centre Group** • Members gain individually • Reframing of staff–user relationship (Louise–group) • Talk about and aim to get involved in centre matters	**Other centre users** • Individual incidents of self-advocacy • Formal suggestions and/or complaints made (suggestion box) • Ambitions of some to be in Centre Group

Figure 7.4 Potential relationships between the Centre Group, users and the advocacy project

> therapist who has worked with the group to produce a poster on 'abuse'. The poster has been put up around centres in the locality, highlighting yet again the group's wider links.
>
> (Fourth meeting)

> Patricia is sick of the big words used in the minutes from the advocacy organization meetings. Next time she will ask that they use short words and pictures.
>
> (Fourth meeting)

The Centre Group appeared to have formed a number of relationships with potential practical outcomes (see Figure 7.4). There is, however, a danger that this figure paints an overly positive picture, ignoring disabling barriers (Barnes 1990). Problems undoubtedly did occur when meetings ended and members went back to the larger centre context. This institutionalized discrimination was hard to break through (Khan 1985; Oliver 1990). At least in the group, members had a safe haven in which to speak out for themselves.

> I said hello to everyone. I asked where Dorothy was. Dorothy is in her seventies. At the last meeting she had proudly told me about going to college and showed me a printout of her name that she had typed up in computer class. Louise, the advisor, stepped in. Dorothy had died. Lesley had represented the group at Dorothy's funeral.
>
> (Sixth and final meeting)

The Social Group: the merging of independence and professionalism

At Lanley Day Centre in the late 1980s, users got together for the annual 'Shouting Out' days organized by the local health and social authorities. These have continued to this day, though a number of users decided that they wanted to meet as a separate group away from the centre and staff. A lecturer from the local university, interested in self-advocacy, was taken on as the group's supporter. The first meeting was held in late 1991 at Lanley Town Hall. People talked about work and pay, where they lived and what they did for themselves. They also voted on how often they would meet (every two weeks) and where (a local pub). By the next meeting the supporter had managed to get hold of a small sum of money from the local health authority. The group proceeded to vote in a chairperson, treasurer and secretary. The Midland Bank was chosen for the group's account. By the third meeting, it was decided that meetings would take place monthly, and the 'Social Group' was named. Over the next year, an open social evening was held, links were made with local and national People First groups and a service manager was invited along. Eventually the venue was changed to a quieter and more private social club. (This group history was obtained from Jurgen, who is one of the advisors.)

The social club is just off the main road and within walking distance of the bus station in Lanley, a small market town in the north-east of England. Inside the social club, just off to the left of the bar area, is a small room where the group meets. It is partitioned off from an adjacent room where various union and political pressure groups get together:

> I was one of the first to arrive. Two members were sat outside of the meeting room chatting together. A supporter stood at the bar with Christopher's dad – a jovial chap who met and greeted members of the group as they made their way in before he left to drive home. Eventually we were all beckoned into the meeting room by Jurgen, one of the supporters.
>
> (First meeting)

Members take a break half way through meetings:

> The bar staff are friendly. Members of the group order orange, coke, bitter shandies and packets of crisps and nuts. Other punters can be distant . . . The noise level was like any busy pub as members congregated around the bar. Another meeting was being held in the snug area of the bar. Someone from this meeting asked the staff to pull down the shutters 'because of the noise'. Karen, the comedian of the Social Group, shouted over, 'We making too much noise for you then?!!'
>
> (First and fourth meetings combined)

The Social Group transcends group types presented in the typology literature (Crawley 1982, 1988, 1990; McKenna 1986; Simons 1992; Dowson and Whittaker 1993). Up to 17 members attend evening meetings for two hours every three weeks. Members make their way to meetings by foot, taxi and bus, or get lifts from supporters and parents. The group has no formal ties with parental or professional organizations. It meets in an independent, non service-based context and members attend voluntarily. Membership was built up by word of mouth through members and supporters. However, some service and divisional ties exist in the support offered to the group. Two members of staff from local services voluntarily offer support in their own time: Virginia (a service manager) and Neil (a key worker to two of the members). Advocacy assistance is represented by Sheila, who is setting up an advocacy project just outside Lanley, and was sitting in on the group to 'learn about advocacy' (as she informed me, third meeting). 'Independent' advice is provided by Jurgen (who in addition works in an unpaid capacity with Virginia in supporting self-advocacy in Lanley centres) and June (an employee of British Rail). Up to five supporters could be present at a meeting. The group pays for the rent of the room out of its modest funds, which it has received from Lanley Health Authority and a local business. During my involvement, Christopher, who had been voted in as chairperson by the group for the past two years, chaired meetings. Ken was vice chairperson and took over when Chris could not attend. Jurgen wrote an agenda in his notebook at the start of the meeting, which he used to keep track of what members had to say:

> Jurgen asked Chris to open the meeting. Then Jurgen asked members if they had anything that they wanted to say. Stories of outdoor pursuits, birthdays, nights out and accidents were offered. Jurgen asked the contributors not to go into detail until they were asked later by Chris.
>
> (First meeting)

> Vice-chair Ken was in the hot seat tonight. When all possible topics for discussion were collected in, Jurgen asked him to choose someone to speak. He immediately plumped for Cliff his housemate who was upset.
>
> (Fifth meeting)

In addition to weekly meetings, members know each other from centres, homes and other service-based 'Speak Out' groups. Jurgen and Virginia have ensured that the Social Group is represented at a number of user consultation meetings in Lanley. General group dynamics are highlighted in the depiction of social group meetings as a sociogram (Figure 7.5).

Jurgen was one supporter who played a central role in the running of the group: collecting the news and views of members at the start, supporting the chairperson Chris, applying for money, looking after incoming mail and the

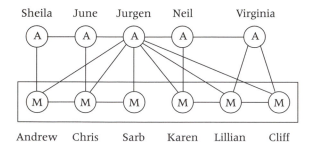

Figure 7.5 The Social Group's structure

group's bank account. He was a focal point for members when they divulged information or made requests. The ratio of advisors to members appeared to fragment the lines of communication into working pairs or groups of supporter–member(s). A contributing factor may have been the professional–client relationships that were exported into the group, for example, in the case of Neil being Karen's key worker at the centre. In addition, there was a lot of debate and communication among advisors during the meetings.

Similar to the Centre Group, solidarity was evident among members (despite the advisor–member relationships). At first sight the Social Group's sociogram approximates the 'advisor(s)-oriented' group structure (Figure 7.1). However, delving deeper into group processes highlights the complexities of support and the interdependence of members.

The Social Group and previous literature

Claim 4: Voluntary staff supporters bring their work with them to the group
Self-advocacy literature has viewed staff support as a paradoxical and contradictory venture, though these appraisals focus on staff advising in service-based groups (Crawley 1990). In contrast, the Social Group combined an independent, non-service context for meetings (social club) with *voluntary* support from two professionals. When professionals offer their support outside of the service system this invites questions about the standing of previous literature on the 'staff advisor'.

A point of caution should be made at this stage. Schatzman and Strauss (1973: 127) warn against the inevitable pinning down of observations into discrete analytical categories. Perhaps I was sensitized to view Virginia and Neil's interactions as directly reflecting their staff roles. Perhaps I saw more than was really there. Moreover, it is difficult to say what members really made of their supporters' professional credentials, or indeed whether members were consistently aware of or bothered about their supporters' staff roles. However, there were a number of incidents that could be seen as examples of staff advisors bringing their work along with them to the group. One of the key criticisms of staff advising is the clash of accountabilities to the group and to colleagues and services (Hanna 1978). For Worrel (1987, 1988) groups can be stifled when members pick up on supporters' conflict of interests (see Vincent and Warren 1997):

> *Karen:* Staff say one thing and then they say another. You don't know which way to go. Now if they want to see me they should come to my house, not me traipse back and forward to their offices.

> *Angie:* Yeah, I hate one of the staff, she said . . . [eyeing advisors]. Well, I'd best not say.
>
> (Paraphrased and written after fifth meeting)

A general air of 'professionalism' seemed to have been brought into the group:

I observed a number of occasions when staff supporters audibly shared comments about members present in the room – how members were getting on at their new houses, what jobs they were doing, when members were next due to meet up with staff. This was especially evident between Virginia and Neil, colleagues at a local Centre.

(Sixth meeting)

Max explained to the group that he had hit a member of staff. Neil, a key worker in the daytime, obviously worried that this might become a new sport among service users, took the moral high ground, 'It's wrong to hit anyone.'

(Seventh meeting)

In the latter vignette Virginia employed what may be termed an advisor-centred intervention (see Chapter 8). Rather than talking through the incident with Max to see if he had good reason for his outburst, a service-based programme was offered. Further evidence appears to support the idea of staff bringing their work along with them:

The group meeting was made up of five supporters and six members. The members sat quietly for about five minutes as the supporters talked among themselves. Then Karen, one of the members, piped up, 'It's like a staff meeting in here.' Jurgen, one of the culprits, acknowledged Karen's remarks: 'Yes supporters – shut up.' Ken, who had looked particularly uninterested, turned to me, winked and remarked, 'You'll sleep well tonight, Danny.'

(Sixth meeting)

Conversely, when an esprit de corps among a staff body disappears this may have ramifications for self-advocates:

Andrew asked Virginia to have a word with a member of staff at the centre who was making his life a misery. Although Virginia obviously felt for Andrew her professional relationships were complicated: 'I would do Andy but we don't speak to each other any more, we had a row.'

(Eighth meeting)

Rosenhan (1973: 258) concluded in his classic study 'On being sane in insane places':

Our overwhelming impression of the staff was of people who really cared, were committed and were uncommonly intelligent. Where they failed, as they sometimes did painfully, it would be more accurate to attribute those failures to the environment in which they, too, found themselves than to personal callousness. In a more benign environment, one less attached to global diagnosis, their behaviours and judgements might have been more benign or effective.

Perhaps, at times, Virginia and Neil couldn't get out of their 'work roles' by the time they had got to meetings of the Social Group. If this is the case then, paradoxically, this inability was at times advantageous to the group:

It's difficult to understand what Sarb is saying. Jurgen suggested that if I couldn't understand Sarb then I should ask him to repeat what he had said. Vacant stares and 'eh . . . yesss' irritate him . . . I couldn't understand Sarb tonight. He was frustrated with me so turned to Virginia, a long-time staff-acquaintance in various service settings and she repeated what he had said.

> (First and fourth meetings combined).

Virginia and Jurgen brought in the draft of their user-accessible leaflet on service consultations. Over the next 45 minutes they went through the leaflet. Members responded to the points that were made, pictures were picked out, and anecdotes presented.

> (Fifth meeting)

Virginia's high-profile job and Jurgen and Neil's service links allowed information to seep quickly into the group. They told members about changes in services and bounced back and forth ideas between the Social Group and other self-advocacy groups (including working and tenants groups in Lanley centres and homes). However, a question mark remains over the relative benefits of supporters' staff status to self-advocates involved in non service-based groups.

Claim 5: Groups that function as social groups are not 'real' self-advocacy groups

Worrel (1988) warns against self-advocacy groups that are organized around social or leisure activities. The Social Group can be seen as such a collective. However, what is chaotic to an outsider may be organized for the insider (see, for example, Marsh *et al.* 1978). Corbett (1991) argues that it is easier to pin notions of disorder and abnormality on to minority groupings. Often the Social Group was not unlike a night out in the pub, but because members of the Social Group have learning difficulties there was an urge to see something shambolic. For devalued people, society rules that indelicate behaviour must be reprimanded and sanctioned (Booth 1990: 31). Fortunately, the Social Group appeared to provide a context away from the surveillance of others:

> Tonight, as usual, people were shouting, teasing, laughing, discussing and arguing. Sarb decided to join me in a New Year drink. Instead of his usual pint of orange he had a lager. Some twenty minutes later he seemed quite pissed . . . Lillian told me about the problems she's having in her house. 'It's no good to bottle things up', she concluded . . . Ken got his pint of bitter shandy in at the bar. 'They don't like me drinking', he told me about the staff in his house.
>
> (Fourth, third and fifth meetings combined)

Worrel (1988: 16) notes that people who have been labelled are often very alone in their personal lives. The Social Group provided members with extra opportunities to make friends:

Cliff is very demonstrative and affectionate. He often grabs your hand, holds your leg or puts his arm around you. Sometimes he smacks you playfully on the head. Some people don't like such displays of affection. Like the chap at the bar, fag in mouth, pint in hand, obviously distressed by Cliff rubbing away on his bald head! Another member, Carol, is very quiet and a great listener. Cliff came up and grabbed her face. She laughed and put her hands on his face as well. 'What are you doing?', Cliff smiled. They sat together.

(Second meeting)

Ken and Cliff fell out. Cliff told Ken to 'piss off'. Afterwards Ken informed me, 'I do feel sorry for Cliff. I go and see my mother every weekend, but he only sees his family now and again'.

(Sixth meeting)

Begum (cited in Campbell and Oliver 1996: 96) notes that a failing of the wider disability movement has been the lack of opportunities for people to meet up socially and develop support systems for one another. Having a culture develops identity and the confidence to open up (Whittemore *et al.* 1986; Goode 1992; Todis 1992):

At the last three meetings Jarrod has told me exactly the same things, 'I'm Jarrod, I work at Kwiksave in the warehouse, I like trams, do you? I went to France, to Paris and Bordeaux with my mother 33 years ago, have you been abroad?' This meeting Jarrod told me about his trip to the countryside.

(Eighth meeting)

The Social Group was not just about having a pint with friends. The meetings appeared to provide an accepting environment where personal concerns could be shared (Simons 1994):

Ken told the group that on Thursdays the staff in his house collect 'his wages' from work at the local college and give him a bit every day. At first, the supporter, Jurgen, put this down to Ken's misunderstanding – 'You don't get wages, Ken' – then twigged, 'Ken, did you know that the money you get is from your benefits?' 'No', replied Ken. He has never seen his post office book and didn't know he had one – 'The staff must have it', he realized . . . Sarb's brother 'minds his wages' for him . . . Jarrod gets paid for working at Kwiksave but it goes straight into his bank account opened by his Mum. Jarrrod doesn't know how much he gets a week.

(Sixth meeting)

Lillian wants her own flat. She hates the group home, the staff treat her like a child and tenants pick on her. 'Wouldn't you be lonely?', asked Neil. 'No I'd have me cat' . . . Cliff and Ken don't have keys to their house. Sarb and Max do, but the latch is left off for them by their brother and Mum . . . Karen said that the staff watch her having a bath.

(Fourth and fifth meetings)

The chance to socialize was appreciated (mentioned in group discussion), which in time raised important elements of self-advocacy. To denounce the Social Group as not a real self-advocacy group ignores the importance of friendship (Taylor and Bogdan 1989) and the positive implications of group identity (Campbell and Oliver 1996). That said, as with all friendship groups and meetings, tensions emerged in the Social Group:

> Sarb is easily bored. When members chat away he is prone to put his head in his hands, sigh loudly, shout 'Boring' or walk out into the bar. However, he contributes a lot, draws up leaflets introducing the group and wants 'to talk about work and money but not rubbish.'
>
> (Fourth meeting)

Similar tensions emerged in all groups.

Claim 6: Independence is necessary for 'true' self-advocacy
The Social Group exemplified the pros and cons identified in the literature about self-advocacy groups that meet in independent contexts without financial or organizational accountabilities to carer, professional or advocacy groups (Crawley 1982, 1988, 1990; McKenna 1986; Simons 1992; Dowson and Whittaker 1993). Members appreciated meeting outside of service settings, including group homes – as Karen put it, 'You can talk to people away from home' (group discussion) – and appeared at ease with themselves and the supporters:

> Chris was talking about his views on services. Jurgen, apparently assuming that Chris was addressing only him, said, 'Tell your views to the whole group.' 'I am speaking to the group thank you very much', Chris replied.
>
> (Ninth meeting)

> Jurgen asked the group to name places where people had treated them well. Andrew told the group about a brilliant pizza he had had at Pizzaland. Jurgen, the supporter, responded, 'That's nice, but we're talking about places which have treated you well, not which places are good to eat in.' 'I know', replied Andrew. 'Let me finish. The staff are lovely in Pizzaland. They always make me feel welcome.'
>
> (Ninth meeting)

Side by side with these shows of confidence were the pragmatic limitations imposed by the group's independence. Previous literature has recognized the financial struggles and lacking resources of 'independent groups' (e.g. Simons 1992). The Social Group highlighted other factors. First, in contrast to the Centre Group, the Social Group's monthly meetings meant that roles were vaguely defined and unpractised:

> Chris, the chair, is continuously prompted by advisors to keep the group in order . . . Chris was back tonight – he's missed the last few meetings – so Jurgen reminded him of the format of the meetings.
>
> (First and seventh meetings)

Second, transport was a problem – with some members not attending the group because staff or carers had forgotten to book taxis. Third, the group's limited funds prevented them from achieving certain ambitions:

> Chris suggested that the group should have a Christmas meal in a restaurant, which could be paid out of the group's kitty. Jurgen reported that the group only had £65.
>
> (Fifth meeting)

Fourth, picking up on Sutcliffe and Simons (1993: 80–1), members only had a short amount of time in which to speak up:

> During 'news' an advisor told Cliff, 'You've had your turn – now give others a go.' Are staff pushy? Well, perhaps they too feel the limits imposed by only meeting every three weeks.
>
> (Third meeting)

Fifth, progress was slow and practical outcomes were little. Whereas the Centre Group pushed for issues to be put in the centre curriculum, supporters of the Social Group were often frustrated:

> Graham is being picked on at work . . . Lillian is sick of being treated like a child by staff . . . Cliff and Ken still have their benefits given out in small sums by the staff. At the Xmas meal, which cost a fiver and clearly pointed out in the letter sent to their house, they arrived with only 3 quid each . . . Jurgen asked, 'What can we do to help?'
>
> (First, third, fourth, sixth meetings)

Paradoxically, when formal, practical and measurable outcomes of the group were observed, this appeared to be linked to the non-independent elements of the group's structure:

> Virginia is carrying out some in-house evaluation of the centre she manages. She asked if members got anything out of the group . . . Virginia and Jurgen have produced a user-friendly booklet on consultation procedures for new services. They went through this with the group. Members agreed with many of the points, especially the bit which read 'Everyone should say what they want to do during the day no matter where they live', which was met with a resounding 'YES!' . . . Jurgen sent a letter to the centre outlining a member's complaints with staff.
>
> (Third, fourth, fifth and sixth meetings)

In a number of specific ways, those supporters with professional status brought with them the potential to act upon self-advocates' concerns about service-related issues (see Figure 7.6). However, these relationships can falter if self-advocacy becomes lost in the system:

> A user consultation meeting was called to launch Lanley's Social Services, Health Commission and Health Care Trust consultation plans for voluntary groups, carers, staff and users. Social Group members were

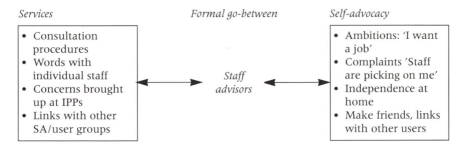

Figure 7.6 Potential relationships between the Social Group, professionals and services

represented twice – as a voluntary group and as individual users. Although service provision plans have already been drafted, and are to be put into practice in three months' time, Lanley authorities aim to 'consult' (after the event). At no time were users with learning diffi-culties adequately addressed. Language used in the meeting by authority representatives included 'fait accompli', 'participative communica-tion', 'consultation membership', 'passive recipients' and 'logistics of communication'.

> (User consultation meeting)

At the next meeting Jurgen asked those that had attended what they remembered. Max looked around the room and pointed, 'I remember speaking to you Cliff, how are yer?'

> (Sixth meeting)

Involvement with the Social Group highlighted the positive and negative effects of being both independent and linked to service systems. To assume the desirability of independence (or to suggest that it can actually exist) may cloud over deeper dynamics within groups.

The Advocacy-supported Group: divisional links

In 1993, Bill Shankling moved 20 miles from his home town to a group home in Cotshom. He quickly made friends with the other residents. Bill stood out, not only because of his outgoing nature but also because of his long-standing involvement with a self-advocacy group in his old town. He was instrumental in setting up a residents' committee in this new house. By chance, two workers from a local advocacy project – John and Paul – had been in contact with Bill's old self-advocacy group. They were told that Bill had recently moved to Cotshom. The two workers were interested in developing self-advo-cacy links and met up with Bill soon afterwards. They offered to support a self-advocacy group that would meet separately from the residents committee. It was not long into 1993 before the Advocacy-supported Group got off the ground, also meeting in Bill's house.

Bill's experience would prove to be invaluable. He and his housemates Rudi and Guy put up posters in local centres inviting people to join the group. Consequently, a number of new members joined, including residents from a local 'autistic community'. Before long, some members from the original residents committee who had joined at the start had now left, so a new venue was sought. Bill, Rudi and Guy looked over a number of places before plumping for the youth club, handily located just down the road from their home. (This group history was obtained from John, one of the advisors.)

The Advocacy-supported Group meets in a quiet village in the Midlands. Cotshom village is Old England – winding, tree-lined roads, Victorian era property, listed buildings and church spires.

> I park up, I'm early by 20 minutes. One of the members pops his head out of a window, 'Hello, are you Danny?' he asks. After checking with the group, Bill shows me in. As I walk in 'news' is just finishing. Each member talks about what they have been up to. Everyone has loads to say. I apologize for being early. Members put me at ease with greetings from every side of the room. I find a seat, just back from the circle of chairs, not too intrusive, while Bill asks for introductions. It is Erica's turn to be chairperson tonight and she skilfully goes around the room eliciting a piece of information from us all.
>
> (First meeting)

Only the Advocacy-supported Group meets on Thursday nights in the youth club, situated behind a pub and close to Cotshom village church. The group has divisional links (with an advocacy project) and shares a number of characteristics with 'autonomous type' groups identified in the literature (Crawley 1982, 1988, 1990; McKenna 1986; Simons 1992; Dowson and Whittaker 1993). Eleven hard-core members voluntarily attend evening meetings once a month for two hours in the independent setting of the youth club. The group has three advisors. John and Paul support the group as part of their jobs as advocacy project workers and take it in turns to attend alternate meetings. George, a nurse in the daytime, offers voluntary and independent support every meeting. His primary job is minute taker. Membership has been built up by word of mouth in homes, centres and advocacy project activities. Members pay 'subs' each meeting to pay for the rent of the youth club. Meetings start with the writing of an agenda on a flip-chart:

> Becca wrote down the agenda on the flip chart paper, including 'News', 'Annual report' (of the advocacy project) and 'AOB'. 'What's AOB stand for?' asked Paul. 'Any other business', replied some of the members in chorus.
>
> (Third meeting)

The chairperson job is shared. Each member is assigned a meeting to chair once a year:

John put up a flip-chart with dates of meetings for the next year. Members shouted up when they would like to chair a meeting and John wrote up names by the dates.

(Fifth meeting)

During my involvement Guy held the treasurer position and was assisted by his housemate Rudi:

Towards the end of the meeting, Guy tacked up a piece of flip-chart paper on the wall. On the paper he had written details of the group's Post Office account which he went through for the benefit of members: how much they had before the meeting, deductions for milk and biscuits, additions for subs, accounts at close of meeting.

(Fifth meeting)

A number of residents of Cotshom Village attend the group, like Bill, who shares a house with Rudi and Guy and lives next door to his brother Richard. In addition, up to five residents from a local 'autistic community' arrived at the doors of the youth club in the community mini-van. Close friendship groups abound as members share homes, services and activities offered by the advocacy project, such as the drama group, sports club and project committee meetings. The group had invited a musician along to a meeting where a group song was written which 'expressed the group's theme' (taken from minutes obtained from treasurer at the fourth meeting).

Before we delve into the group processes of the Advocacy-supported Group, a number of group dynamics can be highlighted by a sociogram (Figure 7.7). An initial facet of group dynamics that I picked up on was the interdependence and solidarity among members:

When coffee break came, members made their way over to the kitchen hatch where Richard was asking for requests for tea or coffee. Over the next 15 minutes people sat and chatted. No one spoke to me. It was great.

(Fourth meeting)

These close ties appeared to exist regardless of advisors' interventions. In contrast to the Social Group, I did not pick up on any obvious advisor–member

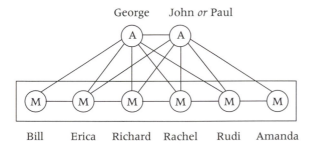

Figure 7.7 The Advocacy-supported Group's structure

working relationships. Instead, lines of communication between advisors and members were prominent when members requested information or support. Involvement with the Advocacy-supported Group highlighted some gaps between the assertions in the literature and the realities of group dynamics.

The Advocacy-supported Group and previous literature

Claim 7: Advocacy supporters are prone to advocate rather than support self-advocacy

Worrel (1988) and Dowson and Whittaker (1993) warn against advisors lapsing into advocacy. Sutcliffe and Simons (1993) call this the problem of the 'balancing act'. There is a fine line between encouraging people to be assertive and being assertive for them; a good organizer pushes to get things done but does not do for other people (Worrel 1988: 52). Daniels (1982) identified problems in the transition from parent advocacy to self-advocacy, with advocates finding it hard to relinquish power to those they were committed to speak up for. Following this line of enquiry, does a professional advocate status create problems for advisors dealing with the aforementioned balancing act? I noted a few occasions when supporters jumped the gun:

> Rudi said that he has helped to make a video on residents' rights.[4] John directed Guy to put down in the minutes that 'Rudi will bring the video to the next meeting.' Rudi was not asked, he stopped talking and the advisors discussed the possibility of getting a video player.
>
> (Fifth meeting)
>
> George is a sentence finisher. When Erica speaks she does so in a long . . . right . . . brok . . . right . . . en . . . okay . . . mann . . . hmmm . . . er. George tends to get in there before she has finished.
>
> (Third meeting)

These vignettes highlight the superficiality of the 'advocate advisor equals advocating advising' relationship. First, George's voluntary independent status indicates that advocacy interventions can come from any advisor regardless of status. I observed advisors enacting what could be termed 'advocacy interventions' across all four groups (see Chapter 8). Second, the above vignettes show advisors pushing the group along. While this may seem problematic, the group only met monthly. With time as valuable as it was, it seems premature to write off supporters' actions when they were trying to ensure that everyone had a say and that things got done. Third, when literature highlights the impact of forceful advisors, the actions of self-advocates may be forgotten:

> Tonight, deciding who would chair each meeting and when, Amanda was asked when she wanted to be in the hot seat. 'Well I'd rather not, thank you very much, my concentration wanders.' Even when pushed Amanda remained resolute.
>
> (Third meeting)

I observed a number of interventions by advisors in which the skills of advocates emerged:

> Graham likes Disney films. At Christmas he got a book on Walt Disney which he brought along to a group meeting. Graham told the group, 'The book alleges that he was prejudiced, anti-Semitic and an aid to the FBI in putting his workers forward to the board of un-American Activities.'[5] After this articulate summary, Graham asked, 'What do people think about that?' Silence. John looked bemused, as did others, but carefully brought the situation around by asking who had seen any Disney films. Jane had seen *101 Dalmatians*. Others joined in. Then the advisor asked the group what prejudice meant, a discussion ensued.
>
> (Third meeting)

> Towards the end of our phone conversation about me coming down to the group, Paul demanded that I feedback some of my findings to the group. I mentioned the possibility of talking with individual members to which Paul replied, 'Hold it! You're saying something different now.'
>
> (Telephone conversation, notes taken afterwards)

If advocacy status is to be accepted as an impacting factor then why should it be negative? Booth (1991: 27) asserts that advocacy partnerships can act as an effective antidote to the power of professionals and the authority of service staff. John and Paul's formal divisional links may have equipped them with the confidence and back-up to challenge institutions, whether they be ser-vice-based or not:

> John the advisor announced that following the group's letters to Cotshom council yellow lines are going to be put down to prevent the many parked cars which the group believe are hazards for people crossing the road.
>
> (Fifth meeting)

The financing and training of workers may promote an ethos that embraces self-advocacy (Wolfensberger 1972a). Moreover, an advocacy base provides advisors with a professional network that overcomes isolation and allows for the sharing of anxieties, ideas and strategies (Sutcliffe and Simons 1993: 88). However, from my observations, the 'advocate advisor equals advocacy relationship' appears only to scratch the surface of group dynamics. Interven-tions of advisors and members existed underneath labels that appeared to be associated with advocacy support.

Claim 8: Divisional groups are too sophisticated
Advocates' voices are strong (Braddock 1994; Tyne 1994). Dangers exist in sophisticated others speaking over and for vulnerable people (Daniels 1982; Flynn and Ward 1991). The advocacy project's 'sophistication' appeared to have an impact when the group dissolved into the larger organization:

> At the advocacy organization AGM, John, the advisor, addressed the audience. He then gave a convoluted spiel about advocacy falling into

'three key issues': (1) short-term advocacy, (2) develop consultation between users and services and (3) self-advocacy projects. I hope others understood because I didn't. Later, the treasurer's report – the chap made a science out of accounting and spoke of 'these people' advocacy is helping. He asked for a vote on the finances, about what I can't say, members with learning difficulties looked bemused, voting cards in hand.

(Advocacy project AGM)

In this sense 'sophistication' is actually equated with inaccessibility or exclusion (Sutcliffe 1990: 28; Sutcliffe and Simons 1993: 104). Back inside the group, divisional status appeared to have less significance. Members considered many issues in accessible ways:

Jane shouted to the group 'Manchester . . . bombing, bombing.' Within seconds Paul had picked up on this, asking the group, 'You know what Jane is talking about? The Manchester bombing?' Rudi said that he had seen it on TV, 'It makes me wild.' It was decided that the group would talk about the bombing later on in the meeting, this was recorded in the minutes – 'Bill asked the group their feelings. Guy had relatives in Manchester and his first thoughts were for their safety. Rudi's anger showed through and he asked why people cannot live in peace . . . The group feel the introduction of CCTV is helping to reduce the acts of violence . . . lots of ideas but no easy answers' . . . Soon the talk moved to the general point of 'nasty people'. Rudi said that it's not always difficult to walk away from nasty people, others agreed, citing incidents of bullying and abuse. Paul wound up the discussion for the group, 'You are all saying how it is not always easy to stick up for yourself.'

(Minutes obtained from supporter and notes from fifth meeting)

In the group, members included one another, at the AGM their interdependence took second place. Claim 8 appears to have authenticity with respect to wider group links. However, read superficially it may downplay self-advocates' actions within self-advocacy groups.

Claim 9: The ambitions of the self-advocacy group get lost in the wider ambitions of advocacy organizations

Organizations for disabled people can be criticized on the grounds of the interests that they actually serve – whether they be of the establishment, the careers of professionals involved or the personal aggrandisement of key individuals through the honours system (Oliver 1990: 115). Advocacy organizations may be prone to similar failings:

At the end of the meeting one of the group's advisors stood up and thanked the local MP for coming along. After that, the manager of the advocacy organisation, the staff at the local ATCs and SECs and the volunteer advocates, were called upon and applauded for 'all their hard work.' No one thanked people with learning difficulties.

(Notes from AGM)

By contrast, a number of incidents in the Advocacy-supported Group highlight the congruence of some advocacy and self-advocacy issues. For example:

> The advisor brought in a report on the new Disability Discrimination Act. The treasurer, Guy, said it was a good idea and sent off for 20 more so that every member could have a copy . . . Paul is completing the annual report for the advocacy project and wanted to know what people get out of the group.
>
> (Fourth and fifth meetings)

Members got to know each other in a wide variety of contexts like drama, football and music clubs set up by the Advocacy Project. This interdependence appeared to be channelled back into the group:

> Rachel smells her hands, rubs her face, says nothing. Paul asked her if she wanted to be chairperson, we waited . . . 'Yes, she does', says Erica her housemate. 'She just winked.'
>
> (Sixth meeting)

News is greeted with empathy. Unhappy tales are met with empathic sighs and encouragement – 'You'll be fine.' Happy anecdotes are given a round of applause.

> (First meeting)

According to Oliver (1990: 113), incidents of self-help are characteristic of the new disability movement, which is culturally innovative in the part it plays in struggles for genuine democracy, equality and justice. Consequently, claim 9 can be turned on its head (see Figure 7.8). A key analytical point that emerges is the extent to which the Advocacy-supported Group is affected by the wider advocacy project. Outside of the group, the project had both negative (e.g. exclusion at the AGM) and positive effects (e.g. providing opportunities for people to make friends). However, as with the Centre Group, intra-group dynamics appeared to be more the result of particular advisor and member interventions. These dynamics exist behind the superficial organizational ties which typology literature attaches so much importance to.

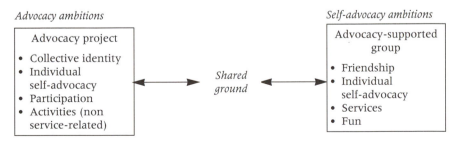

Figure 7.8 Potential relationships between the Advocacy-supported Group and the advocacy project

Ethnography highlights group processes that are not easily placed into discrete organizational categories.

The Independent Group: professional self-advocacy

The Independent Group is based in an office in Blaketon town centre in the north of England. The group's office is a two-up, two-down terraced house, which contains a computer, photocopier, telephones, fax, kitchen and four meeting rooms. Previously the group had met in a building owned by social services, which was situated some three miles outside Blaketon. The new office is not owned by services and is conveniently placed close to the bus station. A leaflet obtained from the group provides a brief history and introduction:

> The Independent Group is an innovative, independent self-advocacy project based in Blaketon. The project is run and managed by people with a learning difficulty, supported by three part-time workers. There are only a handful like it in the country. The main aim of the group is to support adults with learning difficulties in speaking out, making choices and decisions, becoming aware of their rights and to manage the Independent Group themselves. In early 1992 a group of people got together to form a steering group to set up the Independent Group – five people with a learning difficulty, a member of Blaketon Coalition for Disabled People, a person who worked for MENCAP and two people from Blaketonshire Centre for Integrated Living (BCIL) who were holding the money obtained from voluntary services. The steering group drew up a person specification for the job of project support worker, interviews were held and presentations given. Members with learning difficulties on the interview panel could not separate two people. They suggested a job share. They [Dennis and Julia] agreed and started in late 1992.
>   By mid 1993 there were 10 new members meeting in Blaketon every Thursday. The group provided a training day on making information accessible to non-readers and soon after acquired their own office space in a community building. Computer, phone, copier, fax, TV, video, camcorder and kettle were all acquired. They became active in the Blaketon Coalition of Disabled People to show what things are important to people with learning difficulties and continued to carry out training days on 'self-advocacy' and related issues for service users, students and staff. Presently . . . 20 people are involved in the project.
>   (Official introductory leaflet obtained at first meeting)

My first meeting with the group took place in its 'old office':

> I had spoken to Andy, the vice-chairperson, on the phone about visiting the group. When I arrived I was led into a room by one of the members, where a circle of people including self-advocates, three advisors and a suited chap met me [who turned out to be a representative from BCIL].

Everyone introduced themselves before one of the members gave a 20-minute introduction to the group.

(First meeting)

Other notes taken after this first meeting picked up on themes that ran throughout my involvement (in italics):

The group seems to function in a *professional, business-like manner*. Having its own offices and independent status along with the funding of supporters hints at *bureaucracy*.

(First meeting)

As with all the groups, members and advisors were welcoming:

Supporters remained relatively silent throughout the session. One chap, in his forties [Dennis], was particularly non-intrusive and he introduced himself in an understated and humble way.

(First meeting)

The Independent Group has some characteristics of all the different 'types' identified in the literature (Crawley 1982, 1988, 1990; McKenna 1986; Simons 1992; Dowson and Whittaker 1993). The group has autonomous qualities through its independence in terms of meeting place, status of advisors and voluntary membership of members. Further, service-system links exist in two ways. First, two of the supporters, Dennis and Julia, have both worked for services at some point during their involvement with the Independent Group. This has been problematic for both of them. Julia left her half-time job as care assistant after her line manager accused her of spending too much time with the group (fifth meeting). Dennis has also had confrontations with service management over his attempts to promote self-advocacy:

Dennis told me that in addition to the Independent Group, he was supporting a centre-based group. The members of the latter group had decided that they wanted to have their meetings outside of the centre. They arranged to meet in a social club and Dennis told them that they were to phone if they needed him. Some days afterwards the centre manager called Dennis into her office and demanded to know why the group had met outside: 'They could have been run over.' Dennis had replied, 'I could also have been run over – is that a problem? Should I have stayed indoors?'

(Fourth meeting)

Second, Blaketon County Council offers the group as an alternative to day centre services. The group receives a sum of money from the council that pays for the lease of the office premises and Dennis and Julie's salaries ('paid (by group) independents'). Accountability to the county council became particularly evident when the council requested an independent evaluation of the group during my involvement (the group asked me to undertake the evaluation).

There are also divisional origins. The group received an initial sum of money from Blaketon Voluntary Services, MENCAP was represented on the initial steering group and charity money pays the salary of a third supporter (Matthew). During my time with the group, grants from the county council and charities were either coming to an end or being reassessed. The group was therefore in the process of applying for National Lottery money (it was eventually successful in the bid). Finally, the group has a number of coalition relationships, as the above excerpt from the official leaflet points out, with Blaketon Coalition of Disabled People and BCIL. The latter group is represented on the Independent Group's management committee, which meets three or four times a year. However, as Robert pointed out to me, the group has become progressively independent and separated from BCIL, especially since taking on and employing three independent supporters (fourth meeting).

The majority of my contact time with the Independent Group was during its 'drop in' days (my term). These sessions were attended by up to 12 members and all three advisors on various days of the week from mid-morning to mid-afternoon. No meeting was organized; instead members would chat over coffee and packed lunches, help out with photocopying and answer the phone. During the days I attended, members also prepared for executive committee meetings that took place every Tuesday from 10 a.m. to 3 p.m. at Blaketon Town Hall and for training sessions that the group gets paid for:

> Andy was preparing the agenda for the meeting on Tuesday. The TV was on in the other room, Imran and Matthew [the supporter] chatted together over lunch, Colin told me about his organ lessons . . . Robert showed me the flip-chart that he had used along with Andy and Dennis [supporter] at a recent training day.
>
> (Third and fourth meetings)

> Agenda items of executive committee meeting, June 13th 1996: (1) New Office, (2) Workers [supporters] Wages, (3) Funding, (4) AOB [including writing of Annual Report, upcoming Training Days].
>
> (taken from agenda obtained from executive)

The elected members of the executive committee were Robert (chairperson), Andy (vice chairperson), Jane (secretary) and Jonny (treasurer). I was to attend one executive meeting and spoke with two organizations that had received training from the Independent Group. In terms of the organizational structure, the Independent Group had a hierarchy of positions held by members (see Figure 7.9).

The sociogram in Figure 7.9 closely approximates Worrel's (1988) favoured 'member-oriented' form of organization (see Figure 7.2). A number of general points emerged. First, advisors had to deal with a clash of accountabilities to the group as a business (for example, in the long-winded application for funds), to the executive committee (with whom much time was spent preparing agendas and training programmes) and to the general membership (who

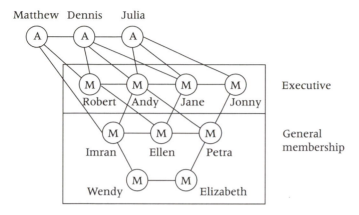

Matthew   Dennis   Julia

Robert   Andy   Jane   Jonny   Executive

Imran   Ellen   Petra   General membership

Wendy   Elizabeth

Figure 7.9 The Independent Group's structure

dropped into the group instead of day centres). Second, the membership was split into executive and general membership groups. While both groups made up the self-advocate base and supported one another, tensions associated with representation and meaningfulness of group membership emerged in this hierarchy. Third, the general memberships' lack of involvement with regular meetings (of the executive) raised questions over what and whom the group was for. The Independent Group exemplifies what could be termed the bureaucratization or professionalization of self-advocacy.

The Independent Group and previous literature

Claim 10: Paid Independent advisors threaten the development of independence in a group
Dowson and Whittaker (1993) are sceptical about paid support, seeing it as contravening a key aim of the advisor's role – to work oneself out of a job. Oliver (1990: 115) is equally suspicious of those who are paid to support disabled people. How can supporters overcome the conflicting interests of non-intrusive support (at best doing little) with the fact that they are paid to support (which at worst is tied to career advancement and creating dependency)? When members of the Independent Group were asked for their views on paid supporters there were no objections: 'I think it's jolly good we pay them, they earn their money, it's intense work' (group discussion).

Without wanting to downplay members' views, I observed a number of incidents that highlighted the dilemmas of paid support. First, commendable though it was, I wrote in my field notes about the possibilities of advisors following a work ethic congruent with their paid performative roles and a professional ethos (Vincent and Warren 1997: 147):

> Dennis and Julia share the supporters job, him coming in half the week, her the other. They both fill their time with as much as possible. Is there

a danger that their 'doing' becomes 'doing it for people' which is not the point?

(Fifth meeting)

Being paid for support may lead advisors to focus on their own personal (career) development:

Matthew enthused to me about his job, 'I've learnt to use the computer, its great' . . . Julia told me that she will concentrate on supporting the group since she resigned from the her job as a careworker.

(Third and fourth meetings)

Second, members were concerned that if no funding was received then the group would fold (mentioned in group discussion). One of the main reasons for seeking funding was to pay for supporters, as made explicit in the group constitution:

The group would be in a position to help Blaketon County Council fulfil objectives two and three of its Community Care Plan for Services for people with a learning difficulty for 1995–6 . . . The group is different from a Day Centre in that all members are equal . . . workers [supporters] are told what to do by members and are there to support people to be in control of the group. They are needed to be an advocacy voice and if required do administration and continuity work.

(Extract from Constitution obtained at first meeting)

The 'official-speak' in this document also illustrates what different parties expect from paid advisors. The last sentence (apparently written for the county council) describes support which sounds very much like professionalized notions of advocacy and work for people with learning difficulties or what Vincent and Warren (1997: 158) term 'performative management' by professionals. Third, because of the pressures of trying to get supporters' posts funded, the executive committee and supporters spent a lot of time considering possible funding bodies:

Julia and Dennis spent much of last week sat in a room of the [new] office filling out the National Lotteries Charity board application form. Matthew spent his time downstairs with the members . . . Half of the meeting was spent talking about funding, bank details and payment methods for supporters' wages.

(Eighth meeting and executive committee)

It seems somewhat paradoxical for a self-advocacy group to rely on the payment of supporters. On the positive side, paying advisors for day-to-day support provided advisors with long-term and frequent opportunities to conceptualize their support:

At the next training day offered by the group, Dennis is to sit next to Andy and prompt him with key-words so he can talk about his experiences of staff attitudes towards sex and people with learning difficulties.

(Third meeting)

Meanwhile, executive power over supporters was also displayed:

> The executive took a vote on the windows of the office being cleaned every week. Robert asked why Dennis was not voting. 'He can't vote he's a supporter', reminded Ellen . . . The group are changing the payment arrangements for the supporters. Now wages come directly from the group's bank account . . . 'The committee needs to think about whether to give a cost of living pay rise to supporters' . . . the group offer a training day on 'what is a good supporter?' Their supporters are involved in drafting up the agenda for the day.
>
> (Seventh, executive committee meeting and extract from agenda)

Opportunities exist for groups to develop the job specifications of paid supporters. The executive committee members, along with the help of other members and supporters, had prepared written documentation outlining what constituted 'a good advisor':

> A good support worker is: patient, helps people to choose, put yourself in someone else's shoes, action – to make things happen, power, where to go can let someone take risks . . . A bad support worker: doing it for other people, people who think they know best, playing god, not listening, no time to give, heart not in it, telling people what to do.
>
> (Taken from training notes, obtained at sixth meeting)

Finally, in keeping with observations of advisors' interventions across all four groups, advisors supported members in empowering ways:

> Imran's father doesn't want him to come to the group. He would prefer to see him at the centre. Petra acknowledged that she would have to ask her keyworker if she could come along to the training day. Dennis spoke with them both about how they could resolve these constraints.
>
> (Eighth meeting)

> At the meeting with Norma and John from the county council, Dennis appeared to avoid eye contact with them. When they posed questions, Dennis would look over to Robert and Andy – alerting everyone present to the two people who represented the Independent Group.
>
> (First meeting for evaluation report)

However, a question mark remains over the relative benefits of groups paying for support.

Claim 11: Member-oriented groups are the best
In the light of the similarities between the Independent Group (Figure 7.9) and Worrel's (1988) 'member-oriented' group (Figure 7.2), a number of arguments presented by Worrel in favour of this group can be appraised (Worrel 1988; see particularly 49–51). First, the advisors' main point of call in the Independent Group was the executive committee. This was particularly the case between Dennis, Julia and executive committee members Robert and Andy:

Dennis had spent the week with Robert and Andy preparing for the meeting today . . . at various times throughout the meeting, the three would consult one another. Dennis still took very much of a back seat.
(Meeting with county council representatives and Independent Group)

In addition, the third supporter Matthew appeared to spend most of his time with the general membership who dropped in: 'Matthew was having "the craic" with Imran and Carol. He's really natural with everyone' (fourth and sixth meetings).

Second, while there were strong links between the members and the executive, these were not perfect. For example, it appeared that only a select few benefited from the executive and general membership hierarchy:

Ellen thought that a room in the new offices would be ideal for the photocopier. Robert reminded her that such decisions have to go to the management committee . . . Imran asked to join the Tuesday meetings. He was informed by Dennis [supporter] that he would have to be voted on to the committee.

(Seventh and eighth meetings)

Friday appears to be mainly about preparing for Monday – although some only drop in on this day. Andy [vice chair] appreciates the executive meetings: 'I get to talk to my friends rather than key workers.' For Andy, Friday is when he winds down from the week.

(Third meeting)

The general membership was separated from the executive, which met away from the offices in the Town Hall. Third, the group had an air of formality that appears at odds with Worrel's point about solidarity being bred through the 'member-oriented' structure (see Figure 7.2). The Independent Group's hierarchy and formal structure were evident in the strict adoption of certain rules during 'drop-in days':

Matthew told Jonny not to interrupt when he was speaking, then he apologized to Jonny, explaining that the rule is to let people speak. There would seem to be structure even over small talk . . . Petra, a member of the executive, reminded Imran about the not shouting rule.

(Third and eighth meetings)

As Fairclough (1989: 64–6) points out, formality in any group setting constrains content of discussion, status of members and group relations. Politeness and preoccupation with rules can undermine the productivity of group decision-making. However, there were many incidents when actions of the executive trickled down among the membership. For example:

Three office premises were visited and videotaped. On the Friday all members came in to view the video and choose which would make the best office.

(Third meeting)

Moreover, the general membership said that they got a lot out of the group (mentioned in group discussion), regardless of the group's hierarchy and formality. There were various levels of personal gain:

> Imran loves coming in on Friday. It's a lot better than the centre, which he maintains is 'boring' . . . so as not to fall out with his parents he has told the taxi-driver that on Fridays he goes to the Independent Group, but to 'keep it quiet'. He also got one of the members to help him write a note to the centre telling them why he wasn't there.
>
> (Fifth and eighth meetings)

Formally, the executive got on with running the group, which dealt with the problems of time identified in the Social and Advocacy-supported Groups, and the general membership benefited accordingly. Informally, I observed interdependence between executive and non-executive members. Below the bureaucratic surface, self-advocates supported one another and gained in various ways.

Claim 12: Professional self-advocacy is the way forward
The Independent Group represents a particular type of self-advocacy that is described in the literature: professional self-advocacy (see, for example, Sutcliffe and Simons 1993: 103–10). Links with BCIL (which produces self-advocacy literature and offers training) and funding aspirations (including accountabilities to current funding bodies) have meant that the group's activities are wide-ranging:

> Members of the Independent Group attend disabled people's forum meetings, work with social services, health, community education, other voluntary organisations, take part in sexual and emotional needs training and training with BCIL. As well as learning new skills and getting better at old skills, members are getting more confident in speaking up, more confident in getting information, making choices, making changes, meeting new people, challenging people using jargon instead of simple words, and enjoying themselves! The members are also developing skills as managers of a project, speaking out skills – such as in meetings, doing training, giving information, chairing meetings, taking minutes, doing the petty cash, accounts, office skills, using equipment, challenging how meetings are run and how people are treated, how minutes are written, with big words and jargon.
>
> (Official introductory leaflet)

The other three groups in this study had little money and tended to be organized around meetings and social, centre or advocacy activities. By contrast, the Independent Group was well funded and spent a lot of time organizing training programmes. The group benefited in a number of ways by offering training. First, by referring to training, the group could show in a practical, formal and measurable way what funding bodies were getting for their money. Hence, the county council asked for feedback from organizations that had received training to be included in the evaluation report. Second, the group's preoccupation with maintaining a high level of funding was served through the income generated from training:

> Andy told me that the group receives £300 for a day's training . . . 'South Blaketon Advocacy have asked us if we will do some work at Blaketon hall for two days on a ward.'
>
> (Third meeting and extract from agenda to executive committee meeting)

Organizations that had received training from the Independent Group were very positive in their feedback. For one, a representative of 'Do it Now', an advocacy organization, the Independent Group had challenged her own role as an advocate:

> She remarked that there was perhaps a tendency for advocacy workers to think they are doing the right thing and to feel smug with themselves. The Independent Group made her think more deeply about many aspects of her job . . . the group's dislike of 'jargon' illuminated the inaccessibility of much advocacy work.
>
> (Extract from feedback)

Similarly, Blaketon College's Special Needs Department has used the group to inform its self-advocacy courses. The group constitution had made Julie Bently, a lecturer on the course, more aware of non-readers and people with visual and hearing impairments (extract from feedback). The quality of the training programme may have been enhanced by the group's divisional links:

> I got a chance to leaf through a folder on self-advocacy written by BCIL that was on top of the filing cabinet . . . some members have done training with BCIL training department, one Independent Group member is now a trained counsellor as part of BCIL's counselling service.
>
> (Fourth meeting and extract from introductory leaflet)

Potentially, then, the Independent Group has a number of organizational relationships (see Figure 7.10).

Yet while the group strives for these business-like relationships, what about the general membership who choose the group instead of a day centre? Members are proud of the group: 'The first we had was owned by social services, we chose this and we love it, it's beautiful, lovely – it's our office' (extract from group discussion). Membership for some, particularly those on the executive, was about having a job to do:

> I asked Andy why he had joined the group and he told me, 'I'm doing it for a change. I'll probably try and work with old people at some time.' Jonny told me that he works at the local ATC's garden centre, making furniture. He gets £5 a week but has to pay £6.50 a day centre charges.
>
> (Fourth meeting)

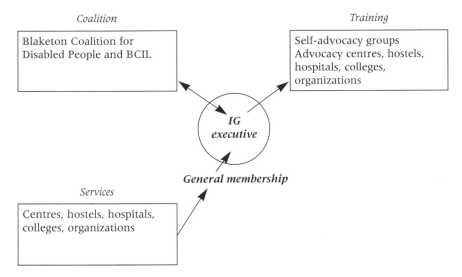

Figure 7.10 Potential relationships between the Independent Group (IG) and various organizations and services

Other members talked about what they got out of being in the group as an alternative or addition to other activities.

> At the centre I'm working with this man who cannot speak or talk but he's a joy to work with . . . You do what you do instead of what they want you to do . . . there's more friends here than at the centre.
>
> (Extract from group discussion)

Page and Aspis (1997) suggest that self-advocacy has become an industry open to the exploitation of services and professionals. The Independent Group may also be open to exploitation by services that offer token gestures to self-advocacy by getting the group in to do a day's training. Below these formal business-like relationships, executive and general members gain in different but personally important ways. The Independent Group presents different levels of organized self-advocacy.

Conclusions: dynamics over typologies

This chapter has described and appraised some of the group dynamics and processes in four self-advocacy groups. A number of general conclusions can be drawn from the above analysis. First, all groups to varying extents transcend group 'types' identified in the literature. The organization of self-advocacy draws upon a number of characteristics of service, divisional, coalition and autonomous group types. Second, it has been shown that there is often a gap between previous literature and the realities of group processes. While this does not mean that previous literature is redundant, group dynamics are complex, messy and not easily categorized – raising questions about the deeper workings of groups. Third, the four groups present four different, albeit overlapping, ways of organized collective self-advocacy, each with advantages and disadvantages. Some of the members I spoke to were involved in more than one self-advocacy group, while users of the Quarry Village Centre who were not involved with the Centre Group may well have been involved with other self-advocacy groups. Sutcliffe and Simons (1993: 17) suggest that 'there is value in diversity and in having a wide range of opportunities open to people.' In the self-advocacy movement, groups have the potential to serve different areas of life: 'Even though their capacity to overthrow power structure is minimal, they have begun to introduce a new language of critical discourse that departs profoundly from the theory and practice of conventional politics' (Boggs 1996: 22).

Fourth, previous appraisals that have pointed out 'good' and 'bad' ways of organizing self-advocacy ignore what self-advocates get out of being in groups. For example, it seems analytically simplistic to say that the Independent Group was better than the Centre Group when members of both groups got something out of being involved with collective self-advocacy. There were many incidents of members getting as much out of the groups as they could. 'Type' did not necessarily prevent members gaining from involvement, nor did it prevent advisors putting in as much as they did to the groups. Fifth, groups may provide a catalyst for members to develop self-help, friendships and confidence. For two of the groups, members met only once a month; the other two groups met weekly. Consequently, groups can provide temporary contexts in which more permanent relationships are formed in relationship to the group and outside. Sixth, self-advocacy was not organized by groups in therapeutic, educational or libertarian ways. For the narrators in Part II of this book, self-advocacy appeared to be about people choosing to embrace a context in which to make friends, gain confidence and try out new things. Groups had built up relationships with other groups, services, divisional and coalition organizations. However, the salient dynamics within groups appeared to lie in the interdependence among self-advocates. Seventh, groups can be seen as reformist, some more than others, as they work within the system, often in collaboration with potentially exclusionary partners. However, what may be reformist to the outsider is radical to the insider. Members provided one another with support and promoted frameworks of meaning and self-reference that contrasted with outsider assumptions of inability (Vincent 1998). Finally, opportunities for shared membership have been illustrated, alongside the threat posed by wider disabling environments. Though the Centre Group existed as a pocket of resistance in the wider centre context, this wider exclusive zone existed none the less.

Sutcliffe and Simons (1993: 17) conclude that 'There is no "right" or prescribed form of self-advocacy.' The four groups were bound together by various intra-group processes and embraced different concerns from social events to formal training programmes. As the stories of Part II of this book recognized, previous literature's search for a 'right form' – a perfect organizational base for self-advocacy – ignores the spaces for resistance and self-empowerment that emerge often in the apparently imperfect contexts. The question remaining is: what aids the creation of these spaces? The next chapter attempts to answer this question by delving deeper into the relational nature of self-advocacy in action, across groups, by considering and conceptualizing the support offered by advisors and self-advocates.

Notes

1 All names of places and people have been changed throughout Part III. Fictional names are used for towns.
2 Unless otherwise stated, indented notes are extracts from observational field notes, taken after each meeting.
3 For all group sociograms only some of the members are represented.
4 This illustrated another criterion that could be used in identifying group 'types' – members' links with other self-advocacy groups.
5 Graham was rather a character. Well spoken and intense, he would often draw me into a long discussion on current affairs. The last time I spoke to him, he was concerned about Tony Blair's 'New Labour'.

 **8**

Across self-advocacy groups: support and models of disability

This chapter takes further the challenge of appraising self-advocacy in action by examining the notion of support offered by advisors and self-advocates. It is suggested that previous literature has failed to account for the multifaceted nature of support. This failure has resulted in simplistic attacks on professional (staff) advisors (or supporters) and a lack of conceptualizations of support that are grounded in models of disability, and has ignored the self-determination of self-advocates with learning difficulties themselves. Presented in this chapter are vignettes of support ('interventions') offered by advisors that can be seen as either empowering or disempowering. Interventions are understood in terms of where they lie on a continuum of support, where at one end is the social model of disability and at the other end is the individual model of disability. Five pairs of intervention are presented, reflecting polar ends of the social–individual model continuum. With reference to disability theory, it is argued that those interventions that are drawn towards the social model end of the continuum offer a more authentic means of promoting self-advocacy skills inside groups. Finally, in addition to the support of advisors, the inter-support networks of self-advocates are presented. By looking across groups it is concluded that collective self-advocacy reflects dynamics that are made up of various interactions, which in turn can be understood as reflecting different discourses of disability.[1]

The advisor role: interventions and discourses of disability

The previous chapter problematized understandings of advisors espoused in previous literature on a number of levels. These problems were particularly evident in the case of 'staff advisors':

1 To assert that staff advisors' support is inevitably limited by their professional status does a disservice to the individuals who exist behind that label. For example, while the staff advisors in the Social Group, Neil and Virginia, appeared to bring their work with them to the group at times, they did not always 'act like staff'. Moreover, Louise's actions in the Centre Group failed to fit the characteristics drawn up in the literature about staff support(ers).

2 Previous analysis about staff advising is static and conservative. It holds not only that structure basically positions people to behave in a certain way (staff role – bad advising), but that resistance to exclusive or oppressive structures is impossible (staff advisors are only part of the paternalistic control of people with learning difficulties). It appears that the logical conclusion of this analysis is to do away with staff supporters altogether. However, as this book has shown so far, staff advising is a reality and requires understanding.

3 Resilience of self-advocates in the face of adversity is ignored. It is assumed that a particular type of support will causally result in a particular type of self-advocacy – people with learning difficulties benefiting or suffering accordingly – but what of the input by self-advocates?

In this chapter these three problems are broached in the following ways. First, rather than considering the advisor's role as a direct reflection of a particular 'type' (e.g. staff advisor), I present how advisors are open to different types of actions or interventions (Dowson and Whittaker 1993). Second, one way of trying to draw together what these interventions mean for self-advocacy is to analyse how they reflect different understandings or discourses of disability. Therefore, I consider interventions as a reflection of discourses or practices (see Fairclough 1989) associated with two models of disability: the individual and social models (Barnes 1990; Oliver 1990, 1996; Morris 1996).

Finally, advisors' actions are not considered alone. I also refer to the actions of self-advocates themselves that occurred, in addition to advisor interventions, and that augmented the development and organization of self-advocacy. I specifically focus on those actions that encouraged the progression of self-advocacy within the group – actions that reflect discourses of self-help, collective identity and social action (aspects of the social model). Their impact on the 'doing of self-advocacy' was as important as the actions of advisors.

So to conceptualizing support. The idea of 'intervention' has been proposed by Dowson and Whittaker (1993: 31–2), who identified six categories of action which may be employed by the advisor:

- Prescriptive interventions – aim to give advice, recommend a behaviour or course of action.
- Informative interventions – aim to give knowledge or information.
- Confronting interventions – challenge attitudes, beliefs or behaviours.
- Cathartic interventions – provoke a release of tension.
- Catalytic interventions – elicit information or opinion from the group.
- Supportive interventions – affirm the value or worth of the group.

Building on the notion of intervention, the subsequent analysis links together the actions of advisors (and later self-advocates) with models of disability. Chapter 3 introduced how dominant discourses of disability inform understandings of what causes 'learning difficulties', how it is experienced, through to the ways in which it is treated. To understand disability in terms of 'discourse' ties together subjectivity and practice (Skrtic 1995a). According to Fairclough (1989: 23), discourses are social phenomena in the sense that whenever people speak, listen, write, read or act, they do so in ways that are determined socially and have social impacts:

> How a discourse exerts power is through individuals who become its carriers by adopting the forms of subjectivity and the meanings and values which it propounds. This theory provides an understanding of where our experience comes from and can explain why so many of our experiences and opinions are sometimes incoherent and contradictory.
>
> (Sidell 1989: 268)

Moreover, a relationship exists between social events and more durable social structures that shape and are shaped by these events. Discourses and practices are inseparable (Fairclough 1989: 28): both refer to either what people are doing on a particular occasion or what people habitually do given a certain sort of occasion. That is, both can refer to either (linguistic) action or convention:

> The social nature of discourse and practice always implies social conventions – any discourse or practice implies social conventional types of discourse or practice . . . people are enabled through being constrained: they are able to act on condition that they act within the constraints of types of practice – or of discourse. However, this makes social practice sound more rigid than it is . . . being socially constrained does not preclude being creative.
>
> (*Ibid.*)

This last sentence links into an important point about discourse and practice: that where there is power there is also resistance (Foucault 1975). This notion of resistance to oppressive discourses recognizes a key issue associated with power. People are not simply empty vessels receiving powerfulness or powerlessness, people reproduce power in various ways, with good or bad effects upon themselves and others (Parker and the Bolton Discourse Network 1999). Oliver (1996: 144) points out that: 'Understanding societal responses to long-term disability is no simple task and requires us to analyse ourselves and the discourses we use in order to talk about our world.'

For Cicourel (1980), when researchers are accounting for discursive and social interactions they need to make explicit reference to broader cultural beliefs. Taking advisors' interventions within groups, this chapter examines how these interventions reflect and reproduce discourses and practices of disability. It appeared that advisors were open to reversing, changing, moving, building upon and rejecting all together their interventions with self-advocates.

Throughout my ethnography it was as if 'good' and 'bad' interventions were available to advisors, just as different discourses float above and between people, with meanings slipping and sliding (Howe 1994: 522). There appeared to be some advisors who were prone to draw upon discourses of disability that assumed individual pathology, while others seemed more able to link practice clearly with assumptions of competence. However, all advisors' interventions were fluid and ever-changing. Following Skrtic (1995b: 42), the disciplinary power of disabling discourses can lead supporters unconsciously or unintentionally to operate under the taken-for-granted contentions and customs of their 'knowledge tradition'. Conversely, other discourses can be embraced which inform more empowering practice. So what are these discourses?

As outlined in Chapter 3, learning difficulties, and disability in general, have largely been understood in terms of individual naturalized impairment. Consequently, impairment, whether it be physical, or 'of mind', is perceived as creating disability (WHO 1992). This understanding of learning difficulties (and disability in general) embraces what has been called the individual model of disability or 'personal tragedy perspective' (Oliver 1990). Discourses originating from the individual model locate disability within the individual, and his or her impairment. Further discourses and practices emerge of personal pathology, of individual difficulties and of dependency in the face of care. Moreover, people so labelled are required to adjust to their environments and be the recipient of professional expertise and medical dominance, and are the focus of policy that at best intervenes and at worse controls (see Oliver 1996). By placing disability resolutely in the realms of personal tragedy, the individual model perpetuates a culture of dependency and non-acceptance. As with most dominant regulatory discourses, it is hard for people to break through and away from the concept of learning difficulties as individual pathology. Consequently, those that step out of this socially prescribed role flout the rules, challenge dominant hegemony and threaten the very foundations of society's understanding of disability. When people with learning difficulties step out of the passive role assigned by society, and take up the active role of *self-advocate*, the resulting drama is unfamiliar. Consequently, if the actions of advisors are embedded in an individual model of disability then their support appears to be at odds with facilitating the self-determination of self-advocates (Goodley 1997).

In opposition to the dominant individual perspective that locates disability in the realms of individual impairment, the alternative social model of disability attends to the ways in which society disables (see, for example, Barnes 1990; Oliver 1990; Morris 1991, 1996; Swain *et al.* 1993). To find the dominant origins of disability we are encouraged to turn attention away from the individual on to a society that excludes. Disabled people are disabled by a social, economic, cultural and political contemporary climate. The application of the social model of disability permits a different way of conceptualizing and practising self-advocacy. The discourses and practices of the social model address notions of social problems, of societal/environmental barriers and of in(ter)dependence and capacity. Moreover, there are demands for societal adjustment and calls for individual and collective responsibility of all societal members to redress disabling environments (see Oliver 1996). Now when people with learning difficulties step out of the passive role assigned by society, and take up the active role of self-advocate, this feeds into the political aims of the social model. Where once stood a model of learning difficulties as individual inadequacy now stands a model that embraces individual and collective empowerment (Schlaff 1993). Assumptions are shifted away from what people cannot do, to what people can do. Consequently, if advisors adopt a social model of disability in their support then this appears to be congruent with facilitating the self-determination of self-advocates (Goodley 1997).

Inclusive and exclusive support: individual and social models of intervention

The links made above between discourse, models of disability and the actions of advisors and self-advocates are at this stage speculative. The subsequent analysis therefore delves deeper into the relationship between discourses of disability and the support of advisors. Throughout the chapter particular reference is made to components of the individual and social models.[2] Following Lukes (1974), people are often not consciously aware of the ways in which they (dis)empower others. The same could be said about the advisors in the four research groups in this study. However, by grounding an analysis of their actions in models of disability, I aim to provide a framework for uncovering the meaning and effects of interventions. Five pairs of interventions are considered, each pair reflecting polar ends of the individual–social model continuum. While many of the vignettes from Chapter 7 could be included in this analysis of support, additional vignettes are the main focus of this chapter.

'Advisor-centred' versus 'self-advocate-centred' interventions

Those interventions that are drawn towards the *advisor-centred* end of this first continuum can be seen as practices of an individual model of disability. Typically advisors respond to the requests of self-advocates with 'I'll have a chat with someone on your behalf' or 'Don't worry yourself, I'll sort out your problem.'

> Jim lives in a group home and is very unhappy with his bed: 'It is too narrow.' One of the supporters, a manager of one of the nearby ATCs, told Jim, 'That's being sorted out for you.'
>
> (Social Group, third meeting)

> Karen mentioned that she was worried about her 'sick note' that she needs to collect her benefits. One of the supporters, who happens to be Karen's key worker, told her, 'Someone's sorting you out with that.'
>
> (Social Group, seventh meeting)

Matthew the advisor has a tendency to tell off members. He told people to be quiet because he wanted to talk to Robert. There is a fine line between group rules on 'not talking when others are' and disciplining people.

(Independent Group, third meeting)

Here support was individualized in terms of 'staff–client' like relationships. Issues and concerns that others may share, or may later have to deal with, were not made public within the group. Instead there was fragmentation into 'working pairs' and the group did not collectively deal with a member's concerns. As Worrel (1988: 39) observes, 'Professionals are trained to see members as clients . . . to deal with people one-to-one with measurable and predictable results. This approach doesn't work with a group that is growing and evolving as it goes along.'

Advisor-centred interventions may uphold professional ethics and a preoccupation with 'client needs' (Gilbert and Specht 1976). Moreover, an expert advisor culture of paternalism may be bred (see Khan 1985) and self-advocates may find it difficult to challenge inadequate interventions alone. In this culture, the self-advocate asking for support may feel intimidated. Those benefiting are primarily the advisors: 'It flatters our ego to feel we are needed, it is often so much easier and quicker to do things ourselves' (Dowson and Whittaker 1993: 14); 'It is tempting to let this attention go to our heads' (Worrel 1987: 34). Advisor-centred interventions may also build up or give an appearance of an *esprit de corps* with other 'professionals'. This can dissuade self-advocates from criticizing 'fellow professionals' and other advisors. Examples of this are typified by the advisor reacting to criticisms of professionals with 'Well they're doing their best' responses. Bachrach and Baratz (1970: 6; cited in Lukes 1974: 18) observe that power may be, and often is, exercised by confining the scope of decision making to relatively 'safe' issues:

Members were talking about their key workers. Karen said that she was unhappy with hers: 'He's never there, I don't know why he bothers.' Ken agreed: 'They come and go.' A supporter reminded Karen that key workers work shifts. Karen later went on to say her key worker was like 'a guardian angel'.

(Social Group, fifth meeting)

No attempt was made by the supporter to discover whether or not Karen had good reason for being unhappy with the absence of her key worker. It was assumed that the key worker's presence was only dependent on her shift-work (her competency stifled by structure), and the implication was that Karen failed to understand shift-work (Karen's incompetence). Supporters conveyed the notion that the job of a professional is an important but difficult one. Consequently, typical of the individual model of disability, professional work was accepted unquestionably and people with learning difficulties' experiences were ignored (Barnes 1990; Oliver 1996):

I had been asked by the group to write up and illustrate a leaflet introducing their group. Cliff had asked me to write, 'Some of our supervisors are treating us badly.' Presenting the leaflet at the next meeting Cliff gave me a 'thumbs up' for putting his comments down. Two advisors seemed to take a different perspective: 'That bit about the supervisors sounds awful', said June. The other, Virginia, put her head in her hands.

(Social Group, fourth meeting)

Whether or not Cliff's comments 'sound awful' did not appear to be the point – they were after all his opinions. In defence of the advisors, they did not suggest that the comments be taken out of the leaflet, but, if such concerns are shared by advisors, how can self-advocates feel comfortable in criticizing staff and in turn build a collective identity intertwined with dissent (see T. Shakespeare 1993; Campbell and Oliver 1996)? At worst, an atmosphere of untouchable 'expert authority' is bred, and others' ineptitude is justified by being ignored. There seems to be a tacit notion that supporters of all kinds should be praised, not criticized. Such ideas heighten the vulnerability of people with learning difficulties (Brechin and Walmsley 1989).

As Lindow (1993: 185) argues, there are still too many people who accept paternalistic services and are therefore grateful to be noticed at all – 'We can let them know that they deserve better.' In accordance with this I observed many interventions that appeared to be drawn towards the *self-advocate-centred* end of the continuum. These were characterised by 'Why don't we have a chat with someone' or 'I'll support you tackling your problem' responses to requests. Three vignettes from the Centre Group highlight this:

Dorothy is sick of people pushing in front of her in the dinner queue. The advisor suggested that they could 'Have a chat with the staff on dinner duty.'

(Third meeting)

Denise was interested in the story of a couple with learning difficulties who had bought their own house. 'I'd love to do that', she told the group. The advisor suggested to Denise that she should talk about it at her IPP.

(Third meeting)

Lesley told the group she wasn't interested in going to the local advocacy project meeting because as a 'non-reader' she finds it difficult to read the minutes – 'They should use pictures.' Louise suggested to Lesley, 'You should have a quiet word with the people there to see if they will change the format of the minutes.'

(Fifth meeting)

In these interventions the advisor appeared to act in ways that did not enforce her authority over the group. Over time, through encouraging members to speak out, the support that one self-advocate receives may be passed between peers. This links into the interdependent aspect of the social model (Oliver 1996). Issues and concerns that others may share, or may later have to deal with, were made public within the group. Advisors made it known that they were there for members to offer support and back up their ambitions.

The dynamics of this intervention can go further, with advisors sustaining self-advocates' criticism of (fellow) professionals. These interventions were evident in the Centre Group, as presented in Chapter 7:

> Lesley is sick of a certain member of staff picking on her. Louise, the advisor, suggested she go see the manager and put in a complaint. She would go with her if Lesley wanted her to.
>
> (Third meeting)

There were occasions when interventions fell into the mid-ground, between advisor-centred and member-centred. For example, some members sought out advisors for one-to-one chats:

> Lillian told me that she was having problems at home. 'People won't pull their fingers out.' She mentioned to me, and later to the group, that she 'Can't get a word in edgeways' [Lillian felt so strongly about this that she also mentioned it in the group discussion] with the group and prefers to talk with one of the advisors, Jurgen, at breaktimes.
>
> (Social Group, fourth meeting)

> Imran spends most of his time with Matthew the supporter. They are inseparable.
>
> (Independent Group, second meeting)

These interventions share characteristics of a client–staff relationship. While not ideal, there was often only so much time for dealing with individual concerns in the group meetings. Action could be taken far more quickly on a one-to-one basis. Moreover, people may not want to talk in front of a larger group, preferring a one-to-one, though later they may gain the confidence to do so. One-to-one relationships provide a strong counterbalance to the general tendency of services to treat people with learning difficulties in a blanket way (Flynn and Ward 1991). However, according to Dowson and Whittaker (1993: 10), they should exist for self-advocates and not for advisors. When interventions fell into this mid-ground, questions remained over who benefited the most from the intervention. Advisors themselves may learn how to support self-advocates through these 'working pairs' and eventually translate this to the larger group. There may be times when it is only right to advocate for someone who feels powerless, lacks speech or asks for advocacy (Booth 1991). However, those interventions which pull towards the 'self-advocate-centred' end of the continuum appeared to be more readily compatible with the promotion of collective self-advocacy and less aligned with professional definitions of need and individual problem-solving (Vincent and Warren 1997: 158).

'Deficit' versus 'capacity' interventions

At one end of this continuum of support, *deficit*, advisors lean too far towards presuming incompetence on the part of self-advocates (Booth and Booth

1992: 65). This is an intrinsic part of oppressive discourses that position disability in the realms of individual pathology, personal problem and individual incapability (see Booth and Booth 1994). Koegel (1986) pessimistically observes that there is a tendency to assume incompetent behaviour on the part of people with learning difficulties and to attribute this exclusively to physiological causes. For Safilios-Rothschild (1981), supporters who view incompetence in others help to enhance their own rewards of 'helping' and 'caring'. When someone is unable to do something, we will do it for him or her, we feel needed, but our control increases as a result. This was evident in the Social Group:

> Cliff has reported to the group many times of being bullied by supervisors at work and staff in his group home. Tonight he mentioned it again. One day after work, the taxi did not turn up as had been ordered, and he told the group how he angrily reacted to this lack of punctuality by hitting a staff member. One of the staff advisors said to another, though loud enough so the group and Cliff could hear, that 'Cliff is always taking out his anger on others.' She told him that she would put him down for a place on the new 'anger management course' run at one of the centres where she works.

> (Seventh meeting)

> Ken told the group that he had asked one of the staff members in his house if he could make a cup of tea. He had said yes but on boiling the kettle another member of staff came in and told Ken to stop. Ken said this was because they thought he might scald himself. The advisors suggested that he ask the staff in his home to show him how to make a cup of tea.

> (Fifth meeting)

No one asked Cliff why he reacted like he did, or took into account the frustrations he had been feeling. The supporters might have considered what had made him feel so angry and perhaps supported him in bringing up his grievances at his workplace and home. No one asked Ken if he had made a cup of tea before. There was a focus immediately on what he couldn't do, and ways and means of remedying these deficits. Ken's capabilities were not considered. When I asked him if he had made tea before he replied, 'Oh yes, I make it for the mother when I saw her at weekends.' Probing wider social reasons for someone's actions opens up numerous causes (Guskin 1963; Koegel 1986; Booth and Booth 1992). Ken later told me that he had been in institutions for 22 years and was on the same ward with Cliff, who is some ten years older, suggesting an even longer spell of incarceration. These life experiences may explain Cliff's anger and perhaps he just wanted someone to be on his side. Friedman-Lambert's (1987) profile of Martin Levine, a Canadian self-advocate, is relevant here. Levine recalls punching a fellow (non-disabled) employee at a work placement after being the butt of some hostile ridicule. As Friedman-Lambert tried to suggest some alternative ways by which Levine could have handled the situation, Levine replied: 'Come on Phil, what would you do?' (*ibid.*: 16).

Cliff continued to get a hard time from some of the supporters. There appeared to be a generally pervasive assumption of his 'deficits':

> Cliff told the group that he had fainted at work because of the heat and nearly fallen into one of the machines. June, a supporter, asked, 'Is that because you were in the wrong room?'
>
> (Social Group, eighth meeting)

This understanding of people as incompetent can potentially suppress the formation of a valued collective identity within the group (see Campbell and Oliver 1996). When self-advocates are trying to help one another, assuming inabilities can disturb supportive interactions between peers, discourage risk-taking and self-belief, and reinforce self-appraisals which augment deficits (Wilson 1992: 31):

> Lillian said she needed to phone a taxi to get home. One of the members, Karen, offered to sort it out. 'What's the address Lil?', she asked. '24 Coathall Lane', replied Lillian. Off Karen went but one of the supporters, Jurgen, was not happy. 'She'll confuse that with her own address', he warned another supporter. Karen returned and was asked which address she had given on the phone, replying '24 Coathall Lane'. Even this was not enough for another supporter, June, who now questioned Lillian's knowledge: 'I'd best ring Lillian's house to see that address is right.' 'No it is', shouted up Jurgen.
>
> (Social Group, ninth meeting)

I also fell into the trap of treating people as stupid:

> Imran found an old lighter in my car. He asked me if he could have it. I gave it to him with a patronizing warning: 'Now don't go burning down your mother's house will you?!' He looked at me with despair and retorted, 'I'm not fucking stupid you know'.
>
> (Independent Group, sixth meeting)

In contrast, there were many occasions when advisors opposed pathological assumptions of inability, sometimes espoused by self-advocates, taking a *capacity* perspective (Booth and Booth 1994):

> As the meeting went on a young Asian man stood outside peering through and knocking on the window. The members shouted at him to 'go away'. The advisor suggested that he was trying to get their attention because he wanted to join the group. One of the members exclaimed, 'He wouldn't understand.' The advisor replied, 'You don't know what he understands.'
>
> (Centre Group, fourth meeting)

This alerted members in the group to the notion that a person's abilities are not a mere reflection of some assumed 'impairment'. Moreover, the social bases of a person's 'problems', an important construction of the social model of disability, are reiterated:

> One of the members, Denise, said that a particular user in the centre was 'being a right pain'. The advisor reminded Denise, 'He has a lot of problems at home you know. You should bear that in mind.'
>
> (Centre Group, fifth meeting)

> Virginia explained 'problem behaviour' as when people have a bad day or get upset and then might feel angry. Jarrord asked, 'What like hitting you?' 'That's right', replied Virginia.
>
> (Social Group, fourth meeting)

> Rudi admitted, 'It's not always easy to stick up for yourself against nasty people.' Paul [supporter] agreed, 'Yes some people don't listen do they?'
>
> (Advocacy-supported Group, fifth meeting)

To reiterate the views of the Canadian self-advocate, Pat Worth, it is important that advisors reject a focus on supposed deficits and emphasise competence: 'The major barrier is *attitude*. People see our disability only, they don't see our ability. We may have a handicap but we're not the handicap' (quoted in Yarmol 1987: 28).

'Talking over' versus 'talking with'

Supporters can take on the role of advocate and speak for others. This becomes problematic when it takes on expertise and care components of the individual model (Oliver 1996: 34) and becomes *talking over*:

> I asked Robert how the group had got on with the training day they gave some weeks back. He was helpful enough to get out the flip-chart that they used as the agenda for the day and started to talk me through it. Unfortunately, Matthew, the supporter, jumped in, 'I'll explain that shall I Robert?', and took over.
>
> (Independent Group, third meeting)

> Jurgen the advisor insisted that the group move on to another topic of discussion, even though they had failed to resolve a previous issue. June, the other advisor, laughed, 'Well they weren't interested in that anyway!'
>
> (Social Group, eighth meeting)

These actions were unhelpful because they downplayed the motivation of people to speak up for themselves. This relates to a personal tragedy discourse, where the voices of those with socially ascribed power override the voices of the powerless (Barnes 1990). Simone Aspis of People First London warns that accountability is paramount: 'People with learning difficulties must be asked what changes they would like, then the professionals should be supporting us, involving us, and making sure what's being said is accessible' (quoted in George 1995: 17). When this does not occur, for Wise (1973) advocating can take on an inappropriately confrontational slant:

> Ken was talking to Andrew about his work. At the same time, the group was discussing a questionnaire that had recently arrived. Jurgen, the advisor, asked Chris, the chairperson, to 'tell Ken to be quiet'.
>
> *Chris*:   Be quiet Ken.
> *Ken*:   Okay.
> *Chris*:   Sorry Ken.
> *Ken*:   That's okay.
>
> (Fifth meeting)

Having to tell off Ken was obviously uncomfortable for Chris. The only way Chris could do it was by later appealing to his friend. Here advocacy went too far, the voice of the supporter dominating, but in this case self-advocates were still able to maintain cohesion. Instead, *talking with* assumes the collective and individual responsibility elements of a social model of disability (Oliver 1996). Advocacy constitutes a new helping relationship (Taylor and Bogdan 1989). From this, relationships may emerge between advocating advisors and self-advocates:

> I heard Lillian tell the supporter Neil, 'The group aren't listening to me.' She wanted to talk about the way staff treat her in her house. Neil started to tell the group that Lillian was unhappy, from this Lillian butted in, 'They don't treat me proper, they treat me like a child.'
>
> (Social Group, fifth meeting)

Neil's intervention was positive as it brought in a shy member of the group into the process of their own advocacy – dispersing the issues under attention throughout the group. At the same time, naivety promoted by an exclusive society can be challenged by providing information (Worrel 1987, 1988):

> Louise asked if the members had received the letter on green paper from the county council. Some members said they had received it but had not had a chance to read it. Others knew nothing about it. The council is now going to charge 75 pence a day for transport to and from college, the centre and other places. The members were furious. Carol said that all members of the centre and staff should have a big meeting to talk about these new charges.
>
> (Centre Group, second meeting)

> Dennis and Julia showed the group the completed application form for Lottery funding that they had just finished.
>
> (Independent Group, third meeting)

Two supporters have written a leaflet on the new consultation document for services for people with learning disabilities. Part of the meeting was spent discussing these issues. Members felt the leaflet was a good idea and well presented – the pictures were particularly helpful.

(Social Group, fifth meeting)

'Talking with' links into a particular conceptual understanding of independence. As Elsa (in Campling 1981: 85) puts it:

> It annoys me when able bodied people hold forth about how we should be as independent as possible. Of course we should be but I'd like to hear some talk about the able-bodied being a bit more independent too – how many of them cut their own hair, for goodness sake?

Similarly for French (1993), ideas of 'independence' applied to disabled people have gone too far, individualizing disability, pushing people to be as independent as possible, even when impairment or lack of experience prevent people from doing things they may never be able to do. Some people will never be able to read, others may never have enough confidence to speak out in a large group, while certain individuals will lack experience of finding out about their own rights (Simons 1992). Numerous environmental deficiencies give rise to a multitude of inabilities (Booth and Booth 1994). Here, then, independence should be substituted for interdependence (Oliver 1996) – something that historically the non-disabled have had an innate right to while disabled people have had it denied in line with misplaced notions that 'They need their independence.' These miscomprehensions were sensitively challenged through advocacy by many of the supporters I observed, and respectful climates were encouraged.

'Expertise' versus 'experience'

The two ends of this continuum could also be described as: 'forgetting why you are there in the first place' versus 'knowing why you are there'. The former can lead people to ignore the original reasons for their support, like at the AGM of a larger advocacy organization, which the Advocacy-supported Group attended (see Chapter 7). Supporting the advocacy skills of another can be fraught with problems (see Wise 1973). Not being self-critical can promote an 'us and them' mentality, emphasizing *expert* opinion of which self-advocates are aware, as shown at a 'service users consultation meeting' attended by members of the Social Group:

> Virginia, one of the group's advisors, stood up to introduce herself. 'I'm at Binglay lane hostel', 'IN CHARGE', shouted one of the self-advocates!
>
> (User consultation meeting)

To be fair, many of the supporters showed reflexive qualities when examining their actions. A bad intervention could be reversed:

> At the start of the meeting it was Becca's turn as chairperson. Becca was writing out the agenda and asked, 'How do you spell "news"?' Erica, a

fellow member, shouted up, 'I know Becca, n . . . e . . .' George the supporter ignored Erica, interrupting, 'It's n . . . e . . . w . . . s.' Later Becca
asked how to spell 'annual'. Erica started to answer, George interrupted,
but seeing the error of his ways encouraged her: 'Sorry Erica go on.'

> (Advocacy supported group, third meeting)

Addressing difficulties from a social model of disability reaffirms the human
nature of people over their purported 'difference'. This leads us to the 'knowing why you are there in the first place' stance – the *experience* position (Oliver
1996) – typified by supporters giving primacy to the experiences of self-advocates. Take, for example, this vignette:

> The British Telecom engineer walked into the office. Looking around the
> room his gaze finally fell upon Julia [the supporter]. 'I've come to sort the
> phones out, is that right?', he asked. Julia shrugged her shoulders
> and looked over to one of the members, Robert. 'What d'yer reckon?',
> she asked Robert. 'Yes that's right, we need the phones fitted upstairs
> and downstairs', Robert replied. The engineer and Robert went upstairs
> and were still chatting away half an hour later.
>
> (Independent Group, sixth meeting)

Julia's skilful prodding of Robert ensured that he took on the role of negotia-
tor. The engineer changed in his interaction from a chap unsure of how to act,
to someone who felt comfortable to chat away. A similar incident occurred
with the same group but a different supporter:

> Robert, Jonny and Andy went to the bank to pay in some money. We
> were stood at the counter, along with Dennis the supporter. The clerk
> looked up to catch the eye of Dennis. However, Dennis must have antici-
> pated this and was looking over at Robert. The clerk noticed this and
> asked Robert what she could do for him.
>
> (Sixth meeting)

When advisors remembered why they were there this appeared to be
associated with maintaining acceptance, tolerance and understanding. However, this meant that potential conflicts with self-advocates could occur:

> The advisor asked the group what prejudice meant. Amanda said it was
> like a black woman and a white man getting married. 'You see many of
> 'em around.' John, the advisor, replied, 'Yes and people don't think it's
> right, do they?' Amanda's reaction was unexpected: 'No I don't think it's
> right.' When asked why, Amanda replied, 'It's difficult to explain.' John
> asked Amanda if she would, accept that people should have the choice.
> 'Yes I do, it's up to people innit?', replied Amanda generously.
>
> (Advocacy supported group, third meeting)

Dowson and Whittaker (1993: 31) put forward the 'confronting intervention'
as a way of tackling members' intolerance. An example of this would be:
'After we've talked so much about respecting people, I feel really angry about

the way you just spoke, Sally.' By contrast, the above vignette in the Advocacy-supported Group shows the advisor embracing Amanda's perspective without prescribing how she should think. Giving space and time for people to speak out is a necessary part of self-advocacy's beginnings (Downer and Ferns 1993: 142–3). To knock down others because their opinions are incongruent with your own can prevent people from even starting to self-advocate. Another difficult issue was that of the 'dominant member'. A number of advisors appeared to be more than able to handle this difficulty:

> Lesley was being rather self-righteous with Carol: 'You shouldn't push in the queue Carol, it's wrong.' Louise stepped in marvellously: 'Well, you can't blame Carol for trying!' The group laughed. Lesley responded, 'I didn't shout at her.' Louise asked Carol, 'Is that right, she didn't shout at you?'
>
> (Centre Group, sixth meeting)

This links into the collective responsibility and identity component of the social model (Finkelstein 1993, Oliver 1996, Morris 1996) – forging bonds and commonalties with one another, challenging actions that are destructive. Diffusion tactics encouraged others to have a say in ways that did not disempower others.

'Missing the point(s)' versus 'addressing the point(s)'

There were many complex ways in which supporters threatened to stifle the self-determination of members. At times, this was linked to focusing on the trivial, or *missing the point* (see Worrel 1987: 34):

> Sarb had spent a lot of time making posters for the group. He had stencilled in the group's name and cut out some pictures from a trade union brochure. This finished draft had been photocopied on to A3 paper and presented a striking poster for the group. One of the supporters made only one comment, 'You'll have to take out the trade union name for copyright reasons.' No other comments, good or bad, were given.
>
> (Social Group, second meeting)

> Chris got out a pen from his bag, and asked me, 'Do you like it? It's new.' June, the supporter, was seated nearby listening and asked Chris in a patronizing drawl, 'Is that a new pen?' Chris looked bemused. Later Sarb went to the bar for a drink. He returned, as always, with a pint of lager and sat down beside Chris. June looked up and asked, 'Are you thirsty Sarb?'
>
> (Social Group, ninth meeting)

This was very similar to my own ridiculous comments to Jim:

> Jim was reading a magazine on car tyres. I asked him what he was reading and he replied, 'A magazine on tyres.' He then turned away, probably

concerned that he might catch my 'asking stupid questions deficit disorder'.

(Social Group, second meeting)

While these interactions now seem laughable they are actually potentially harmful. Treating people as 'retarded' has the knock-on effect that 'acting like the retard becomes second nature' (Guskin 1963). For Worrel (1988: 55) an ignorant advisor misses the first and most important step of support. Without listening carefully and assisting people to express themselves, advisors may miss out on important questions that people are asking themselves:

Sarb is sick of having no money. June asked, 'What is it about not having any money that you don't like?' 'Not having any', Sarb replied.

(Social Group, seventh meeting)

Similarly, salient issues associated with choice are ignored.

Carol has been told that she and her colleagues are moving workplaces. Advisors asked what work she'd be doing there, one of them reassured Carol, 'You'll like it there.'

(Social Group, fourth meeting)

Advisors did not find out if Carol was asked if she would like to move. Instead it was tacitly accepted that others had made decisions for her and these were the right decisions. Self-advocates may need to be reminded of their own rights and resources, thus, advisors *address the point(s)* (Worrel 1988). Too often the failure of others to recognize the self-determination of people with learning difficulties suppresses their sense of worth (Atkinson and Williams 1990). On occasions too numerous to mention, many of the members of all four groups I observed would ask a supporter, or me, if they could go to the toilet. My response was, 'You don't have to ask me.' In addition, many of the advisors (and self-advocates) had wonderfully delicate ways of prodding people into opening up. Supporters would often reply to members' cathartic expressions ('You obviously feel really strongly about that', 'You seem to be angry'), thus reinforcing people's concerns as important (as with Dowson and Whittaker's 'cathartic intervention'). Both advisors and self-advocates appeared to be skilled at this:

Imran suggested that the group keep a record of the phone calls they have made. Matthew [the supporter] went around the office telling people about Imran's 'brilliant idea'.

(Independent Group, fourth meeting)

Jane often repeats things verbatim from the TV. 'Now go over to Gillian Shepherd . . . what do you think Mrs Shepherd . . . education.' Paul [a supporter] noted, 'That's a good point about education Jane, did you see it on the news?' Jane replied, 'Yes.' 'Good', continued Paul. 'What do others think about education?'

(Advocacy-supported Group, fifth meeting)

There was movement away from the specific to the general – from the periphery to the centre of self-advocacy. In the latter vignette, Jane's views were validated and the debate was extended to others. One of Jane's peers, Bill, recognized the use of Jane's commentaries: 'It's good because Jane tells us news we have missed' (Advocacy-supported Group, fifth meeting).

Two other vignettes from the Social Group highlight how simple questions from advisors can address basic human rights, from risk-taking to independence:

> Virginia asked the group if they had their own keys to their homes. Adam said he had. Virginia asked him, 'Do you let yourself in when you get home?' 'No', said Adam, 'my mother leaves the door open for me.'
>
> (Social Group, fifth meeting)

> Lillian said that she's not allowed to use the stove at home. Virginia asked, 'Why? Have you used it before? Will the staff let you?' Lillian replied, 'No they won't because I burnt myself.'
>
> (Social Group, fifth meeting)

Addressing concerns of self-advocates can help to build up collective identity of the group – an important aspect of the social model (Finkelstein 1993; Morris 1996; Oliver 1996). More about this below.

Not just advising: self-advocates supporting one another

It would appear that the support of advisors is changeable. As with Chapter 7, which rejected previous literature's preoccupation with group 'type', this chapter so far has brought into question the relationship between advisor status and 'good' and 'bad' support. In contrast to previous literature, my ethnography suggests that types of support do not fit neatly with types of advisor. Instead, the fluidity of support means that advisors can support in good and bad ways, and these interventions can be understood as reflecting positions on individual–social model continuums. In addition to advisor interventions, self-advocates themselves created a group setting that facilitated the development of self-advocacy. Their actions magnify the self-help element of a social model of disability, where disabled people move towards personal and social action through the resource of collective identity (T. Shakespeare 1993; Hales 1996). As Crawley (1988) points out, self-advocates are a lot more able to promote the empowerment of their 'less-able' peers than even the most well meaning advisor. Goode (1992: 205) suggests that interdependence among people with learning difficulties overrides notions of incompetence held by others. In his case study of Bobby, a 50-year-old man with learning difficulties, videotaped recordings of Bobby with his friends showed Bobby behaving 'more competently' than when he was in the company of staff and researchers. This, Goode concluded, was the direct consequence of friends not seeing any problems with the way Bobby acted. Similarly, Schapiro's (1976) account of the advocacy support lent by senior citizens to a collection of deinstitutionalized people supports the viability of informal (self-)advocacy relationships. My observations picked up on many supportive skills of members, though I am not trying to paint a perfect picture. Some members openly disliked one another, some were bossy, others dismissive. Yet considerations of support would be lacking without attention to the ways in which self-advocates themselves bolstered group cohesion and encouraged one another to speak out for themselves. It is worthwhile to include these vignettes, as they suggest that there is more to promoting self-advocacy than advising (Siegel and Kantor 1982). Support can therefore be understood, revamped and changed, in accordance with what self-advocates can do for themselves.

First is challenging advisors' interventions. People with learning difficulties are not passive in the doing of self-advocacy and are able to offer 'instrumental' (practical) and 'expressive' (emotional) support to their peers. In my ethnography, members knew when advisors were starting to take over:

> Louise mentioned that the tape recordings they have made of the meetings are very difficult on the ear. These tapes are used, first, for writing up the minutes and, second, are available for 'clients' in the centre. She suggested that in future, one of the members, like Simon, could go into a quiet room and read out the main points from the minutes, which would be taped. The recording would be a lot clearer and so allowing other clients the chance to hear what had been talked about in the working group. Lesley, the chair, stepped in, 'Hold on – what about other people reading the minutes out as well as Simon?' The advisor agreed and said she had only used Simon as a 'for instance'.
>
> (Centre Group, fourth meeting)

> Matthew [a supporter] swore and the members in the room at that time shouted him down – 'You know the rules Matt, no swearing.'
>
> (Independent Group, third meeting)

Here members themselves were resilient enough to challenge dominant supporters. As Ken from the social group put it, during a period of advisor dominance, 'Even Danny's falling asleep, you'll sleep well tonight Danny!' (sixth meeting).

Second, sometimes members *resisted assumptions of deficit*, inability, incompetence or inappropriateness that were held by others:

> Karen had recently had a meeting with an educational psychologist because, she joked, 'I'm dumb in the head.' A supporter who works at the college suggested that this meeting be arranged because Karen 'was not joining in in class'. Karen disagreed – 'No, I were bored.'
>
> (Social Group, seventh meeting)

> Virginia [an advisor] suggested that members in the group should be taught how to cook. At the back Karen piped up, 'I can cook already.'
>
> (Social Group, fourth meeting)

One member's father doesn't like him coming to the group and would prefer him to be in the centre. 'Centre's fucking boring – I prefer the group', he explained. To avoid conflict with his dad and the centre staff, he told me that he took away the dates of the next meeting – one for the centre and one for the taxi driver – to take him to the group not the centre.

(Independent Group, fifth meeting)

Even at formal meetings self-advocates were skilled at challenging others' prejudices:

> Karen spoke for the group to an audience of staff, parents and 'users': 'In our group we talk about out hobbies, interests and worries we have. People with learning difficulties are just like anyone else you know.'
>
> (Social Group, Users' consultation meeting)

Representatives from the local council suggested that in order for me to canvass the opinions of members smaller groups should be used, so that 'People with speaking problems have a chance to talk.' Robert agreed: 'Yes, some us never shut up and others can't get a word in.'

(Independent Group, meeting with council)

Some of the members of the group are actors and dancers in a drama group. Towards the end of the meeting they came to the front and performed a new play they have been working on. Afterwards, with the musical accompaniment of supporters, they wrote a song. Clive shouted out, 'Hold on to your dreams don't let them go.'

(Advocacy-supported Group, advocacy project's
annual general meeting)

Third, self-advocates themselves encouraged one another to open up, accept, listen and *share skills, experiences and self-help strategies*. Being in centres or houses together ensured that people know one another's foibles:

> Sarb is having problems at home. His brother picks on him and tells him what to do. Karen agreed, she hates it when staff watch her having a bath.
>
> (Social Group, sixth meeting)

It was Bill's turn to chair the meeting. Around the group members offered their news and views. Erica took her time to think about what she had done, 'I'm just thinking.' The group waited patiently. Bill gave her time to speak and skilfully moved on to the next person. 'Thank you for that Erica, now Rachel what have you been up to?'

(Advocacy supported group, second meeting)

Jane jumped up out of her seat and lashed out at Erica. Erica was shook up, 'You did make me jump.' Then Jane got up and went over to apologize, kissing Erica on the cheek. Erica responded, 'That's good of you Jane – well done.'

(Advocacy supported group, sixth meeting)

This acceptance spread to potential members. Membership of certain groups was open, unconditional and encouraged:

Guy told the group that a woman at his centre wanted to come down to the group. He asked the members what they thought. Richard was honest but fair: 'Well she's a bit of a pain sometimes, but why not?' Bill was not happy: 'She's naughty.' Guy was defensive: 'Yes she was, but she's changed.'

(Advocacy-supported Group, fourth meeting)

At the executive committee meeting, members were discussing the work that one of the supporters, Matthew, does for another self-advocacy group. Andy argued, 'That group needs more training, they didn't even know what "self-advocacy" meant.' Ellen defended the group: 'Yes, but Matt doesn't use that long word with them they use short words like "speaking out".' 'Oh, I'm sorry', replied Andy.

(Independent Group, executive meeting)

Fourth is *advocacy among self-advocates*, where friends know friends:

Rachel does not speak often. She spends her time quietly and apparently contentedly smelling her fingers and looking around the room. At break-time Bill asked her if she would like a cup of coffee or tea. Erica, who lives with Rachel, replied, 'She likes coffee don't you Rachel?' Bill looked at Rachel. 'Coffee then?'

(Advocacy-supported Group, fifth meeting)

Whatever the group, some members are more articulate than others and skills can be distributed so others benefit. Ferguson (1987: 56) argues that more should be spoken about interdependent living and cooperative work as opposed to independent living and competitiveness. Paradoxically, the path to greater independence is one that reinforces the idea of interdependence and cooperation (Williams 1989:257):

Robert suggested that any documents on the new office premises should be photocopied and circulated to all members.

(Independent Group, fourth meeting)

Guy, the treasurer, shares the group's accounts with the members by referring to the flip-chart on which the balance of the account before and after the meeting is presented.

(Advocacy-supported Group, fifth meeting)

Every Friday Robert, Andy, Jonny and Petra sort out the agenda for the meeting on Monday (which uses words and pictures), write and post letters and sort out the finances.

(Independent Group, second meeting)

Andy decided that details about the annual costs for the new offices should be photocopied and given out to all members.

(Independent Group, third meeting)

This advocacy also meant that peers *provided encouragement and humour*, link-ing into the process of deciding, a process that is as important as the outcome of a decision (Worrel 1987: 32):

Each time a member gives their news brings the reaction of a loud and enthusiastic round of applause. By the end, the room is full of smiles. At one meeting Becca was ecstatic: 'Danny – Rudi thinks I'm doing a really good job as chairperson.'

(Advocacy-supported Group, first meeting)

Lesley goes to the advocacy development project. She suggested that someone else could come with her and she'd support them.

(Centre Group, third meeting)

At the executive committee meeting Robert went round the group to ask how many times a week the office windows should be cleaned. Some weeks before, the group was moving to their new offices. Imran has difficulty walking so the others put belongings in the van. Andy told everyone, 'Imran makes an excellent supervisor.'

(Independent Group, executive meeting)

One of the residents in Lillian's house is violent towards her. Jarrord suggested, 'You should stick up to them. I do – I shout out loud until someone comes.'

(Social Group, fifth meeting)

In all four groups, there were particular members who fulfilled the role of group comedian, able to make people laugh and put others at ease:

Karen looked depressed. As it came to her turn to give her 'news' she told everyone that she had to go to the dentist the following day. 'Are you okay?', asked one of the supporters. 'Yes', said Karen, 'my appointment's at tooth hurty!'

(Social Group, ninth meeting)

One of Imran's favourite sayings is 'Get real'. A number of the members and I were walking around the town to get some shopping and as we passed the market, a chap on the 'fruit and veg' stall shouted, '50p for a pound of toms'. 'Get real!', shouted back Imran.

(Independent Group, sixth meeting)

Graham was chatting away as usual. Becca turned to Bill, looked up and joked, 'Eeee, that Graham's like a tin of marbles!'

(Advocacy-supported group, third meeting)

As I entered the room Lesley greeted me with an enthusiastic rendition of 'Oh, Danny boy'. Members thought this was a scream, falling about laughing hysterically.

(Centre Group, second meeting)

Rudi has broken his arm. 'No weight lifting for a while – eh Rudi!', somebody shouted from the back.

(Advocacy supported group, sixth meeting)

Conclusion: conceptualizing support in practice

This chapter has conceptualized some of the interventions of advisors in terms of their position on five social–individual model continua of support. In addition, some aspects of the solidarity among self-advocates have been presented. This exploration of advisor and self-advocate interventions has highlighted the complexities of support and delved further into the group dynamics presented in Chapter 7. Lukes (1986: 14) asks that we turn attention to the person: 'Who takes the big decision, those that are irreversible, whose consequences risk being prolonged indefinitely, and being experienced by all the collectivity's members.'

In the four groups, advisors had the power to take big decisions but self-advocates were not powerless. By understanding the link between actions and discourses of disability it is possible to become aware of the larger implications. Those advisors and members that supported well, listened and acted in ways that challenged the discourses that silenced and disabled. There is more to advising than status or position. Self-advocates can be powerful but this needs to be recognized and reinforced. In terms of applications for policy makers, service-providers and supporters, two general points emerge. First, following Means and Smith (1994), in the contemporary culture of 'user empowerment' and widespread adoption of self-advocacy, there may be a tendency to become obsessed with the changing elements of service provision and support. However, as this chapter has indicated, there may still be a need to consider the basic assumptions that underlie the way we address, talk and act with oppressed groups such as people with learning difficulties. Second, people of any (oppressed) social group are capable of individual and collective determination. Consequently, there may be a need to move away from paternalistic notions of 'empowering' people to practices that incorporate those self-empowering actions that already exist. Self-advocates can be supported, by listening and acting in ways that challenge those discourses that silence and disable.

Notes

1 An abridged version of this chapter can be found in Goodley (1998a); the chapter builds upon a theoretical paper about discourse, models of disability and support (Goodley 1997).
2 A useful summary of the continuum between the two models is provided by Mike Oliver (1996: 133–4).

 PART **IV**

SELF-ADVOCACY REVISITED

 **9**

Conclusions: the politics of resilience

As she dressed that morning, Sophie didn't know that a clinical psychologist had written in her case notes that she 'would be unable to learn to cross the road'. She left her room and walked down the stairs, greeting the few house mates who had decided to wake early on this Saturday morning. Most of the residents of the large group home were still asleep. She stood in the foyer until she heard the car horn of the taxi. For four years the same taxi firm had picked her up to drive her the walkable distance to the meeting of the self-advocacy group that she attended. The taxi driver mumbled 'hello' as he opened the door for Sophie to clamber into the back seat before they set off. It was raining and the car made unhealthy noises as it stood at the traffic lights. Within a couple of minutes she had arrived . . . The taxi pulled in close to the pavement on the right side of the road. Sophie got out, making her way to the entrance of the building. Suddenly and with obvious practice, Sophie turned around and walked back to the curb, looking up the road to the right, to check where her taxi had got to. As it turned out of sight, Sophie looked right, then left, and crossed the road. On the other side she made her way to the newsagents on Dominick Street. She had to get the milk and biscuits for the coffee break. She was after all, the group's designated 'shopping manager'. She died this year. The position hasn't yet been filled.

(A story of a friend)

This chapter takes stock in the light of the preceding analysis of the storied and enacted elements of self-advocacy. The first section draws together a number of analytical connections from the empirical sections of the book. These include resilience of people with learning difficulties, variation and complexity in the movement, the impacts of group 'type' and organizational dynamics, supporting self-advocacy, groups as a context for furthering self-advocacy, self-advocacy and self-definition, interdependence and culture and the need for self-advocates to call the shots. The second section presents a number of questions that remain unanswered and therefore point ways forward for future research. These include self-advocacy and impairment, commonality between self-advocates and other disabled activists, the self-advocacy movement and the disability movement, leaving self-advocacy and the need to embrace the different forms that self-advocacy may take. The third section considers the implications of this appraisal with respect to supporting self-advocacy, policy-making, service provision and professional practice. The fourth and final section takes a critical look at the research undertaken for this book in the light of debates associated with participatory and emancipatory research, suggesting ways forward in which theory and practice are brought more closely together.

Making analytical connections

A number of themes emerge as a consequence of examining the impact and workings of self-advocacy.

The resilience of people with learning difficulties

> Although 'enacted stigma' or overt discrimination seems a pervasive aspect of the lives of people with learning disabilities, there exists a body of research which reveals that people with learning disabilities do not necessarily see themselves as disqualified from a variety of roles . . . while it is typically assumed that this denotes the strength of their convictions, there is a lack of data on how these convictions are informed or supported.
>
> (Todd and Shearn 1997: 344)

Chamberlin (1990: 323) notes that only when a group begins to emerge from subjugation can it begin to reclaim its own history. The self-advocacy literature presented in Chapter 2 tended to focus on the self-determination of people with learning difficulties in terms of membership of self-advocacy groups. This book has shown that self-advocacy of people with learning difficulties may exist prior to and as the consequence of joining groups (see Chapter 6), alongside group structure (Chapter 7) and with the support of advisors (Chapter 8). Resilience appeared to exist despite disablement – as pointed out by proponents of the social model of disability (Chapter 3). The accounts presented in this book suggest that people so labelled are resilient and determined throughout their lives. Consequently, the term 'self-advocate' may emphasize 'otherness' and give the impression that people with learning difficulties only exhibit self-advocacy in self-advocacy groups. Likewise, the identification of resilience raises questions about empowering research and other forms of intervention on the part of professionals and policy makers. For example, should research or the philosophies of service providers aim to 'empower' oppressed groups or does such an aim reinforce the victim status of people within these groups (Bhavnani 1990)? Moreover, when people empower themselves, how do researchers and professionals stand in relation to such self-empowerment – are research projects or user empowerment initiatives a help or hindrance?

To answer these questions, it is necessary to consider the meaning of resilience in the lives of people with learning difficulties represented in this book. A number of things appear to characterize resilience. First, it is *contextualized*, looming in a variety of socio-political and interrelational contexts. Families, professionals, schools and work influence and shape its emergence. For some of the narrators in Chapter 5, their very experiences of disablement appeared to inform their subsequent resilience. For others, inclusive relationships with family and professionals were necessary in encouraging self-determination. When Marx (1832) wrote in *The German Ideology* that 'life determines consciousness' he was aware of the contradictory social conditions of oppression and resistance from which comes forth sensuous awareness of individuality and society. Later, in *Theses on Feuerbach* (1845), he observed that human essence is 'the ensemble of social relations . . . [belonging] to a particular form of society'. Similarly, self-advocacy groups have the potential to invite the development of a consciousness that is sensitized to disabling *and* enabling conditions from which resilience emerges. In this sense, then, resilience allows us some explanatory value in assessing the impact of social contexts upon people with learning difficulties. The doing of self-advocacy may provide access to social networks that help resilience to germinate from potential to action. In this sense, resilience seems to reside in the space between structure and individuality. It is not an individual attribute or a structural product. Hence, and second, resilience is *complicating*. It is anti-essentialist as it troubles notions of naturalized impairment and opposes crude structuralist takes on disablement. It appears to be associated with the mid-ground of theorizing social life, flirting with notions of pre-existing potential for personal and collective resistance, while locating understandings in social contexts. Third, it is *optimistic*. It is related to the capacity of human nature to resist oppression, challenging the tendency to underestimate people with the label of learning difficulties. Resilience as a phenomenon questions how we understand the concept of learning difficulties. There is a need for supporters, professionals, researchers and policy makers to assume the potential for resilient lives when developing collaborative work with people with learning difficulties. Fourth, it is *interpersonal*, open to various forms of intervention and social interaction, highlighting the support of others that enables or denies. Finally, resilience is *indicative of disablement*. Alongside shows of resistance, this book has revealed stories and observational vignettes of disabling ideologies, environments, attitudes and actions that permeate the lives of self-advocates. There is a danger of romanticizing the 'autonomy' of self-advocates if we ignore their day-to-day experiences of oppression. Self-advocacy groups appear to provide a place in which self-advocacy can potentially be supported. For some people, like Patrick Burke, joining a group is instrumental in recognizing and developing self-determination (Chapters 5 and 6): from damaging environments to embracing groups. Members of research groups (Chapters 7 and 8) made similar points about the changes that occurred for them when they joined their group: 'We were allowed to speak our minds' (Colin, Independent

Group, group discussion). This book has recognized both resistance to and the continuing prevalence of disabling barriers.

The impacts of group 'type' and deeper organizational dynamics

Chapter 7 addressed the complexities of group organization. Various in-group dynamics of the Centre, Social, Advocacy-supported and Independent Groups were described. A number of findings emerged from this ethnography that went some way to explain how self-advocates and advisors were affected by the organizational form of their groups. First, the four groups illustrate the overlap of group types. The Independent Group, for example, while seemingly autonomous, had characteristics of all four types identified in Chapter 2. Second, organizational links appeared to have some effects upon the running of groups. Members of the Centre Group, for example, were stifled by the wider centre context; the Social Group appeared to have a hidden organizational limitation in the form of staff advisors bringing their work with them into group meetings; and the Advocacy-supported Group was restrained by time constraints of meeting times. However, delving into group processes uncovered deeper dynamics that appeared to have greater impacts upon the workings of the group. The third conclusion was that members' actions appeared to transcend superficial aspects of group organization.

For example, while the Centre Group was restrained by the centre context, members appeared to gain much from membership, with the group providing a safe haven. Although the Social Group was limited in terms of time and money, members used meetings to build up(on) friendship groups and publicly present grievances, while integrating themselves in the culture of the social club: a culture much more expansive than those of service and group settings. Therefore, fourth, rather than being dependent on 'typology', the organization of groups was grounded in the relational ties between group members, alongside the varying support of advisors.

Supporting self-advocacy

Chapter 8 continued to examine the organization of groups by focusing on the support of advisors and self-advocates. A number of themes emerged. First, the usefulness of applying models of disability in conceptualizing support was displayed. Plotting advisor interventions on social–individual model continua captured some of the styles and effects of support and provided an analytical technique for identifying good and bad practice. In this sense, the relevance of the social model to the lives of people with learning difficulties was demonstrated, building upon the call for an inclusive model laid out in Chapter 3. Second, following on from a rejection of 'type' as *the* determining factor in the formulation of self-advocacy (Chapter 7), it was shown that the tendency of previous literature to dismiss professionalized support and uphold independent support was simplistic, unhelpful and inauthentic. Instead, third, support was specific, fluid and open to change by advisors in their interventions.

Chapter 8 turned away from conceptualizations of the bad or good advisor (presented in some of the advisor and typology literature, e.g. Worrel 1987, 1988) to incidents of bad (individual model) and good (social model) interventions (Dowson and Whittaker 1993). Through the use of conceptual frameworks of discourse as action (Fairclough 1989, 1992), this analytical turn reflected Jackie Downer's assertion that: 'Some professionals are . . . *professionals*, others are ace – they know where the users are coming from . . . it depends on the person' (Jackie Downer, Chapter 5).

A number of continua were presented, including 'advisor-centred' versus 'self-advocacy-centred', 'deficit' versus 'capacity', 'talking over' versus 'talking with', 'expertise' versus 'experience' and 'missing the point' versus 'addressing the point'. This analysis contrasts with Mitchell's (1998) findings, which emphasize the constraints of services and professional identity upon advising. Instead, a poststructuralist turn to the spaces inhabited by discourse and action, between structure and individual, provides a way of understanding support and interdependence as dynamic. An MPhil study by Harrison focuses solely on advisors. It will be interesting to see how the findings from this study compare with those from this book and Mitchell's (1997, 1998) research. Fourth, the support of advisors was not the only contributing factor to the development of self-determination within. In addition, the ethnography highlighted the support offered by self-advocates, a theme that also emerged from an analysis of the life stories (see Chapter 6). Self-advocates challenged advisors' interventions, resisted assumptions of deficit, shared experiences and self-help strategies, advocated for and encouraged one another and provided necessary humour to break paternalistic discourse (Chapter 8). The self-empowering actions of people with learning difficulties constitute a major recurring theme of this book.

Groups as a context for furthering self-advocacy

> You see her sometimes silent with her head pressed against the window, looking at the girls in the street. It's as if she wanted to join in. But no-one's going to come knocking on the door to ask her out.
>
> (A mother describing Bernice, her 21-year-old daughter with learning difficulties, cited in Todd and Shearn 1997: 348)

Chapter 6 indicated that self-advocacy groups provided the five narrators with a context for defining self-determination and a place to support one another, allowed friendships to blossom and offered opportunities for practical gains. Stepping into the workings of groups supported these conclusions (Chapters 7 and 8). Members of the four research groups seemed to use groups as a context for self-expression, even when the group was organized around service-based issues (Centre Group) or took on the appearance of a 'trivial' social event (Social Group). Valued members took on valued roles.

Nevertheless, tensions exist within groups, as with the breakdown of friendships (see Anya Souza's experiences, Chapter 5), and in the hierarchies that appeared to exclude some but not others (see Centre Group and Independent Group, Chapter 7). Further problems occurred when supporters assumed incompetence on the part of self-advocates (see Chapter 8), ignored self-determination ('missing the point') and took too much of a 'hands on' approach (Social Group, Chapter 8). Such findings will resonate with readers' own experience of social groups. We are reminded that searching for purity in collectives of disabled people (for example, the 'true' autonomous self-advocacy group; see Chapter 2) may contribute to the 'othering' of disabled people: where such collectives are not afforded the right to enjoy or endure group dynamics. A continuation of such perceptions will contribute to the exclusion of disabled people, where waiting by the window, looking at other (non-disabled) individuals is seen as an indicator of tragedy rather than curiosity. This book has recognized the influential role of the self-advocacy group on the development of members' self-advocacy, where doors are knocked upon and peers invited out to join in with the activities of a group.

Self-advocacy groups and self-definition

This book has touched upon issues of identity. In 1963, Howard Becker wrote that:

> The person who is thus labeled an outsider may have a different view of the matter. He [*sic*] may not accept the rule by which he is being judged and may not regard those who view him as either competent or legitimately entitled to do so . . . the rule-breaker may feel his judges are the *outsiders*.
>
> (Becker 1963: 1–2)

The stories and actions presented in this book highlight some issues associated with labelling, self and identity. First, similarities between disabled and non-disabled people were confirmed, like the anxieties of going to school, leaving and getting a job, the importance and difficulties of relationships, and hopes for the future (Chapter 6). Second, and in contrast, difference was also reiterated, though the values that were attached to difference were challenged:

> You've got to keep reminding people – especially on the outside, you've got to remind them all the time that we are different to what they are, which, fair enough, we are. We've all got our own ways of living.
>
> (Patrick Burke, Chapter 5)

This paradoxical point of emphasizing difference and similarity was illustrated in Lloyd Page's poignant commentary: 'We're just ordinary people with learning difficulties' (Chapter 5). Self-advocacy groups have the potential to support members in recognizing and perhaps celebrating their own (understandings of) difference, while also challenging others who, in line with an individual model of disability, understand difference only as an indicator of pathology:

Karen had recently had a meeting with an educational psychologist because, she joked, 'I'm dumb in the head'. A supporter who works at the college suggested that this meeting be arranged because Karen 'was not joining in in class'. Karen disagreed – 'No, I were bored.'

(Social group, seventh meeting)

Attending to labelled groups' understandings of labels taps into insider experiences rather than outsider expertise (see Oliver 1996). As Jackie Downer put it, 'Every experience is totally different and you need to go back and ask self-advocates' (Chapter 5). This comment recognizes the complex factors involved in identity formation. In a time of postmodern celebration of identity politics (Burman 1990), it is timely that the narratives of people with learning difficulties are publicized through the activism of self-advocacy, destabilizing the simplicities of pseudo-medicalized notions of identity-as-syndrome.

Interdependence and culture

> Self-advocates who speak out raise important basic issues: freedom, fulfilment and self-determination. Nobody can speak more eloquently on these issues than the people directly concerned.
>
> (Worrel 1988: 13)

A recent appraisal of the disabled people's movement drew out interdependence and collective identity as key components of disabled people's self-organization (Campbell and Oliver 1996):

> It is vital that all disabled people join together in their own organisation so that there is a creative interaction between disabled people who are involved with the politics of disability and disabled people involved in the arts. It is this interaction which can be particularly fruitful in helping us to take the initiative in developing a new disability culture.
>
> (Finkelstein, quoted in *ibid.*: 111–12)

This book found many fruitful, political elements of self-advocacy. Chapter 8 illustrated a number of interventions by self-advocates that promoted cohesion among the self-advocate body. Chapter 6 represented narrators' opinions on whom the self-advocacy group was for and how the movement should develop. While Whittemore *et al.* (1986) assert that people with learning difficulties are denied a culture, this appeared to have been overturned to various extents by the narrators in Part II and the members of the research groups in Part III. Membership of groups appeared to constitute specific, though perhaps not immediately apparent, and therefore hidden, cultures.

First, the culture of each group was 'outed' in a number of settings: at high-profile conferences (1993 People First conference in Canada; see Chapter 6); when groups lobbied the county council over the state of the roads or the inaccessibility of consultation documents (see Advocacy-supported Group,

Chapter 7, and Patrick Burke, Chapter 5); and in meetings of advocacy or ser-vice user consultation meetings (Centre, Social and Advocacy Groups, Chap-ter 7). Second, group actions and narrators' experiences link into a definition of culture as the acquired knowledge that people use to interpret experiences and generate social behaviour (Spradley 1979: 7). Chapter 7 exhibited smaller-scale cultural components, like shared ways of running meetings (sharing the chairperson role, the Advocacy-supported Group), conventions over divulging information (getting members' views written down at the start of the meeting, the Social Group) and in-group preoccupations (sorting out training programmes, the Independent Group). Third, groups appeared to give members access to an alternative framework of sense (Vincent 1998):

> When you've been locked up all your life, you can't make no friends. Now I'm starting to make friends . . . People First . . . [has] helped to bring me out of things that I wanted to be brought out of . . . I could tell you about the past, the future in 15 years' time, how I'm going to cope, will I cope?
>
> (Patrick Burke, Chapter 5).

> By speaking out to other people in the group it gives you confidence to speak to other people.
>
> (Lloyd Page)

> It enables me to talk about my problems and to listen to other people's problems.
>
> (Graham, Advocacy-support Group, group discussion)

Inasmuch as self-advocates were involved in the making of their culture, the larger exclusive, disabling culture continued to threaten their activity and amplify their disabilities. Self-advocacy could be viewed as a cultural artefact of disabling society. Worrel (1988) asserts that people with learning difficulties would no longer need self-advocacy groups in an inclusive culture where all members are each and everyone's advisors.

Nevertheless, there is a point of caution. While groups welcomed develop-ment and individuals gave anecdotes of resistance, experiences of a wide vari-ety of exclusionary social contexts were consistently recalled. Remember Ken, a member of the Social Group (see Chapter 8), who relished the freedom of the group and parental home, while braving the passive, dependent child-like role assigned to him by staff in his group home. Self-advocacy displays inci-dents of resistance in a wider culture that undoubtedly disables and abuses.

> So jail is where you are watched over, inspected, spied on, directed, legis-lated, locked up, caged in, regimented, preached at, controlled, assessed, registered . . . prevented, stripped naked, extorted, pressured, robbed, beaten up, censored, commanded . . . all by creatures that have neither the right nor wisdom nor virtue to do so.
>
> (Adams 1996)

For many people with learning difficulties, we could replace 'jail' with 'society'.

The need for self-advocates to call the shots

> There's a story about three baseball umpires standing behind home
> plate before the start of the game. It seems they were discussing
> their individual methods of calling balls and strikes. 'I calls 'em as
> they are,' said the first umpire, an idealist. The second umpire, a
> realist, said, 'Well, I calls 'em as I see 'em.' The third umpire, a
> pragmatist, shook his head in disagreement and said, 'They ain't
> nuthin' 'til I calls 'em.' The key for developmentally disabled and
> other handicapped people is to be in the position where they are
> 'calling 'em.' The key for anyone wanting to support or participate
> in the People First organization is to help so-called 'handicapped'
> people get behind the plate and then let them 'call 'em' . . . The
> major role of the helper or advisor . . . is simply to help
> handicapped people get 'behind the plate'.
>
> (Hanna 1978: 31)

This book has drawn attention to the self-organization of people with learning difficulties. In Part II, narrators identified those people whom they
thought should be in control of self-advocacy. Joyce Kershaw insisted that
people with learning difficulties should be the ones heading developments
within the movement, for then 'They'd get more people helping them' (my
story). Concerns were also expressed about advisors taking over (Jackie
Downer). Group dynamics appeared to work well when they were mediated
by the actions of self-advocates rather than when they reflected the aims of
some of the higher echelons of linked organizations. For example, in Chapter
7, the Advocacy-supported Group members were ignored at the AGM of their
affiliated advocacy project. This contrasted with the cohesion that was
observed in their meetings. Likewise, the Centre Group provided asylum
away from the ideological constraints of Quarry Village Day Centre. Group
alliances were located in the social relations between self-advocates. In Chapter 8, examples of good support in which advisors' interventions pulled
towards the social model end of the five continua, emphasized supporting
self-advocates in their own self-empowerment (Oliver 1996: 34).

   This point about self-advocates calling the shots resonates with the position
taken by Lloyd Page and Simone Aspis (1997). They argue that the self-advocacy movement must remain in the hands of people with learning difficulties,
instead of becoming a context for promoting tokenistic service interventions
or therapeutic-cum-training programmes for people with learning difficulties.
Self-advocates must call the shots, just as they have done during those times
when they had to self-advocate in discriminating contexts of institutions and
communities (Chapter 6).

Issues for the future

This book leaves many stones unturned. A number of questions remain unanswered and therefore point ways forward for future research. Some of these
questions are outlined below.

Self-advocacy and a social model of impairment

> The next few years are going to be about defining what that model
> [social model of disability] is and what implications it has for our
> own national movements and the international movement.
>   (Richard Wood, director of the BCODP, cited in
>   Campbell and Oliver 1996: 174)

The theoretical model that has underpinned this book, the social model of disability, owes much to the growth of the disabled people's movement in
Britain. For example, as documented in Chapter 3, definitions of impairment
and disability proposed by the Union of the Physically Impaired Against Segregation (UPIAS 1976) have been at the core of social model ever since (Oliver
1990, 1996; Swain *et al.* 1993; Shakespeare and Watson 1997). In addition,
the latter sections of Chapter 3 suggested ways forward for making the social
model even more inclusive for people with learning difficulties. The subsequent empirical work in this book brought up a number of issues associated
with an 'inclusive social model of disability'.

This book illuminated some understandings of the relationship between
identity and impairment held by a few in the self-advocacy movement. In
Chapter 6, it was pointed out how narrators made distinctions between themselves as people with 'learning difficulties' and people with physical impairments. While the former label was critically owned, the latter was viewed as
undesirable:

> Learning disabilities – I don't like that, disability makes you believe that
> we are in wheelchairs and we can't do anything for ourselves, when we
> can. We've got jobs now, we've got paid jobs.
>   (Joyce Kershaw, my story, Appendix 2)

Self-advocates insist on being perceived as people first, fighting against the
denial of humanity itself (Gillman *et al.* 1997: 690); 'I'm lucky I'm not like
people with severe learning difficulties' (Jackie Downer, Chapter 6). In view
of the ubiquitous nature of the individual model of disability, this fight is
hardly surprising. Narrators' reflections lend support to the development of
an inclusive social model of disability that takes on board a social theory of
learning difficulties and impairment (as argued in Chapter 3, following, for
example, Ryan and Thomas 1980; Ferguson 1987). Impairment is a personal
experience (Morris 1996, Oliver 1996). The UPIAS definition may be acceptable to physically impaired people (though it is being challenged: Hughes and
Paterson 1997) but it may reaffirm a denial of humanity for people with
learning difficulties. Questions therefore remain over the appropriateness of
this definition of impairment for self-advocates and, indeed, for physically
impaired people (Hughes and Paterson 1997; Chappell *et al.* forthcoming).

Focusing on impairment could be viewed as watering down the social
model (French 1993; Oliver 1996; Mitchell 1998). However, if one of the key
points about this model is to embrace the experiences of disabled people

(Oliver 1996: 34), then reconsidering the notion of impairment feeds into a wider project. In view of the questions raised about terminology, impairment and definition by self-advocates in this book, it is crucial that the development of a social theory of learning difficulties contributes to the writing of a social critique of impairment; thus remaining accountable to the critical questions put forward by the self-advocacy movement.

Commonality between self-advocates and other disabled activists

While there may be distinctions in terms of impairment between self-advocates and physically impaired activists, this book touches upon commonality, challenging a charity culture that separates disabled people on the basis of impairment groupings (Oliver 1990). A number of disabling experiences previously documented by physically impaired activists were also reflected in the accounts of self-advocates, including institutionalization (Barnes 1990), exclusion from ordinary life experiences (Morris 1991), enforced dependency on benefits (Barnes 1991) and denial of work opportunities (Barnes 1996a). Simultaneously, the actions of self-advocates had parallels with the activities of organizations of disabled people, including shared experience (Finkelstein 1993), activism (Campbell and Oliver 1996), radical actions in reformative collectives (Oliver 1990) and challenging service interventions (Morris 1993a). Further research could draw together experiences from the self-advocacy and wider disability movement, making links and ascertaining shared ground.

The self-advocacy movement and the disability movement

> It is no small challenge to the movement to ensure that barriers are eradicated so that no impaired group are disadvantaged.
>
> (Campbell and Oliver 1996: 96)

This book has only scratched the surface of the relationship between the self-advocacy movement and the disability movement. In Chapter 2 it was suggested that coalition links threatened to place self-advocacy issues in the background as articulate physically impaired activists came to the fore. Difficulties in separating divisional and coalition types of group were demonstrated, following a postal survey, as the overlap was so great (Goodley 1998c). Moreover, Simons (1992: 6–7) reports that few people with learning difficulties become involved in coalitions of disabled people. In Chapter 7, the Independent Group saw its increasing independence from the Blaketon Council for Integrated Living and the Blaketon Council of Disabled People as positive developments. These findings lead only to vague understandings of the relationship between the self-advocacy and disability movements. Further research could assess the relationship between these two groups and see whether or not distinct identities exist, which may possibly lead to prejudice in the disability movement (as argued by Aspis, in Campbell and Oliver 1996) and in the self-advocacy movement (as hinted at in Chapter 6 of this book). The research by Dowse offers some necessary analyses of the relationship between self-advocacy and the disability movement, in the context of Britain (see Dowse, 1999, forthcoming).

Furthermore, questions emerged about the role of the professional in organizations of disabled people. For Oliver (1990, 1996), when professionals become involved in organizations of disabled people, ambitions associated with career advancement and an uncritical acceptance of the individual model of disability threaten the interdependence of disabled activists. The appraisal offered in this book has been less dismissive of professionals who are involved in the self-advocacy movement. While accepting that professionals potentially bring along the baggage of a staff role (see Chapter 7, the Social Group), the ethnography also highlighted a number of supportive interventions that were conducive to the workings of self-advocacy groups and appropriate to the development of members' self-advocacy (Chapters 7 and 8). Further research could follow up the role of the non-disabled supporter in organizations of disabled people, to see if a rejection of such support is hasty or acceptable.

Finally, the bureaucratization of self-advocacy provides possible employment opportunities for people with learning difficulties. Such opportunities take on a salient character in the light of the inadequacy of the Disability Discrimination Act (1995) for promoting real work for disabled people (see Barnes 1996a). For example, while questions were raised over the Independent Group's preoccupation with training staff and others about self-advocacy (Chapter 7), this group highlighted the involvement of disabled people in training policy makers, professionals and carers in disability rights. Still, questions are also raised about whom or what the groups are for (self-help, training, politicization and so on).

Leaving self-advocacy and types of self-advocacy

We are left wanting to know more about those who have left the self-advocacy movement. In Chapter 5, Anya spoke about her fall-out with a group that led to her leaving. In Chapter 7, Andy, the vice chair of the Independent Group, spoke about his reasons for working with the groups: 'I'm doing it for a change. I'll probably try and work with old people at some time.' Finding out why people move on from self-advocacy groups could help to establish the impact of group membership on life chances and how ex-members perceive group relations. Moreover, such a research focus may well broaden understandings of self-advocacy outside of groups. In Chapter 6, self-advocacy was tentatively defined as the public recognition of people with learning difficulties' resilience. This appraisal has focused upon resilience in the publicly observable context of self-advocacy groups. In addition, questions are raised about the membership of various other contexts in which self-advocacy may well occur.

First, people with learning difficulties may boast membership of a number of self-advocacy groups. Bill Shankling from the Advocacy-supported Group was additionally involved with a residents' committee and the advocacy project management committee (Chapter 7). Self-advocates with multiple memberships would make ideal appraisers of the comparative groups. Second, self-advocacy in action can take different formats, including performance arts, drama groups and dance troupes (see Moore and Goodley 1999; DIY Theatre Company and Goodley 1999). Bill Shankling and his peers met together in a drama group (this could be added to Bill's list above) and showcased their performance at the AGM of the advocacy project. Incidentally, their performance was the only part of the meeting in which the presence of people with learning difficulties was acknowledged and made public. Self-expression can be found in many contexts. Third, self-advocates advocating for peers in various contexts could be followed up and supported. Joyce Kershaw's stories showed her shouting up for her peers in the centre (Chapter 5), and Erica spoke up for her non-speaking friend Rachel in the Advocacy-supported Group (Chapters 7 and 8). Self-advocacy as it is couched in the experiences of people with learning difficulties can take on a number of forms.

Points for practice

While various questions are left unanswered by this book, a number of implications are raised that are of relevance to advisors, policy makers, service providers and professionals.

Advisors

The supporters in this book should be applauded for allowing their actions to become the objects of analysis as part of this appraisal. A consequence of their openness allows us to draw together a number of points associated with supporting self-advocacy.

- An openness to the deficiencies of support was welcomed by self-advocates in this study, especially when advisors recognized that their support was unhelpful or unnecessary. Chapter 8 puts forward a challenge for advisors to identify and unpack the assumptions that they may hold about 'learning difficulties'. There are no 'good' or 'bad' advisors. Instead, support is ever-changing, from 'good' practice that conforms to the tenets of the social model of disability to 'bad' that reinforces an individualized and pathological way of interaction with self-advocates.
- This study has drawn attention to the continuing relevance of Crawley's (1988) maxim: that self-advocates are a lot more able to promote the empowerment of their ('less-able') peers than even the most well meaning advisor. Chapters 5, 7 and 8 highlight the interdependence among the self-advocate body. These *a priori* networks of support should be kept in mind before, during and after advisors' interventions. Advisors walk a tightrope,

balancing intervention with standing back in the face of self-advocate inter-dependence.

- Conflict of interests appeared to affect all advisors. Conflicts can be located in the advisor's service affiliations or professional accreditation. In addition, the origins of conflict can reflect the independent advisor taking on the 'advisor role' ('I need to intervene'), and the incongruent relationship that this role has with self-advocates supporting themselves. All advisors have power. The good advisors are very much aware of this.

- The superficiality of previous literature's tendency to tie together a group type with a particular form of self-advocacy has been challenged. Group type is not a prerequisite for how well a group runs or an indicator of the potency of the advisor's support. For example, the group dynamics of an 'independent group' can still be affected by an advisor who views their voluntary role as a job. Advisors cannot hide behind their group type.

- None of the advisors in this study had achieved Dowson and Whittaker's (1993) ultimate goal: to work themselves out of a job. Leaving the group does not mean never seeing the group again. Indeed, members may require advice and support at various times in certain contexts. However, as groups continue to age, it will be interesting to see if and how supporters leave the groups, so that members all take on the 'advisor role'.

- Self-advocates represented in this study have had a hard time when involved with user consultation procedures. Moving from the accessible, supportive, listening context of the group to the often abstract, distant and ignorant places associated with consultation ensured that many in this book felt excluded from the very procedures that were meant to include their views and ambitions, particularly with respect to service provision. Supporters should encourage members, and those purportedly consulting, to use inclusive modes of communication.

- We are reminded that self-advocacy groups are 'members first', not 'advisors first', groups (Goode, quoted in Worrel 1988: 31). Advisors could start by asking why they got involved with self-advocacy in the first place.

Policy-makers and service providers

This book illuminates a hidden history of self-empowerment among the learning difficulties' population continuing to this day, in addition to professionally led models of empowerment, such as normalization and user consultation. Policy makers, service providers and professionals should bear these 'hidden practices' in mind and ask where their own practices stand in relation to those of self-advocates. Professional models of empowerment should be continuously appraised by a user-led perspective. As this study has shown, self-advocates have clear ideas about how services should be developed. A number of related points emerge.

- Participants in this study have pointed out the need to start with assumptions of capability rather than incapability. To work from the latter risks understanding people with learning difficulties in terms of some arbitrary, deficient classification bound up in taken-for-granted notions of 'handicap' (the individual model of disability).

- Remember that self-advocates support one another in augmenting resilience and realizing ambition. Those working with people with learning difficulties should avoid attaching significance to their own support and remember that support networks exist among the self-advocate body regardless of inter- vention (a key component of the social model of disability).

- Inclusive consultation should mean exactly that, not some tokenistic gesture to a climate of 'user empowerment'. As a starting point, the term 'learning difficulties' should be adopted, as people who have been labelled have con- sistently requested (Chapter 5). Second, self-advocates should be treated as the experts that they are of the 'learning difficulties experience'. Week in, week out, self-advocacy groups tap into this expertise. Providers could initi- ate inclusive consultation measures by consulting with, for example, a number of experienced self-advocates who can represent the views of their peers. However, this raises questions associated with listening.

- Self-advocacy groups exemplify the potency of 'listening differently', through the use of accessible language, prose and pictures, and through articulate self-advocates talking for inarticulate peers.

- The social model of disability is not some abstract epistemological turn that is unconnected to the realities of service provision and 'users' lives'. For example, this model provides an analytical tool for assessing the worth of professional intervention (see Chapter 8). Moreover, the basic tenets of this model, which are bound up in the self-empowerment of disabled people, have major implications in relation to the individualized focus of service intervention. The interdependence within self-advocacy groups points to the collective character of self-empowerment. Thus, an inarticu- late person may, through an individualized assessment, exhibit incom- petent and 'handicapped' behaviour. However, the same individual, viewed within the context of a self-advocacy group, can be seen to draw upon the various skills of peers. Following Booth and Booth (1994, 1998), distributed intelligence in self-advocacy groups reminds us that ability is a reflection of support networks rather than some individual quality or deficiency.

- Self-advocacy groups do and can continue to offer expertise in terms of training people who work with people with learning difficulties. Without people so labelled such employment opportunities would not exist. People with learning difficulties are not just users of services, but are effectively the unpaid employers. Professionals would benefit from training by these employers.

Critical reflections on this study: theory, activism and commodities in disability research

> Simply increasing participation and involvement will never by itself constitute emancipatory research unless and until it is disabled

> people themselves who are controlling the research and deciding
> who should be involved and how.
>
> (Zarb 1992: 128)

Following Swain (1995: 77), the appraisal presented in this book was initiated
by me, at my discretion, whereby I had ultimate control. Like many
researchers in the disability studies field I was driven by an adherence to the
theoretically enlightening character and praxis-oriented tenets of the social
model. In one way the social model celebrates radical theorizing, though in
other ways it questions the rights to authorship and ownership of the theorist. Recent writings by key contributors in the field (see Oliver 1996; Barnes
and Mercer 1997; Oliver and Barnes 1997) have further highlighted the tensions between being theoretically radical and also accountable to disabled
people and their organizations in the doing of disability research. Showing
parallels with feminist research of the 1970s and 1980s (see Oakley 1981;
Stanley and Wise 1993), the social model calls for an all-embracing though
contradictory relationship between theoretical developments and political
ambitions of the disabled people's movement. First, often heard are critical
voices against the role of the non-disabled (academic) researcher. Exactly *why*
and *how* do these researchers contribute to the development of an alternative
disability culture that breaks down, deconstructs and eradicates disabling society (see Finkelstein and Stuart 1996)? Moreover, why are so few disabled
people involved in disability research, particularly when they boast ontologi-
cally privileged access to incidents of disablement and resistance (Oliver and
Barnes 1997)? Second, and in contrast, (non-disabled) researchers working
alongside disabled people have drawn attention to the critical distance and
theoretical skills that they bring along to disability research (Moore *et al.* 1998;
Goodley 1999b). Indeed, researchers involved with people with the label of
learning difficulties have argued for the authority they hold in exposing disablement and encouraging resistance in the lives of people whose own ambitions have been consistently suppressed (Booth and Booth 1994; Gillman *et
al.* 1997).

   Although this book is most closely associated with the second research position, a critical reflection upon the research process throws up a number of
emerging themes that probe the distinction between theory and practice,
while re-examining the doing of participatory and emancipatory research.
Research projects capture, as societal microcosms, ideological and interpersonal constructions of disability, intervention, policy and practice. Interro-
gating the conditions of research production contributes to a critique of wider
disabling practices.

Commodification, parody and false domains of research

Research that attempts to adhere to the radical potential of the social model
of disability sits uneasily with the current climate of research production that
mirrors the modes of production of late capitalism. In particular, the commodification of different research domains separates research communities.

One consequence is the distinction created between different 'theory' and 'action' research commodity domains. Lost is praxis (where theory and practice are dialectically linked) and in its place are separated marketable fields of knowledge and expertise. Disability studies are not exempt from this commodification. Indeed, it is possible – through parody – to represent these created social spaces to consider the challenges facing disability theorists and activists. These parodies aim to capture a particularly cynical view of the distinctions between 'theory' and 'practice', a cynicism that is augmented by and a reflection of the current climate of research in late capitalism.

First, I present a parody of the 'disability theorist' and their involvement with 'non-participatory research'. Here disability theory delves into abstracted examinations of the complex relations of disablement. While the social model can be viewed as the disability movement's 'big idea' (Hasler 1993), much of the literature of the social model fits neatly into an academic scholastic tradition (Marx 1845). Here the academy is exploited for its space and relative intellectual freedom (T. Shakespeare 1997b). Theories of disability are brought above ground, from crude activism to intellectual knowing, to assessment from the top down. While the movement boasts its organic intellectuals (e.g. Barnes 1990; Oliver 1990, 1996; Morris 1991, 1993a; T. Shakespeare 1993), dangers exist in research moving away from action and activism, with the consequent loss of disabled people in grand narrative. As Marxist critiques dominate, accusations abound of the structuralist victimization of disabled people (Corker 1998). Abberley (1987) suggests that physically impaired people, in contrast to the non-impaired proletariat, are surplus to revolutionizing practice in the work of Marx and Engels. People with impairments are therefore either conceptualized as products of exploitative, dangerous working conditions (as argued by Engels) or considered to be unable to offer non-alienated value as workers in socialistic societies. Elsewhere, interpretivist research that engages with the 'lived realities' of disabled people – 'giving voice' – can so easily slip back into an objectifying gaze as these 'voices' are swallowed up in analysis (e.g. Ferguson *et al.* 1992; Goodley 1998c). Here, as the researcher enjoys a free rein in relation to analysis, the individualized, rational, bounded individual survives in positions of subject and object. In search of 'voice', the researcher moves nearer and nearer to the therapeutic subject, playing around with a variety of strategies to gain the individual's authentic voice (e.g. Goodley 1998b).

In contrast, a rejection of pseudo-humanistic attempts to 'empower' has invited theorists to 'turn to the text' (see Bhavnani 1990; Burman and Parker 1993). Postmodernists start to enjoy a fashionable position in research, where 'voice' is redundant and deconstruction is employed to pick at the 'psy-complex' that pathologizes and creates abnormality (e.g. Corker 1998; Hughes and Paterson 1997; T. Shakespeare 1998). Judith Butler, Michel Foucault and Jacques Derrida occupy almost 'Third Way' Blairite positions in social scientific discussion: palming us off in response to our requests for political alternatives. The radical character of paralysis, 'never knowing', standing in the naive landscape between individualism and society, promises us everything but provides nothing.

Second, I present a parody of the 'disabled activist' and their attempts to employ 'emancipatory disability research'. Disability activism resonates towards the materialist destruction of micro and macro relations of disablement. The social model was and is the disability movement's 'big idea' (Hasler 1993), though disability studies literature so often loses touch with the daily experiences of oppression and resistance (Barnes 1997; Germon 1998). Here in the 'real world', outside of academia, spaces of resistance are demonstrated and the disability movement's organic intellectuals and activists are thrown together as comrades in order to self-organize. Practice and politics are thrown forward, theories denounced for their fictional and abstracted nature. A model of emancipatory disability research is espoused, where disabled people take the reins and direct the research process in ways that contribute to emancipation. It is far more than 'giving voice'. Instead, research is about doing, acting, changing and contributing – activism masquerading as research. Often there appears to be little to distinguish action, politics and research – so that telling the inappropriately inquisitive doctor to 'fuck off' can be conceptualized as an act of emancipation. Where discussions of disability theorists centre on postmodernism or Marx, here action researchers consider questions put forward by participants: alternative frameworks of meaning are drawn together and celebrated (Vincent 1998); service provision is reappraised (Whittaker *et al.* 1993); and professional practice is critiqued and informed (e.g. Goodley 1998a). While emancipatory research has its own vocabulary and style of presentation, a lot of emphasis is placed on accessibility, meaning and relevance. People First groups have carried out their own appraisals of professionalism and engage in educating the public about the rights of people with learning difficulties. Here a new 'third way' is created, in between revolutionary and party politics, a politics of positive identity. The position of the theorist in all of this becomes opaque: as Marx (1845) would have it, the theorist's work is the stuff only of the scholar and not the revolutionary, though it is to the latter we should always turn.

These parodies do a disservice to the participants of each camp who attempt to bridge the divide and engage in 'praxis'. However, parody is never far from the truth, directly reflecting the false separation of 'theorists' and 'practitioners' as commodities. This separation leads to acrimony between the two camps, one arguing for the virtues of theory over practice, the other the opposite. At times, guilt is expressed from those theorists working from the 'top down' – 'theorizing the oppressed' – though offering no direct political involvement or alternative to discriminatory practices. Meanwhile, those working from the 'bottom up' – 'working with the oppressed' – appear unable to move beyond common-sense understandings of the world or to stand outside of their very work in a critical-reflexive manner. The separation of camps in contemporary disability studies threatens to simplify and deny the cross-fertilization of ideas.

Bridging gaps

This book suffers from being so closely connected to the academy and in its attempts to provide a scholarly, some could argue idealistic, account of self-advocacy. In *Theses on Feuerbach* (1845), Marx challenges the contradictory separation of contemplation (idealism) from activity (materialism). In point II, we are reminded that idealism is particularly apparent in scholarly bourgeois writing; celebrating itself over practice, the latter of which is conceptualized as outside, alien to thought. In VII and IX, he notes that as all social life is practical, those idealistic or contemplative materialist positions that fail to recognize this fact are always prone to contemplate only individuals. Perhaps worryingly, much space is given in this book to *assessing* the actions and stories of people with learning difficulties and the reader is taken through a bizarre journey from pathologized objects (noting how self-advocates are often excluded by a variety of social barriers) to resilient subjects (demonstrating their resilient tales and actions through stories and field notes) back to subjectified and objectified objects (phenomena to be analysed and understood). As Clough and Barton (1998) put it, research so often re-creates the very difficulties it is meant to challenge. However, to conclude so pessimistically is to leave a victimized image of self-advocates who have informed the analyses in this book. In reality, they have necessarily complicated matters, by providing ways of bridging the artificial divide of theory and practice, conceptualization and activism, idealism and materialism. Their actions violate the distinction between commodities, stressing how theory and activism emerge together in places where one would perhaps not expect such actions to take place: putting forward ideas for future research agendas. Two examples of the ways in which self-advocates can inform research can be identified.

First are those occasions when theory emanates from the activism of self-advocates. People with learning difficulties represented in this book have pointed to the fundamental political nature of diagnosis, policy and professional practice. It could be suggested that this research project was emancipatory in the sense that it captured the emancipatory acts that disturb previous dominant theoretical concepts. For example, self-advocates displayed awareness of disabling barriers, though they also presented their resistance. The life stories in Chapter 5 remind us that disabled people are not 'cultural dopes' (Ferguson 1987; Ferguson and Ferguson 1995; Skrtic 1995a). Consequently, research projects that work with self-advocates as co-researchers could help to temper analyses that 'make difficulties' either through emphasizing deficit, inability and passivity as an effect of disablement or by reconstructing disabled people as objects of research (Clough and Barton 1995; Barton and Clough 1998). Instead, self-advocates in this book drew attention to their capacity, ability and activity, thus suggesting that research needs to go even further than celebrating their subjective takes on the world – additionally tapping into and supporting their actions that resist. Second, forms of activism become visible in the theories of self-advocates. The self-advocacy groups represented in this study demonstrated the supportive cultural contexts that they offered to their members. Here, again, this study could be viewed as emancipatory understandings of groups held by self-advocates – theories – that disturb the view that people with learning difficulties are unable to act in ways that are socially bounded, culturized and informative.

For example, the Social Group discussed in Chapter 7 reminds us of the importance of non-service-based contexts in which people with learning difficulties create their own groupings, friendship groups and 'cultural capital': presenting an alternative view of their actions in terms of interdependence and capacity rather than dependency and deficiency. Consequently, research projects that use groups as co-researchers could address some of the problems that have been identified in research with vulnerable and lonely people. In the case of short-term research initiatives, groups could offer research participants (without membership of self-advocacy groups) access to ongoing support networks when research comes to a close. Such inclusive practices could tackle paternalism in empowering research where researchers go into people's lives and then struggle to offer further support (Clough and Barton 1995). Self-advocacy groups as co-researchers could also address the dilemmas of non-disabled researchers being the primary collectors of disabled people's accounts (see Chapter 4). Physically impaired activists and researchers have argued that disability research must remain accountable to physically impaired people in their organizations of disabled people (see special issue on disability research of *Disability, Handicap and Society*, 7(2), 1992). Similarly, self-advocacy groups could be consulted about research with people with learning difficulties. After all, participants in this study were already involved in consultation. Anya had talked about Down's syndrome at conferences and had involvement with the Down's Syndrome Association (Chapter 5). Joyce Kershaw addressed doctors and students (my story, Appendix 2). The Independent Group trained up staff about self-advocacy and Social Group members spoke out at user consultation days (Chapter 7).

It is important to recognize that a number of research projects have already made connections between self-advocacy and research. Services have been evaluated by researchers and self-advocates (Whittaker *et al.* 1991; 1993; Downer and Ferns 1993), a self-advocacy group for parents with learning difficulties developed out of an earlier researcher-led appraisal (Booth and Booth 1994), while self-advocates have been involved as co-researchers in studies of the impacts of self-advocacy on family life (March *et al.* 1997; P. Mitchell 1997, 1998) and the history of learning difficulties and institutionalization (Atkinson *et al.* 1997). Attempts have been made to include people with learning difficulties meaningfully in research, challenging notions of participatory research that have more to do with strengthening dominant ideologies than real shifts of power (Swain 1995: 89). Moreover, participants can use research contexts for their own means – as Joyce Kershaw and some of the research groups did in this study (see Chapter 4). Self-advocacy groups appear to provide a useful starting point not only for the inclusion of people with learning difficulties in research, but also in the planning, carrying out and subsequent analyses of research. Here, then, we can challenge the stifling false distinctions that are made between theory and activism: and in the space between them we see the social phenomenon of 'learning difficulties' being challenged in a variety of ways.

Conclusion

> The materialist doctrine that men [*sic*] are products of circumstances
> and upbringing, and that, therefore, changed men are products of
> other circumstances and changed upbringing, forgets that it's men
> who change circumstances and the educator must himself be
> educated. Hence this doctrine is bound to divide society into two
> parts, one of which is superior to society. The coincidence of the
> changing of circumstances and of human activity can be conceived
> and rationally understood only as revolutionising practice.
>
> (Marx 1845: 28)

An enduring image of this research, for me, was of people identified by an
arbitrary label who, despite often adverse social conditions, were actively
changing their circumstances. Their actions were revolutionizing and far
removed from pervasive assumptions of deficit, incompetence and passivity.
The self-advocacy of people with learning difficulties raises telling points
about conceptions of (in)humanity, the professionalization of disablist culture, the tacit informative discourses of care and pathology, as well as placing
our preconceptions under the microscope. It is hoped that this book has provided a window of opportunity to consider the poignant words of educators
and experts of self-advocacy and disablement, so highlighting the social construction of 'learning difficulties' and the challenge to related discrimination
posed by people so labelled who refuse to be marginalized. We all need to
work out what our own positions are in relation to such incidents of self-
empowerment.

Introductory booklet for narrators

Danny Goodley
PhD Research Student
University of Sheffield

Self-advocacy Stories

I am a research student at the University of Sheffield. A year ago I was lucky enough to get some money from the University to help support my study. My study will look at the **self-advocacy movement** in Great Britain.

I am going to write a 'thesis' (report) on self-advocacy.

In two years time this thesis will be marked by examiners. If the examiners feel that it is good enough (and I hope they do) then I will be awarded the qualification of **'PhD'** by the University of Sheffield.

(HOPEFULLY!)

To help me understand self-advocacy and write my 'thesis' I have done a number of things.

First, I have sent a 'questionnaire' to groups in Great Britain.

From this I will be able to see what groups are like in Great Britain. I will write about the findings in my thesis.

Second, I am going to visit a small number of groups to see how self-advocacy works. I will be talking to self-advocates and supporters in these groups.

Third, I want to hear about the **stories of a number of self-advocates** – this is where **you** come in.

I think that when people read these stories they will understand what self-advocacy is about.

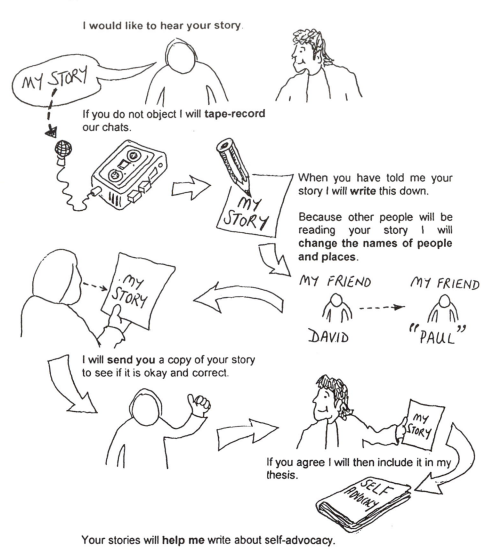

I would like to hear your story.

MY STORY

If you do not object I will **tape-record** our chats.

When you have told me your story I will **write** this down.

Because other people will be reading your story I will **change the names of people and places**.

MY FRIEND DAVID → MY FRIEND "PAUL"

I will **send you** a copy of your story to see if it is okay and correct.

If you agree I will then include it in my thesis.

SELF ADVOCACY

Your stories will **help me** write about self-advocacy.

My thesis will be handed into the University of Sheffield in 1997.

I expect some of my thesis to be **published**

I hope that your stories and my writing will provide an **understanding** of self-advocacy and **help it** in some way.

After I have finished writing the thesis I hope to write a **report** of my findings **for self-advocates**. I expect this to be finished in 1998.

If you do agree to share your story then you will be **helping me** in a big way as your story will help me write my thesis.

But I aim and hope to make sure that **self-advocacy is helped** in some (small) way by my work.

Thank you for your time.

Danny Goodley

APPENDIX **2**

Collaborative life story of Joyce Kershaw

From boarding school to married life

I went to a boarding school for children with epilepsy. They used to wake us up about 5 o'clock in the morning. There used to be a night-nurse on and she used to come and give us a pill and then at 5.30 we used to have to get up and get washed and dressed, clean us teeth and everything. There were two dormitories, one for little ones and at 13 you went in the big dormitory. Down for breakfast for 7.30, with porridge which was like slush or sometimes, if your parents sent you something, you could have that. Mum didn't send me much she was too poor.

After breakfast we used to have to clean the dormitory with like a big 'dummy', like a duster on a stick. At nine o'clock we'd go to school. It was like a proper school, we used to have a teacher there and then we'd come home for our dinner and go back until four. We had our tea then we'd do different things, it just depended what day it was. On Friday we used to do darning. They used to sit us down and we'd darn our black socks and mend sheets, we used to have to do the little girls' sewing. On a Wednesday we'd have bath nights. We used to bath the little ones and sometimes would clear the cupboards out. After we'd done that we'd have a game, either Monopoly or table tennis or anything like that with the nurses. Every Sunday we'd to go to church. That's where I got confirmed.

People could come and visit you every month. I had about one visitor all the time I was there. My Mum said she'd try and send someone to take me out. I soon got used to it, getting dressed up ready to go out. Every year you could come home for a fortnight and then you had to go back afterwards. It was nice coming home, oh it was. I used to stand there and get dressed up when I thought they were coming for me and look out the window. I'd see everyone else going out and there was me with tears running down my eyes. Of course I was only 13 then and when I was 14 I got used to it.

I left school at 16 and came back home to my Mum and Dad's. My father went to Woolworths with me and he explained to this manager that I had epilepsy and that I hadn't had a fit for a long time, for two years. It was a lady manager and she said she'd give me a trial. She was all for people like us, like people who had a learning difficulty, so I went to work in the stores. I met my husband there, he was a soldier. He was on leave. He came into Woolworths and asked if there was a picture place about. I told him there was one. He said 'because I've come from Oldham, I'm just on leave and I don't know where it is.' He was based in Germany, he used to come home on leave. He was a cook in the army, he'd just come over to town and he didn't know his way round – so he said! Anyway he went away but came back again and asked me if I'd show him, if I'd come out with him to the pictures, and I said 'yes'. Then we started seeing each other. I remember we used to go out on a tandem together every weekend. When he was away with the army, I used to write a letter every night and he used to write to me and that. I was married when I was 18 and we had a little house. He left the army, started on the buses as a bus conductor, and eventually ended up as a driver. I stopped working at Woolworths and went in an office for a while until we broke up, me and my husband. He went with my best mate, we'd been mates ever since we were kids. Aye, I was upset.

Caring at home

I'm not frightened of living on my own now but when my husband left it seemed a bit strange. I'd never been on my own before. I'd always been in somebody's company, my mother's or my sister's or someone else's. Even at the boarding school there used to be a lot of girls there and nurses and they were really nice. So my mother and my sister came and took me down to live with them at my mother's. It was a bit weird being at my Mum's after seven years away.

After a while my mother and I went to live with my brother because his wife left him. We used to look after his two lads who were four and ten, my sister's lads who were two and ten, and of course my brother and my sister's husband. We'd have tea ready for them all in the evening. I took the kids to school when they first started and I'd do all the washing. Nothing like the washers are now, scrubbing all the necks of the shirts in a tub. My mother used to bake lovely buns. The children would come in and see the buns on the side that had just come out of the oven. Then when my mother was sat in the living room they'd say 'can we wash our hands Grandma?' and go into the kitchen. After a while my mother went into the kitchen to see what the kids were up to and all the buns had gone! My sister was taken poorly with cancer. She used to live in a prefab but they've pulled all them down now. When she died I brought her children up to our house and put them in bed with the others. Around that time I went into hospital myself to have a cyst taken off and when I came back my mother was taken poorly. I was with her for over a year. I slept on a two seated couch and I used to be up and down the stairs seven or eight times a night to see her. She'd be rattling the legs of the bed with her walking stick, shouting 'Joyce' at the top of her voice. One day I was vacuuming the living room. My mother was sat in her chair watching me and all of a sudden she said she wanted to go to bed. I said that I'd help her when I'd finished cleaning up. When I did finish she had already died. Do you know, I could hear her shouting my name for years after.

My Dad used to visit me and my brother every week. One day on his way back home his legs went. He was in hospital for eight weeks and the doctor said that he couldn't live on his own. He would either have to live in a home or with us. Well my brother said that no way would we leave Dad in a home and he came to stay with us. Soon after moving in he had a stroke in my arms. I ran up and got my brother and it took both of us to get him in the chair. There I was running up and down to the neighbours in my nightie shouting 'can you phone the doctor!' When he was dying, the day he died, the Doctor said 'he's really poorly'. I said, 'I've been telling you that all week.' All he gave me were these prescriptions so I gave him them back.

I was at the centre then. I started when my mother had already died and I've been going ever since for 21 years. I stopped working to be at home, to help with the kids, and then my father got poorly. Before he got really poorly he said I could do with someone to help me, so he went somewhere, and these people used to come and see me. They got me into this place, the centre.

The centre and staff

You used to have to call the staff by their last name but they used to call us by our first names. Also when we went for our dinner there used to be two members of staff stood up and three rows of us. They used to say 'this row' and that row used to get up and go off. And if people were talking they used to say 'Right this row go because you're talking.' Also the staff used to go in a little room for dinner. I asked the centre manager 'Aren't we good enough to eat with?' and he said that of course we were. So I asked him why the staff ate in a separate room and he told me that it had always been like that. So I said that *we* thought they should eat with us, that it didn't look right. It was as though we weren't good enough to eat with. And he told me he'd bring it up at the next meeting. Also I wanted us to be able to call them by their first names. So I went round all the staff asking them if we could. At first some said no so I told them they could call me Mrs Kershaw from then on. And when they called me Joyce I wouldn't answer them.

The centres were bad then. We didn't used to get jobs or group homes. They started getting group homes when *we* started to say where we'd like to live. I've got my own house but some lived in the old institutions, others with their mothers, foster carers and like that, but they were mostly in these hostels. In the centres they used to play hell with you if you did anything wrong. I used to take no notice of them but some used to cry. There was one girl called Julie, her and Mary got a house together, and there was one lad Pete and he was always picking on her. I told her that the more she took notice of him the more he could see that he was upsetting her, and the more he saw that he was upsetting her the more he'd do it.

Some staff were all right with you, others weren't. If I was talking to one of the staff another one of the staff would come up and interrupt me. It was all right for them to interrupt us but if we did it, even if it was something important that we needed to say, even if we said excuse me, they'd say 'We're talking it's ignorant to interrupt when we're talking.' So once when I was talking to one of the staff another one of the staff, who always used to be interrupting, came up and started talking. I said 'Excuse me do you mind I'm talking – it's ignorant to interrupt when people are talking.' Well he couldn't say anything because he was the one who'd said that to me the day before!

Also if we pushed in the queue for dinner the staff would send us to the back. One day one of the staff was at the front of the queue, I was watching him, and he was just about to push in so I went down to him. I told him that we had been waiting and he had only just come in. He said that he was talking to his mate but he had a plate in his hand. So I said 'You won't be needing this then', took the plate off him and sent him to the back of the queue. Another time these two staff came into the games room and these two lads were playing table tennis. They couldn't play properly, they were quiet, they weren't bothering anybody and they were fair having fun playing their little game by themselves. Then one of the staff said, 'Right can we have a go now', and the lads gave them the bats and sat down. Anyway the next day me and this lass were on the table and these two staff came up and said 'Can we have a game?' I told them we were playing a game and that they could have a go after we'd finished. So they sat down and when we'd finished one game they got out their seats. But I made my friend play another game, and then another, and the staff were getting fair annoyed. They kept getting up every time they thought we'd finished and then sitting down again. I only did it to teach them a lesson. I kept my eye on the clock and we finished just before it was time to go back to our groups. I said 'Oh look at the time we'll have to stop.

Anyway it was good that' and they looked and went 'tut'. I was doing it so they would-
n't do it to other people. I said to them 'It's how you ask, "can I have a go" not "can I
have a go after you've finished please". You act like you do when you're telling people
to do something – "do that", not "will you do that for me please". You don't ask properly, you frighten them, they give in to you. That's why I played ping-pong like that
from side to side because I've seen you do it.' One of them said 'Oh, I thought I hadn't
seen you playing ping-pong before' and I told them it was surprising what I can play
when I have to! Since then they've *asked* if people can go to the shop, and *asked* if
people can do this, and they've found them jobs.

Starting People First

I've always stuck up for myself even before People First. I stare them in the eye as long
as they stare me in the eye. I started our People First group. At the centre all week we
used to go round everyone in the centre asking if they had any news. There used to be
six of us and we used to write down what people said: if they'd won at bingo, or been
on holiday, got some new clothes, or had a fight with their husbands. We used to put
it all down. Then on a Friday we used to read it out to one of the key workers and he
used to take it home and type it up. He would give us all a page to read and then at
dinner time it used to come over the loudspeaker for everyone to hear. Once one of the
staff had been on holiday and she'd bought some new thermal underwear and we put
that over. Some of the staff said 'Oh let's have a look then!'

One day the centre manager showed me this leaflet he had. It was about people with
learning difficulties, like advocacy groups and that. So I asked to have a look and saw
the address of a group nearby. I decided to write to them and ask if they could help us.
This chap got back in touch with me and I told him that we wanted to start a group. I
asked him what they were called and he said that some were called People First groups,
some were advocacy groups, but theirs was called a People First group. So we asked
one of the staff if she'd do it with us and she said she'd be our advisor. Then we went
and found the centre manager and he told me that there was a room at the Co-op we
could hire for meetings for four pounds. So I went and saw the manager there. I told
him that we didn't get paid so he let us have it for free!

At first there were about ten members. I went round asking them all in the centre if
they'd like to come. They didn't understand what I was talking about. I said that it was
about being independent and sticking up for yourself. I only told them what this fella
had told me. I said 'It's about sticking up for your rights against these big-nobs who put
you down, when they make you feel small you can make them feel small' – which I
have done to a lot of them. That's why they never argue with me.

At the first meeting we were wondering what to do. At first people were nervous but
they soon got into it. The advisor used to write down everything that had happened at
the meeting, and there used to be so many that would go on a Tuesday night to arrange
what kind of fund-raising we could do. It wasn't the big meeting it was a little group and
we used to write letters to people and post them off and read other letters. When we
started we used to ask for help from other groups. I suggested to the advisor one day that
we should have someone to keep the group in order. So I was chairperson at the start.

On advisors

Our first advisor was one of the staff from the centre. She used to make us all feel nervous. We always used to be having five mile walks to raise money. I couldn't do it
and a lot of others couldn't. So I started thinking of something we could all do like

sponsored dominoes and I went and asked all the members if they'd do it and they said they would. So I told them to put their hands up when we voted for it at the next meeting. When it came to the next meeting I mentioned the sponsored dominoes but the advisor thought a walk would be better. 'Hands up who agrees with me and hands up who disagrees with Joyce', she said. She used to stick her hand up and look at them. Gradually she would stare at them and there was only me and another who didn't put our hands up. Then she said 'So hands up who disagrees' and I said 'Well there aren't many more – you've frightened them all into putting their hands up. You frighten them into it instead of explaining, you just take it all on your own. The group isn't for you, this is for people with learning difficulties, it isn't for your benefit so you can go on a walk, it's for what *we* can do.' Every meeting we'd have an argument over something. She'd always be on to somebody and I'd be sticking up for them, telling her off. I got a card from her when she was on holiday and on it she said how sorry she was about one of the meetings and how it showed I could stick up for myself. I thought 'Aye, I wish a lot more would speak up.'

She wanted it all her own way. She always wanted to be the top dog, she wanted the top job at work. She's left now and is the boss of a home. She got what she wanted. I think there's a problem with advisors who are staff because you see them every day. She was always watching you. It was like when people were shown round the centre and the manager would say 'This is Joyce typing up wage slips.' I said 'I can't do it while people are watching, I can feel you at the back of me.' I think the members saw her first as a staff member. They thought if they said anything wrong she'd take it out on them at work. They found it very difficult to say yes and no. They agreed with her so she wouldn't play hell with them at work.

We like the advisor we've got at the moment. He doesn't tell us what to do, he'll tell us what he's found out but it's up to us whether we want it or not. We have hands up, whereas the other advisor would say 'I think we should do this.' Our advisor now lets everyone have a say. He wants everyone to have a part, something to do in People First, so that everyone feels wanted. Whereas before there was only secretary which was me, treasurer which was me, and an advisor. Now we have lots of officers.

The advisor is there to explain things. People put letters complicated sometimes and we don't understand. They have all these long words so I fold it up and put it away until the advisor comes and we ask him to explain it. The members run the group and they ask the advisor to find out things. If I thought the advisor were taking over, I'd tell him that I don't want him to take over because it's our group. It goes on what we want and say. If you can find out anything we'll listen to you, but it's up to us – you don't do it on your own. Now with England People First they'd already decided and voted themselves in in Canada and the advisors are taking over. England People First should be run by people with learning difficulties with people helping them, advising them, like our advisor's helping us, but they should have the last say what should be done, not the advisors. If it was run by a person with learning difficulties then they'd get more people helping them. But they were doing it and not letting people know what was being said. If you can't read then you should have pictures, like with our feedbacks from the meetings. But with England People First we never heard a word from them. I think they could do a lot for us, get to know a lot of things for us, but if they'd only just do the feedbacks. Not all of us can go to meetings.

Conferences

The first conference I spoke at I was scared stiff. I asked the advisor to write me something down to say, I had two or three pages of notes. It was at a university. They were students and they wanted to know about people with learning difficulties because they were going to be social workers. I went in and they were all looking. There was like a big room and I went up to the front, looked down at my notes and then looked up again, and then when I looked down again I'd lost me blummin' place! I thought 'flippin' find it', so I told everyone 'I'm sorry but I've lost my place. That's that then, terrible writer!' Well they all burst out laughing and when they did that I felt a bit of confidence. Then I just said what I felt, what came out of inside, not what the advisor wanted to say but what *I* wanted to say. So I chucked away the notes that she had written and everybody laughed and clapped and I just started saying what I thought. I said 'People with learning difficulties won't bite you they're just human beings like yourselves.' They all came up afterwards and said they'd fair enjoyed my speech and wanted to know how I did it without any paper. When I was leaving someone gave me a bag of money, they'd had a collection for me they'd enjoyed it so much.

At the 1993 International Conference in Canada, the Canadians sent all the advisors out. They said 'If you're not a person with learning difficulties you're to go out.' Then one got up on stage and he had been falling out with his girlfriend and it had upset him but he was talking rubbish. He was going on because he didn't have his advisor with him. As long as they see the advisor they're not frightened to say anything, when they're put on their own they lose all confidence.

Asking people with learning difficulties

I got asked to do a book. This researcher told me I'd get a thousand pounds afterwards. At first I said that I was too busy but I thought about it, spoke to a few friends and decided to do it. It lasted for three weeks and there were two of us with learning difficulties. We interviewed people one by one in their houses and asked them about their experiences. How they liked it, whether they chose the home, chose the furniture and everything, whether they had a say in anything. That was the first time that anything like that had been done by people with learning difficulties. I asked if they had had a say in the house but they hadn't. People with learning difficulties were not being given a say in their lives.

I told the centre staff that when we get a new key worker we should be allowed to sit in and pick one we like. Because it's us who have got to live with it. People might not like such 'n' such a person whereas they might take to someone straight away. Nothing has come of it. The centre staff said they were going to break us all up and put so many of us into one centre and others into another. They asked us what we thought about it and at first I thought it wasn't a good idea, because people have just learnt how to go on the bus themselves, how to do new jobs, and now we are just having to go back to the beginning. I mean for a start you'll have to show them all again where to catch the bus from. I told them it's not on, it's not fair. Not only that, we've been with one another all these years, we don't want to go and meet some new people we don't know. We're always the last to know when we should be the first to know. It's our lives not theirs. You must ask us what we want, some people are asked but there's still a long way to go.

Talking properly

There's still people who use the word mental handicap and if I hear them I'll pull them up about it. Even if I'm at a conference or a meeting and they use *that word* I'll say 'Do you mind not using that word. Next time you come to it can you use "learning difficulties" please.' Learning disabilities – I don't like that, disability makes you believe that we are in wheel chairs and we can't do anything for ourselves, when we can. We've got jobs now, we've got paid jobs. Like I said when I made that first speech we've all got learning difficulties. I said to everyone you have, you have, you have. You talk posh and all that, it's all right all these big words but you want to say what you mean and talk proper English. Can't people talk proper English?

People have got a learning difficulty in anything they do. If mine wasn't epilepsy it might be arthritis or I might be really slow at reading, slow at writing, you don't know. Men wouldn't like to do a woman's work they'd find it hard. Groups of kids, when we were going for our buses, they used to say 'Oh look they're mental', I used to be bloody heart broken. 'Crackers', 'Are you going back home', 'Is your green bus waiting for you?' It used to fair upset my friends and I told them once 'Just walk straight past, they used to say it to me, but they don't now because I walk straight past them.'

People First teaches you how to stick up for yourself and we do, you don't hear half as many people calling us now. One time me and two friends were having a drink in a café. We were just sat talking, having our drink waiting for the bus and there were these two lads and these two lasses. They just kept looking at us grinning. I noticed them and the girlfriends started saying to the lads 'shhh' but they kept on looking and laughing. So I said to my friends 'Come on let's sit over there I don't like sitting where babies are, let's have a proper grown up talk.' And they looked at us, I just looked at them, they looked, I looked, and one of the lads' girlfriends said 'Come on Jean they're showing us up' and they just walked out!

I don't know why people say those things. They either see it on the telly or they hear their mothers say something like 'don't go near that'. Because there used to be some houses for people with learning difficulties and no one would live near them. The TV sometimes has people with learning difficulties on and sometimes it has people who act you funny, and these men go and knock him about and his brother or father will come up and look after him. I think it frightens people. This woman had put in the local paper 'mentally handicapped are simple and happy people'. I read it and thought the cheeky so-and-so. There was a meeting about it and I went up to her and said 'What do you think about what they put in the paper?' I didn't let her know that I knew she had written it. She said 'Oh I don't know, I'll have to go I've got another meeting.' After a few times of me asking and her refusing to answer me I followed her down the steps and I said 'Excuse me but do you think it's right because I'm one of your simple happy people.' I said 'I'm not always happy and I'm not simple, some of you lot might be by thinking that.' I told her that we all have our off days and we're happy other days. I think people with learning difficulties should be on the TV or in the newspaper to make a speech talking grown up, telling others what we do.

Once when I was talking to students I said 'You want to come and see some of them working in the centre and I bet they'd have to teach you how to do it.' Because we were making masks and you used to have two little buckles, some elastic, you used to have to cut the elastic, thread it through, then put a mask on, so it could go just over your head. And I told those students 'I bet you'd get mixed up doing them buckles. Come and try and do our work and you'll soon find out if you've got a learning difficulty or not.'

I think if you talk to people properly, not baby talk, I think people understand. There was this girl with learning difficulties in the café of the bus station. They'd let her out and she was crying. She said that she'd lost her way home and didn't know which bus to catch. I asked her where she had come from and she told me, and I said 'Oh dear love don't cry.' So I went and told the woman at the counter to phone up for a bus or an ambulance. I sat with her until they came, telling her about myself. She was fair sobbing away but as she listened to me she forgot about it. I missed two buses! Eventually a woman from her home turned up and said 'come on love' and as soon as she saw her she wasn't frightened any more.

Two or three meetings where I've gone and spoke and I've made centre managers look small and there's been folk who talk posh I've said 'Can you tell us what you mean instead of using these big words?' It was the same when I spoke about sex at a university, and this chap said to me 'You come straight out with it.' The younger they tell people with learning difficulties about things like that the better. Because the father might do something to them and tell them they're good girls but not to tell their mams because it's 'their secret'. The staff could do it, in these homes, and tell them they're good and they wouldn't know any different. A woman in the centre came to me and said 'I'm pregnant Joyce.' I said 'What are you talking about?' and she said 'Well Andrew kissed me.' So I said 'Yes go on', and she said that her boyfriend had kissed her so she would be pregnant. I said 'You're pregnant because he kissed you? Who told you that?' and it was her mother. She were fair frightened and she's forty something years old. I said 'Well if you get pregnant like that then I must have a load of children all over the place!' I asked her if she kissed her mother good night, which she did, and said 'Next time tell her you can't because you might get pregnant.' Then I sat down and I told her the facts of life, she was surprised.

Reflecting on People First

I used to be right quiet. When I say that I used to be right quiet and frightened, you know when I was a child, that my brother used to stick up for me, people don't believe it. Oh I wish I'd have known about People First when I was young. Oh I wish I had, I wish I'd have known then. I mean the nurses at the boarding school used to tell us to stick up for ourselves. We need People First for when younger babies come into the world that have got a learning difficulty then they won't be frightened of speaking up for themselves. They've heard of us and they won't be frightened. We've stuck up for ourselves and you can. Babies who haven't been born yet or who have just been born when they grow up and they're frightened of speaking up they can join a People First group and it'll teach them about independence and how to stick up for yourself. Like I said to the centre manager 'Is there a People First in our town?' – he said 'no' and I told him 'Well there is now!' People First is getting stronger every year. More and more people with learning difficulties are sticking up for themselves. All these books are coming out showing what we have done, how we've got on and put people down. They'll be frightened, raise your voice and not be frightened of them and stick up for yourself.

# APPENDIX 3

Introductory booklet for groups

**Danny Goodley
PhD Research Student
University of Sheffield**

Finding out about self-advocacy

I am a research student at the University of Sheffield. A year ago I was lucky enough to get some money from the University to help support my study. My study will look at the **self-advocacy movement** in Great Britain.

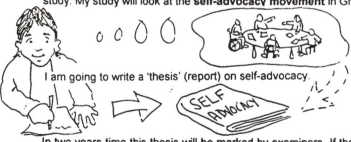

I am going to write a 'thesis' (report) on self-advocacy.

In two years time this thesis will be marked by examiners. If the examiners feel that it is good enough (and I hope they do) then I will be awarded the qualification of **'PhD'** by the University of Sheffield.

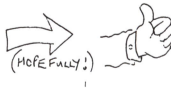

(HOPEFULLY!)

To help me understand self-advocacy and write my 'thesis' I have done a number of things.

First, I have sent a 'questionnaire' to groups in Great Britain.

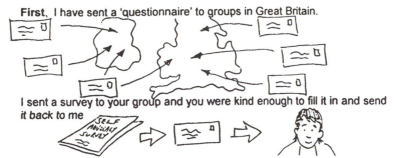

I sent a survey to your group and you were kind enough to fill it in and send it back to me

When I get all the **surveys** back from groups, I will be able to see what groups are like in Great Britain. I will write about the findings in my thesis.

Second, I am going to visit a small number of groups to see how self-advocacy works. I will be talking to self-advocates and supporters in these groups.

This is why I would like to visit **your group**. I would like to **chat** with self-advocates and supporters in your group - so that you can help me understand about self-advocacy.

2

I will meet a number of groups and will write about these visits in my report.

Because other people will be reading my report I will **change the names of groups, places and people mentioned**:

In the report I will **not** give the names of the groups I visit.

I will **not** say in which town the groups are.

I will **not** give names, self-advocates supporters and others.

By writing about the groups I visit I hope that people who read my report *will get to understand what self-advocacy groups are about.*

My thesis will be handed into the University of Sheffield in 2001.

I expect some of my thesis to be **published**

I hope that my thesis (report) will provide an **understanding** of self-advocacy and **help it** in some way.

After I have finished writing the thesis I hope to write another **report** of my findings for self-advocates. I expect this to be finished in 2002.

If you do agree to let me visit your group then you will be **helping me** to write my thesis.

But I **aim** and **hope** to make sure that **self-advocacy is helped** in some (small) way by my work.

Thank you for your time.

Danny Goodley

 THANKS!

References

Abberley, P. (1987) The concept of oppression and the development of a social theory of disability, *Disability, Handicap and Society*, 2(1): 5–19.

Abberley, P. (1992) Measuring disability. Paper presented at the Disability Research National Conference, June.

Abraham, C. (1989) Supporting people with a mental handicap in the community: a social psychological perspective, *Disability, Handicap and Society*, 4(2): 121–9.

Adams, G. (1996) *Before the Dawn: An Autobiography*. London: Mandarin.

Allport, G. W. (1947) *The Use of Personal Documents in Psychological Science*. New York: Social Science Research Council.

Amans, D. and Darbyshire, C. (1989) A voice of our own, in A. Brechin and J. Walmsley (eds) *Making Connections*. London: Hodder & Stoughton.

Angrosino, M. V. (1994) On the bus with Vonnie Lee: explorations in life history and metaphor, *Journal of Contemporary Ethnography*, 23(April): 14–28.

Apple, M. (1982) *Education and Power*. London: Routledge & Kegan Paul.

Aspis, S. (1997) Inclusion and exclusion. Paper presented at the Social History of Learning Disability Conference 'Inclusion and Exclusion', The Open University, Milton Keynes, 10 December.

Atkinson, D. (1989) Research Interviews with people with mental handicaps, *Mental Handicap Research*, 1(1): 75–90.

Atkinson, D. (ed.) (1993a) *Past Times: Older People with Learning Difficulties Look Back on Their Lives*. Buckingham: Open University Press.

Atkinson, D. (1993b) Relating, in P. Shakespeare, D. Atkinson and S. French (eds) *Reflecting on Research Practice: Issues in Health and Social Welfare*. Buckingham: Open University Press.

Atkinson, D., Jackson, M. and Walmsley, J. (eds) (1997) *Forgotten Lives: Exploring the History of Learning Disability*. Plymouth: BILD.

Atkinson, D. and Shakespeare, P. (1993) Introduction, in P. Shakespeare, D. Atkinson and S. French (eds) *Reflecting on Research Practice: Issues in Health and Social Welfare*. Buckingham: Open University Press.

Atkinson, D. and Williams, F. (eds) (1990) *'Know me as I am': An Anthology of Prose, Poetry and Art by People with Learning Difficulties*. Kent: Hodder & Stoughton in association with The Open University and MENCAP.

Bachrach, P. and Baratz, M. S. (1970) *Power and Poverty: Theory and Practice*. New York: Oxford University Press.

Bambrick, M. and Roberts, G. E. (1991) The sterilisation of people with a mental handicap: the views of parents, *Journal of Mental Deficiency Research*, 35(4): 353–63.

Banks, A. and Banks, S. P. (eds) (1998) *Fiction and Social Research: By Ice or Fire*. London: Sage.

Bannister, P., Burman, E., Parker, I., Taylor, M. and Tindall, C. (1994) *Qualitative Research Methods in Psychology: A Research Guide*. Buckingham: Open University Press.

Banton, R., Clifford, P., Lousada, J. and Rosenthal, J. (1985) *The Politics of Mental Health*. London: Macmillan.

Barker, I. and Peck, E. (1987) *Power in Strange Places: User Empowerment in Mental Health Services*. London: Good Practices in Mental Health.

Barnes, C. (1990) *The Cabbage Syndrome: The Social Construction of Dependence*. London: The Falmer Press.

Barnes, C. (1991) *Disabled People in Britain and Discrimination: A Case for Anti-discrimination Legislation*. London: Hurst & Company, University of Calgary Press in Association with the British Council of Organisations of Disabled People.

Barnes, C. (1993) *Disabling Imagery and the Media: An Exploration of the Principles for Media Representations of Disabled People*. Halifax: Ryburn and The British Council of Organisations of Disabled People.

Barnes, C. (1996a) Visual impairment and disability, in G. Hales (ed.) *Beyond Disability: Towards an Enabling Society*. London: Sage.

Barnes, C. (1996b) What next? Disability, the 1995 Disability Discrimination Act and the campaign for disabled people's rights. Paper presented at the Walter Lessing Lecture (Part 2) Skill (National Bureau for Disabled Students) Annual Conference, London.

Barnes, C. (1997) Disability and the myth of the independent researcher, in L. Barton and M. Oliver (eds) *Disability Studies: Past Present and Future*. Leeds: The Disability Press.

Barnes, C. and Oliver, M. (1997) All we're saying is give disabled researchers a chance, *Disability and Society*, 12(5): 811–14.

Barnes, C. and Mercer, G. (eds) (1997) *Doing Disability Research*. Leeds: The Disability Press.

Barnes, M. (1994) Objective research or social interaction? Researching users' views of services, *Research, Policy and Planning*, 12(2): 1–3.

Barnes, M., Prior, D. and Thomas, N. (1990) Social services, in N. Deakin and A. Wright (eds) *Consuming Public Services*. London: Routledge.

Barnes, M. and Wistow, G. (1992a) Research and user involvement: contributions to learning and methods, in M. Barnes and G. Wistow (eds) *Researching User Involvement*. Leeds: The Nuffield Institute for Health Studies.

Barnes, M. and Wistow, G. (eds) (1992b) *Researching User Involvement*. Leeds: The Nuffield Institute for Health Studies.

Barnes, M. and Wistow, G. (1992c) Understanding user involvement, in M. Barnes and G. Wistow (eds) *Researching User Involvement*. Leeds: The Nuffield Institute for Health Studies.

Baron, S. and Haldane, J. (eds) (1992) *Community, Normality and Difference: Meeting Social Needs*. Aberdeen: Aberdeen University Press.

Barton, L. (1996) Inclusion: an emancipatory project or a counter-productive discourse? Paper presented at the Culture, Difference and Inclusion Conference 16–19 February, Rutland Hotel, Sheffield.

Bashford, L., Townsley, R. and Williams, C. (1995) Parallel text: making research accessible to people with intellectual disabilities, *International Journal of Disability, Development and Education*, 42(3): 211–20.

Baxter, E., Poonia, K., Ward, L. and Nadirshaw, Z. (1990) *Double Discrimination: Issues and Services for People with Learning Difficulties from Black and Ethnic Minority Communities*. London: King's Fund Institute.

Bayley, M. (1973) *Mental Handicap and Community Care*. London: Routledge & Kegan Paul.

BCODP (1992) *Introduction to the British Council of Organisations of Disabled People*. Belper: BCODP.

Becker, H. (1963) *Outsiders: Studies in the Sociology of Deviance*. New York: The Free Press.

Beresford, P. (1992) Researching citizen-involvement: a collaborative or colonising enterprise? in M. Barnes and G. Wistow (eds) *Researching User Involvement*. Leeds: The Nuffield Institute for Health Studies.

Beresford, P. and Harding, T. (eds) (1993) *A Challenge to Change: Practical Experiences of Building User-led Services*. London: National Institute for Social Work.

Berger, P. and Luckmann, T. (1987) *The Social Construction of Reality*. London: Pelican Books.

Bersani, H. (1996) Leadership in developmental disabilities: where we've been, where we are, and where we're going, in G. Dybwad and H. Bersani (eds) *New Voices: Self-advocacy by People with Disabilities*. Cambridge, MA: Brookline Books.

Bertaux, D. (ed.) (1981a) *Biography and Society: The Life History Approach in the Social Sciences*. Beverly Hills, CA: Sage.

Bertaux, D. (1981b) From the life-history approach to the transformation of sociological practice, in D. Bertaux (ed.) *Biography and Society: The Life History Approach in the Social Sciences*. Beverly Hills, CA: Sage.

Bertaux-Wiame, I. (1981) The life history approach to the study of internal migration, in D. Bertaux (ed.) *Biography and Society: The Life History Approach in the Social Sciences*. Beverly Hills, CA: Sage.

Bhavnani, K. (1990) What's power got to do with it? Empowerment and social research, in I. Parker and J. Shotter (eds) *Deconstructing Social Psychology*. London: Routledge.

Biklen, D. (1976) Advocacy comes of age, *Exceptional Children*, 42(6): 308–13.

Blumer, H. (1939) *Critiques of Research in the Social Sciences I: An Appraisal of Thomas and Znaniecki's The Polish Peasant in Europe and America*. New York: Social Science Research Council.

Blumer, H. (1962) Society as symbolic interaction, in A. M. Rose (ed.) *Human Behaviour and Social Processes: an Interactive Approach*. London: Routledge.

Blumer, M. (1987) *The Social Basis of Community Care*. London: Unwin Hyman.

Boal, A. (1994) *The Theatre of the Oppressed*. London: Pluto Press.

Bogdan, R. and Taylor, S. (1976) The judged not the judges: an insider's view of mental retardation, *American Psychologist*, 31: 47–52.

Bogdan, R. and Taylor, S. (1982) *Inside Out: The Social Meaning of Mental Retardation*. Toronto: University of Toronto Press.

Boggs, C. (1996) *Social Movements and Political Power*. Philadelphia: Temple University Press.

Booth, T. and Booth, W. (1992) Practice in sexuality, *Mental Handicap*, 20 (June), 64–9.

Booth, T. and Booth, W. (1994) *Parenting under Pressure: Mothers and Fathers with Learning Difficulties*. Buckingham: Open University Press.

Booth, T. and Booth, W. (1998) *Growing up with Parents Who Have Learning Difficulties*. London: Routledge.

Booth, W. (1990) Soapbox, *Social Work Today*, 21(48): 31.

Booth, W. (1991) A cry for help in the wilderness, *Health Service Journal*, 14 February: 26–7.

Booth, W. and Booth, T. (1993) Family undoing, *Mental Handicap*, 21 (December): 137–41.

Borthwick, C. (1996) Racism, IQ and Down's syndrome, *Disability and Society*, 11(3): 403–10.

Bourlet, G. (1988) A share of the action for consumers, *Community Living*, April: 20–1.

Bowker, G. (1993) The age of biography is upon us, *Times Higher Education Supplement*, 8 January: 9.

Braddock, D. (1994) Presidential address 1994: new frontiers in mental retardation, *Mental Retardation*, 32(6): 434–43.

Braginsky, D. and Braginsky, B. (1971) *Hansels and Gretels: Studies of Children in Institutions for the Mentally Retarded*. New York: Holt, Reinhart and Winston.

Bramley, J. and Elkins, J. (1988) Some issues in the development of self-advocacy among persons with intellectual disabilities, *Australia and New Zealand Journal of Developmental Disabilities*, 14(2): 147–57.

Brandon, D. and Towe, N. (1989) *Free to Choose: an Introduction to Service Brokerage*. Surrey: Hexagon Publishing.

Branson, J. and Miller, T. (1989) Beyond integration policy: the deconstruction of disability, in L. Barton (ed.) *Integration: Myth or Reality?* London: Falmer Press.

Bratlinger, E. A. (1985) Mildly mentally retarded secondary students: information about attitudes towards sexuality, *Education and Training of the Mentally Retarded*, 20: 99–108.

Brechin, A. (1993) Sharing, in P. Shakespeare, D. Atkinson and S. French (eds) *Reflecting on Research Practice: Issues in Health and Social Welfare*. Buckingham: Open University Press.

Brechin, A., Liddiard, P. and Swain, J. (eds) (1981) *Handicap in a Social World*. Kent: Hodder & Stoughton in association with The Open University.

Brechin, A. and Walmsley, J. (eds) (1989) *Making Connections: Reflecting on the Lives and Experiences of People with Learning Difficulties*. London: Hodder & Stoughton in Association with The Open University.

Breggin, P. (1993) *Toxic Psychiatry*. London: HarperCollins.

Brinckerhoff, L. C. (1993) Self-advocacy: a critical skill for college students with learning disabilities, *Family and Community Health*, 16(3): 23–33.

Brisenden, S. (1989) Young, gifted and disabled: entering the employment market, *Disability, Handicap and Society*, 4(3): 217–20.

Brooks, N. A. (1991) Self-empowerment among adults with severe physical disability: a case study, *Journal of Sociology and Social Welfare*, 18(1): 105–20.

Brown, H. (1994) 'An ordinary sexual life?' A review of the normalisation principle as it applies to the sexual options of people with learning difficulties, *Disability and Society*, 9(2): 123–44.

Brown, H. and Craft, A. (eds) (1989) *Thinking the Unthinkable: Papers on Sexual Abuse and People with Learning Difficulties*. London: Family Planning Association.

Brown, H. and Smith, H. (1992a) Introduction, in H. Brown and H. Smith (eds) *Normalisation: A Reader for the Nineties*. London: Routledge.

Brown, H. and Smith, H. (eds) (1992b) *Normalisation: A Reader for the Nineties*. London: Routledge.

Brown, S. and Wistow, G. (eds) (1990) *The Roles and Tasks of Community Mental Handicap Teams*. Aldershot: Avebury.

Browning, P., Thorin, E. and Rhoades, C. (1984) A national profile of self-help/

self-advocacy groups of people with mental retardation, *Mental Retardation*, 22(5): 226–30.

Bruner, J. (1986) *Actual Minds, Possible Worlds*. Cambridge, MA: Harvard University Press.

Bruner, J. (1987) Life as narrative, *Social Research*, 54 (Spring): 11–32.

Bryman, A. (1988) *Quantity and Quality in Social Research*. London: Unwin Hyman.

Burman, E. and Parker, I. (eds) (1993) *Discourse Analytic Research: Repertoires and Readings of Texts in Action*. London: Routledge.

Burrell, G. and Morgan, G. (1979) *Sociological Paradigms and Organizational Analysis*. London: Heinemann.

Burstow, B. and Weitz, D. (eds) (1988) *Shrink Resistant*. Vancouver: New Star Books.

Butler, J. (1990) *Gender Trouble: Feminism and the Subversion of Identity*. New York: Routledge.

Butler, J. (1993) *Bodies that Matter: On the Discursive Limits of 'Sex'*. New York: Routledge.

Cameron, D., Frazer, E., Harvey, P., Rampton, M. B. H. and Richardson, K. (eds) (1992) *Researching Language: Issues of Power and Method*. London: Routledge.

Campbell, J. and Oliver, M. (1996) *Disability Politics: Understanding our Past, Changing Our Future*. London: Routledge.

Campling, J. (ed.) (1981) *Images of Ourselves: Women with Disabilities Talking*. London: Routledge & Kegan Paul.

Carabello, B. J. and Siegel, J. F. (1996) Self-advocacy at the crossroads, in G. Dybwad and H. Bersani (eds) *New Voices: Self-advocacy by People with Disabilities*. Cambridge, MA: Brookline.

Chadwick, A. (1996) Knowledge, power and the Disability Discrimination Act, *Disability and Society*, 11(1): 25–40.

Chamberlin, J. (1989) *On Our Own*. London: MIND.

Chamberlin, J. (1990) The ex-patients' movement: where we've been and where we're going, *Journal of Mind and Behaviour*, 11(2): 323–36.

Chappell, A. (1998) Still out in the cold: people with learning difficulties and the social model of disability, in T. Shakespeare (ed.) *The Disability Reader: Social Science Perspectives*. London: Cassell.

Chappell, A., Goodley, D. and Lawthom, R. (forthcoming) Applying and revising the social model of disability with people with learning difficulties, *British Journal of Learning Disabilities*.

Charmaz, K. (1995) Grounded theory, in J. A. Smith, R. Harré and L. V. Langenhove (eds) *Rethinking Methods in Psychology*. London: Sage.

Chatman, S. (1993) Story and narrative, in D. Walder (ed.) *Literature in the Modern World*. Oxford: Oxford University Press.

Cheston, R. (1994) The accounts of special education leavers, *Disability and Society*, 9(1): 58–69.

Cicourel, A. V. (1980) Three models of discourse analysis: the role of social structure, *Discourse Processes*, 3(2): 101–31.

Clandinin, D. J. and Connelly, F. M. (1994) Personal experience methods, in N. Denzin and Y. Lincoln (ed.) *Handbook of Qualitative Research*. Thousand Oaks, CA: Sage.

Clare, M. (1990) *Developing Self-advocacy Skills with People with Disabilities and Learning Difficulties*. London: Further Education Unit.

Clegg, J. A. (1993) Putting people first: a social constructionist approach to learning disability, *British Journal of Clinical Psychology*, 32: 389–406.

Clough, P. and Barton, L. (eds) (1995) *Making Difficulties: Research and the Construction of Special Educational Needs*. London: Paul Chapman.

Clough, P. and Barton, L. (eds) (1998) *Articulating with Difficulty: Research Voices in Special Education*. London: Paul Chapman.

Cobb, H. (1972) *The Forecast of Fulfilment: A Review of Research on Predictive Assessment of the Adult Retarded for Social and Vocational Adjustment*. New York: Teachers College Press.

Cohler, B. J. (1991) The life story and the study of resilience and response to adversity, *Journal of Narrative and Life History*, 1(2–3): 169–200.

Cooks, L. M. and Hale, C. L. (1992) A feminist approach to the empowerment of women mediators, *Discourse and Society*, 3(3): 277–300.

Cooper, D. and Hersov, J. (1986) *We Can Change the Future*. London: National Bureau for Handicapped Students.

Corbett, J. (1991) So, who wants to be normal?, *Disability, Handicap and Society*, 6(3): 259–60.

Corbett, J. (1998) Promoting an inclusive culture in a climate of fear and stress. Paper presented at the Policy, Failure and Difference seminar, Ranmoor Hall, Sheffield.

Corker, M. (1998) Disability discourse in a postmodern world, in T. Shakespeare (ed.) *The Disability Reader: Social Science Perspectives*. London: Cassell.

Corker, M. and French, S. (eds) (1998) *Disability Discourse*. Buckingham: Open University Press.

Cornwell, J. (1984) *Hard Earned Lives: Accounts of Health and Illness*. London: Tavistock.

Corradi, C. (1991) Text, context and individual meaning: rethinking life stories in a hermeneutic framework, *Discourse and Society*, 2(1): 105–18.

Craft, A. (ed.) (1987) *Mental Handicap and Sexuality*. Kent: Costello.

Crawley, B. (1982) The feasibility of trainee committees as a means of self-advocacy in adult training centres in England and Wales. Unpublished PhD, Manchester.

Crawley, B. (1988) *The Growing Voice: A Survey of Self-advocacy Groups in Adult Training Centres and Hospitals in Great Britain*. London: Values into Action.

Crawley, B. (1990) Advocacy as a threat or ally in professional practice, in S. Brown and G. Wistow (eds) *The Roles and Tasks of Community Mental Handicap Teams*. Aldershot: Avebury.

Cuff, E. C., Sharrock, W. W. and Francis, D. W. (1990) *Perspectives in Sociology*. London: Unwin Hyman.

Curtis, C. (1995) The changing role of the People First advisor. *American Rehabilitation*, cited on website http://www.independentliving.org/toolsforpower/tools29.html

Dagnan, D., Dennis, S. and Wood, H. (1994) A pilot study of the satisfaction of people with learning disabilities with the services they receive from community psychology services, *British Journal of Developmental Disabilities*, 40(1): 38–44.

Dahrendorf, R. (1990) Decade of the citizen, *Guardian*, 1 August.

Dalley, G. (1989) Community care: the ideal and the reality, in A. Brechin and J. Walmsley (eds) *Making Connections: Reflecting on the Lives and Experiences of People with Learning Difficulties*. London: Hodder & Stoughton in Association with The Open University.

Daniels, S. M. (1982) From parent-advocacy to self-advocacy: a problem of transition, *Exceptional Education Quarterly*, 3(2): 25–32.

Davis, A. (1992) Who needs user research? Service users as research subjects or participants, implications for user involvement in service contracting, in M. Barnes and G. Wistow (eds) *Researching User Involvement*. Leeds: The Nuffield Institute for Health Studies.

Deacon, J. (1974) *Tongue Tied*. London: MENCAP.

Deakin, N. and Wright, A. (eds) (1990) *Consuming Public Services*. London: Routledge.

Dean, J. and Foote-Whyte, W. (1978) How do you know if the informant is telling the truth? in J. Bynner and K. M. Stribley (eds) *Social Research: Principles and Procedures*. London: Longman.

DeNora, T. and Mehan, H. (1994) Genius: a social construction, the case of Beethoven's initial recognition, in T. R. Sarbin and J. I. Kitsuse (eds) *Constructing the Social*. London: Sage.

Denzin, N. K. (1970) *The Research Act in Sociology*. London: Allen & Unwin.

Denzin, N. K. (1992) Deconstructing the biographical method. Paper presented at the American Educational Research Association Annual Meeting, San Francisco.

Dexter, L. A. (1956) Towards a sociology of the mentally defective, *American Journal of Mental Deficiency*, 61: 10–16.

Dexter, L. A. (1958) A social theory of mental deficiency, *Journal of Mental Deficiency*, 62: 920–8.

Di Terlizzi, M. (1994) Life history: the impact of a changing service provision on an individual with learning disabilities, *Disability and Society*, 9(4): 501–17.

Didion, J. (1979) *The White Album*. New York: Simon and Schuster.

Dingham, H. F. (1968) A plea for social research in mental retardation, *Journal of Mental Deficiency*, 73(1): 2–4.

DIY Theatre Company and Goodley, D. (1999) People with learning difficulties share views on their involvement in a performing arts group, *Community, Work and Family*, 1(3): 329–34.

Doddington, K., Jones, R. S. P. and Miller, Y. (1994) Are attitudes to people with learning disabilities negatively influenced by charity advertising? An experimental analysis, *Disability and Society*, 9(2): 123–44.

Downer, J. and Ferns, P. (1993) Self-advocacy by black people with learning difficulties, in P. Beresford and T. Harding (eds) *A Challenge to Change: Practical Experiences of Building User-led Services*. London: National Institute for Social Work.

Dowse, L. (1999) On the margins of the movement: people with learning difficulties and disability activism in the UK. Paper presented at the Society for Disability Studies 12th Annual Meeting, Washington, DC, 27–30 May.

Dowse, L. (forthcoming) Contesting practices, challenging codes: self advocacy, disability politics and the social model, *Disability and Society*.

Dowson, S. and Whittaker, A. (1993) *On One Side: The Role of the Advisor in Supporting People with Learning Difficulties in Self-advocacy Groups*. London: Values into Action in association with the King's Fund Centre.

Drake, F. (1992) Consumer participation: the voluntary sector and the concept of power, *Disability, Handicap and Society*, 7(3): 267–78.

DTI (1996) *Small Businesses*. London: HMSO.

Dybwad, G. (1996) Setting the stage historically, in G. Dybwad and H. Bersani (eds) *New Voices: Self-advocacy by People with Disabilities*. Cambridge, MA: Brookline Books.

Dybwad, G. and Bersani, H. (eds) (1996) *New Voices: Self-advocacy by People with Disabilities*. Cambridge, MA: Brookline Books.

Eagleton, T. (1983) *Literary Theory*. London: Blackwell.

Edgerton, R. B. (1967) *The Cloak of Competence: Stigma in the Lives of the Mentally Retarded*. Berkeley: University of California Press.

Edgerton, R. (1976) *Deviance: A Cross-cultural Perspective*. London: Benjamin/Cummings.

Edgerton, R. B. (1984a) Introduction, in R. B. Edgerton (ed.) *Lives in Process: Mentally Retarded Adults in a Large City*. Washington, DC: Monograph 6, American Association on Mental Deficiency.

Edgerton, R. B. (1984b) The participant-observer approach to research in mental retardation, *American Journal of Mental Deficiency*, 88(5): 498–505.

Edgerton, R. and Bercovici, S. (1976) The cloak of competence: years later, *American Journal of Mental Deficiency*, 80(5): 485–97.

Emerson, E. (1992) What is normalisation? in H. Brown and H. Smith (eds) *Normalisation: A Reader for the Nineties*. London: Routledge.

Emerson, E. (1995) *Challenging Behaviour: Analysis and Intervention in People with Learning Disabilities*. Cambridge: Cambridge University Press.

Erlandson, D. A., Harris, E. L., Skipper, B. L. and Allen, S. D. (1993) *Doing Naturalistic Inquiry*. Newbury Park, CA: Sage.

Evans, C. (1995) Empower the people, *Community Care*, 24–30 August: 1.

Fairclough, N. (1989) *Language and Power*. London: Longman.

Fairclough, N. (1992) *Discourse and Social Change*. Cambridge: Polity Press.

Ferguson, P. M. (1987) The social construction of mental retardation, *Social Policy*, 18: 51–6.

Ferguson, P. M. and Ferguson, D. L. (1995) The interpretivist view of special education and disability: the value of telling stories, in T. M. Skrtic (ed.) *Disability and Democracy: Reconstructing (Special) Education for Postmodernity*. New York: Teachers College Press.

Ferguson, P. M., Ferguson, D. L. and Taylor, S. J. (1992a) The future of interpretivism in disability studies, in P. M. Ferguson, D. L. Ferguson and S. J. Taylor (eds) *Interpreting Disability: A Qualitative Reader*. New York: Teachers College Press.

Ferguson, P. M., Ferguson, D. L. and Taylor, S. J. (eds) (1992b) *Interpreting Disability: A Qualitative Reader*. New York: Teachers College Press.

Ferguson, P. M., Ferguson, D. L. and Taylor, S. J. (1992c) Introduction, in P. M. Ferguson, D. L. Ferguson and S. J. Taylor (eds) *Interpreting Disability: A Qualitative Reader*. New York: Teachers College Press.

Fernald, W. E. (1912) The burden of feeble-mindedness, *Journal of Psychoasthenics*, 17: 87–111.

Fido, R. and Potts, M. (1989) 'It's not true what was written down!' Experiences of life in a mental handicap institution, *Oral History*, Autumn: 31–5.

Finkelhor, D. and Korbin, J. (1988) Child abuse as an international issue, *Child Abuse and Neglect*, 12: 3–23.

Finkelstein, V. (1981) To deny or not to deny disabilities, in A. Brechin, P. Liddiard and J. Swain (eds) *Handicap in a Social World*. London: Hodder & Stoughton.

Finkelstein, V. (1993) The commonality of disability, in J. Swain, V. Finkelstein, S. French and M. Oliver (eds) *Disabling Barriers – Enabling Environments*. London: Sage.

Finkelstein, V. and Stuart, O. (1996) Developing new services, in G. Hales (ed.) *Beyond Disability: Towards an Enabling Society*. London: Sage.

Flynn, M. and Ward, L. (1991) 'We can change the future': self and citizen advocacy, in S. S. Segal and V. P. Varma (eds) *Prospects for People with Learning Difficulties*. London: David Fulton Publishers.

Flynn, M. C. (1986) Adults who are mentally handicapped as consumers: issues and guidelines for interviewing, *Journal of Mental Deficiency Research*, 30: 369–77.

Flynn, M. C. and Saleem, J. K. (1986) Adults who are mentally handicapped and living with their parents: satisfaction and perceptions regarding their lives and circumstances, *Journal of Mental Deficiency*, 30: 379–87.

Ford, S. (1996) Learning difficulties, in G. Hales (ed.) *Beyond Disability: Towards an Enabling Society*. London: Sage/The Open University.

Foucault, M. (1970) *The Order of Things*. London: Tavistock Publications.

Foucault, M. (1975) *Discipline and Punish*. London: Allen Lane.

Foucault, M. (1983) The subject and power, in H. L. Dreyfus and P. Rabinov (eds) *Michael Foucault: Beyond Structuralism and Hermeneutics*. Chicago: University of Chicago Press.

Freire, P. (1970) *Pedagogy of the Oppressed*. London: Penguin.

French, J. and Kuczaj, E. (1992) Working through loss and change with people with learning difficulties, *Mental Handicap*, 20, September: 108–11.

French, S. (1993) Disability, impairment or something in between? in J. Swain, V.

Finkelstein, S. French and M. Oliver (eds) *Disabling Barriers – Enabling Environments*. London: Sage.

Friedman-Lambert, P. (1987) How would you like it? *Entourage*, 2(2): 15–17.

Gagnon, N. (1981) On the analysis of life accounts, in D. Bertaux (ed.) *Biography and Society: The Life History Approach in the Social Sciences*. Beverly Hills, CA: Sage.

Galton, F. (1869) *Hereditary Genius: an Enquiry into Its Laws and Consequences*. Cleveland: World Publishing.

Garfinkel, H. (1967) *Studies in Ethnomethodology*. Englewood Cliffs, NJ: Prentice Hall.

Garfinkel, H. (1968) Common-sense knowledge of social structures, in C. Gordon and K. Gergen (eds) *The Self in Social Interaction*. New York: Wiley.

George, M. (1995) Rules of engagement, *Community Care*, 7–13 September: 17.

Gerber, D. A. (1990) Listening to disabled people: the problem of voice and authority, in Robert B. Edgerton's *The Cloak of Competence*, *Disability, Handicap and Society*, 5(1): 3–23.

Gergen, K. J. (1988) If persons are texts, in L. A. Sass and R. A. Woolfolk (eds) *Hermeutics and Psychological Theory*. New Brunswick, NJ: Rutgers University Press.

Gergen, K. J. and Gergen, M. M. (1988) Narrative and the self as relationship, *Advances in Experimental Psychology*, 21: 17–56.

Gergen, M. (1994) The social construction of personal histories: gendered lives in popular autobiographies, in T. R. Sarbin and J. I. Kitsuse (eds) *Constructing the Social*. London: Sage.

Germon, P. (1998) Activists and academics: part of the same or a world apart? in T. Shakespeare (ed.) *The Disability Reader: Social Science Perspectives*. London: Cassell.

Gilbert, N. and Specht, H. (1976) Advocacy and professional ethics, *Social Work*, 21(4): 288–92.

Gillespie, T. (1994) Feminist research: reclaiming objectivity, *Research, Policy and Planning*, 12(2): 23–5.

Gillman, M., Swain, J. and Heyman, B. (1997) Life history or 'care history': the objectification of people with learning difficulties through the tyranny of professional discourses, *Disability and Society*, 12(5): 675–94.

Glaser, B. G. and Strauss, A. L. (1967) *The Discovery of Grounded Theory*. Hawthorne: Aldine.

Goffman, E. (1961) *Asylums*. New York: Doubleday.

Goffman, E. (1963) *Stigma: Some Notes on the Management of Spoiled Identity*. Harmondsworth: Penguin.

Goode, D. A. (1992) Who is Bobby? Ideology and Method in the discovery of a Down syndrome person's competence, in P. M. Ferguson, D. L. Ferguson and S. J. Taylor (eds) *Interpreting Disability: A Qualitative Reader*. New York: Teachers College Press.

Goode, D. A. and Gaddy, M. R. (1976) Ascertaining choice with alingual, deaf-blind and retarded clients, *Mental Retardation*, 14(6): 10–12.

Gooding, C. (1995) *Blackstone's Guide to the Disability Discrimination Act 1995*. London: Blackstone.

Goodley, D. (1996a) Tales of hidden lives: a critical examination of life history research with people who have learning difficulties, *Disability and Society*, 11(3): 333–48.

Goodley, D. (1996b) How do you understand learning difficulties? Placing inclusion in a social model of learning difficulties. Paper presented at Culture, Difference and Inclusion Seminar, organized by University of Sheffield, Sheffield, 16–19 February.

Goodley, D. (1997) Locating self-advocacy in models of disability: understanding disability in the support of self-advocates with learning difficulties, *Disability and Society*, 12(3): 367–79.

Goodley, D. (1998a) Supporting people with learning difficulties in self-advocacy groups and models of disability, *Health and Social Care in the Community,* 6(5): 438–46.

Goodley, D. (1998b) Stories about Writing Stories, in L. Barton and P. Clough (eds) *Articulating with Difficulty: Research Voices in Special Education.* London: Paul Chapman Ltd.

Goodley, D. (1998c) Appraising self-advocacy in the lives of people with learning difficulties. Unpublished PhD thesis, University of Sheffield.

Goodley, D. (1998d) Acting out the individual programme plan: performance arts and innovative social policy for and by people with learning difficulties. Paper presented at the Disability Studies Seminar, Edinburgh, 2–4 December.

Goodley, D. (1999a) Disability research and the 'researcher template': reflections on grounded subjectivity in ethnographic research, *Qualitative Inquiry,* 5(1): 24–46.

Goodley, D. (1999b) Action, in I. Parker and the Bolton Discourse Network, *Critical Textwork: An Introduction to Varieties of Discourse and Analysis.* Buckingham: Open University Press.

Goodley, D. (1999c) *Self-advocacy in the Lives of People with Learning Difficulties: An Accessible Summary.* Bolton: Bolton Institute.

Goodley, D. (2000) Collecting the life stories of self-advocates with learning difficulties: crossing the boundary of researcher and researched, in D. Atkinson, J. Walmsley and M. Jackson (eds) *Crossing Boundaries.* Plymouth: BILD.

Goodson, I. F. (1992) Studying teachers' lives: an emergent field of inquiry, in I. F. Goodson (ed.) *Studying Teachers' Lives.* New York: Teachers College Press.

Goodwin, J. (1982) *Sexual Abuse: Incest Victims and Their Families.* Bristol: John Wright.

Grant, G. (1992) Researching user and carer involvement in mental handicap services, in M. Barnes and G. Wistow (eds) *Researching User Involvement.* Leeds: The Nuffield Institute for Health Studies.

Greasley, P. (1995) Individual planning with adults who have learning difficulties: key issues, key sources, *Disability and Society,* 10(3): 353–63.

Griffiths, R. (1988) *Community Care: An Agenda for Action.* London: HMSO.

Groce, N. (1992) 'The town fool': an oral history of a mentally retarded individual in a small town society, in P. M. Ferguson, D. L. Ferguson and S. J. Taylor (ed.) *Interpreting Disability: A Qualitative Reader.* New York: Teachers College Press.

Guardian (1995) Cosmetic surgery for Down's children, *Guardian,* 5 July: 5.

Guardian. (1996a) Zoo refuses entry to disabled people. *Guardian,* 6 July: 4.

Guardian. (1996b) Anger over thousands of disabled set to be 'losers in bonus share deal'. *Guardian,* 5 November: 3.

Guba, E. (1993) Foreword, in D. Erlandson, E. Harris, B. Skipper and S. Allen (eds) *Doing Naturalistic Inquiry.* London: Sage.

Gunn, M. J. (1990) The law and the learning disability, *International Review of Psychiatry,* 2: 13–22.

Guskin, S. (1963) Social psychologies of mental deficiency, in N. R. Ellis (ed.) *Handbook of Mental Deficiency.* New York: McGraw-Hill.

Hales, G. (ed.) (1996) *Beyond Disability: Towards an Enabling Society.* London: Sage/The Open University.

Halfpenny, P. (1984) *Principles of Method.* York: Longman.

Hampson, Y. (1994) Self-advocacy and people with learning difficulties. Unpublished MEd, University of Sheffield.

Hanna, J. (1978) Advisor's role in self-advocacy groups, *American Rehabilitation,* 4(2): 31–2.

Harré, R. (1981) Rituals, rhetoric and social cognition, in J. P. Forgas (ed.) *Social Cognition.* London: Academic Press.

Harris, P. (1995) Who am I? Concepts of disability and their implications for people with learning difficulties, *Disability and Society*, 10(3): 341–51.

Harrison, B. and Stina-Lyon, E. (1993) A note on ethical issues in the use of autobiography in sociological research, *Sociology*, 27(1): 101–9.

Hasler, F. (1993) Developments in the disabled people's movement, in J. Swain, V. Finkelstein, S. French and M. Oliver (eds) *Disabling Barriers – Enabling Environments*. London: Sage.

Hatch, J. A. and Wisniewski, R. (eds) (1995a) *Life History and Narrative*. Lewes: Falmer Press.

Hatch, J. A. and Wisniewski, R. (1995b) Life history and narrative: questions, issues and exemplary works, in J. A. Hatch and R. Wisniewski (eds) *Life History and Narrative*. Lewes: Falmer Press.

Heckel, R. V. (1968) Review of the cloak of competence: stigma in the lives of the mentally retarded, *Mental Hygiene*, 52: 313–14.

Hekman, S. J. (1990) *Gender and Knowledge: Elements of a Postmodern Feminism*. Cambridge: Polity Press.

Herr, S. S. (1979) *From Rights to Realities: Advocacy by and for Retarded People in the 1980s*. Washington DC: President's Committee on Mental Retardation.

Hersov, J. (1996) The rise of self-advocacy in Great Britain, in G. Dybwad and H. Bersani (eds) *New Voices: Self-advocacy by People with Disabilities*. Cambridge, MA: Brookline Books.

Heshusius, L. (1987) Research on perceptions of sexuality by persons labelled mentally retarded, in A. Craft (ed.) *Mental Handicap and Sexuality*. Kent: Costello.

Hevey, D. (1992) *The Creatures Time Forgot: Photography and Disability Imagery*. London: Routledge.

Hisada, N. (1991) A study of the older mentally handicapped person in residential care. Unpublished PhD, University College Swansea.

HMSO (1990) *Community Care in the Next Decade and Beyond: Policy Guidelines*. London: HMSO.

HMSO (1991) Virginia Bottomley opens conference on community care training: Press release, Department of Health, London.

HMSO (1995) *Disability Discrimination Act*. London: HMSO.

Hoffman, L. (1993) *Exchanging Voices: A Collaborative Approach to Family Therapy*. London: Karnac.

Holland, T. P. and Kilpatrick, A. C. (1993) Using narrative techniques to enhance multicultural practice, *Journal of Social Work Education*, 29(3): 302–8.

Hollway, W. (1989) *Subjectivity and Method in Psychology: Gender, Meaning and Science*. London: Routledge.

Holman, B. (1987) Research from the underside, *British Journal of Social Work*, 17: 669–83.

Howe, D. (1994) Modernity, postmodernity and social work, *British Journal of Social Work*, 24: 513–32.

Howie, D., Cuming, J. M. and Raynes, N. V. (1984) Development of tools to facilitate participation of moderately retarded persons in residential evaluation procedures, *British Journal of Mental Subnormality*, 30(2): 92–8.

Huddersfield People First (n.d.) *What Is Huddersfield People First?* Huddersfield: Huddersfield People First, c/o Swallow Street SEC, Swallow Street, Huddersfield, W. Yorkshire.

Hudson, B. (1988) Do people with mental handicaps have rights? *Disability, Handicap and Society*, 3(3): 227–37.

Hughes, B. and Paterson, K. (1997) The social model of disability and the disappearing body: toward a sociology of impairment, *Disability and Society*, 12(2): 325–40.

Humphreys, M., Hill, L. and Valentine, S. (1990) A psychotherapy group for young adults with mental handicaps: problems encountered, *Mental Handicap*, 18 (September): 125–7.

Humphreys, S., Evans, G. and Todd, S. (1987) *Lifelines: An Account of the Life Experiences of Seven People with a Mental Handicap Who Used the NIMROD Service*. London: King Edward's Hospital Fund.

Hunt, M. (1993) *The Story of Psychology*. New York: Anchor Books.

Hunt, N. (1967) *The World of Nigel Hunt*. Beaconsfield: Darwen Finlayson.

Independent on Sunday (1996) CPS 'shrugs off sex attacks on vulnerable'. *Independent on Sunday*, 2 June: 10.

Jahoda, A., Markova, I. and Cattermole, M. (1988) Stigma and the self-concept of people with a mild mental handicap, *Journal of Mental Deficiency Research*, 32: 103–15.

Jenkins, R. (1993) Incompetence and learning difficulties: anthropological perspectives, *Anthropology Today*, 9(3): 16–20.

Johnston, B. (1972) Advocacy for handicapped, *New Outlook for the Blind*, 66(10): 380–3.

Kaufman, S. Z. (1988) *Retarded ISN'T Stupid, Mom!* Baltimore: Paul. H. Brookes.

Kavale, K. and Nye, C. (1981) Identification criteria for learning disabilities: a survey of the research literature, *Learning Disabilities Quarterly*, 4(4): 383–8.

Kennedy, M. (1997) Thoughts about self-advocacy. Article with Bonnie Shoultz, from Internet homepage of the Center on Human Policy, Syracuse University, New York (http://soeweb.syr.edu/).

Khan, R. F. (1985) Mental retardation and paternalistic control, in R. S. Laura and F. Ashman (eds) *Moral Issues in Mental Retardation*. London: Croom Helm.

Kidder, L. H. and Fine, M. (1997) Qualitative inquiry in psychology: a radical approach, in D. Fox and I. Prilleltensky (eds) *Critical Psychology: An Introduction*. London: Sage.

Klockars, C. B. (1977) Field ethics for the life history, in R. S. Weppner (ed.) *Street Ethnography*. Beverly Hills, CA: Sage.

Koegel, P. (1981) Life history: a vehicle towards a holistic understanding of deviance, *Journal of Community Psychology*, 9: 162–176.

Koegel, P. (1986) You are what you drink: evidence of socialised incompetence in the life of a mildly retarded adult, in L. L. Langness and H. G. Levine (eds) *Culture and Retardation*. Kluwer: D. Reidel Publishing Company.

Korbin, J. E. (1986) Sarah: the life course of a Down's syndrome child, in L. L. Langness and H. G. Levine (ed.) *Culture and Retardation*. Kluwer: D. Reidel Publishing Company.

Kumar, K. (1978) *Prophecy and Progress*. Harmondsworth: Penguin.

Kurtz, R. A. (1981) The sociological approach to mental retardation, in A. Brechin, P. Liddiard and J. Swain (eds) *Handicap in a Social World*. Kent: Hodder & Stoughton in association with the Open University Press.

Langness, L. L. and Levine, H. G. (eds) (1986) *Culture and Retardation*. Kluwer: D. Reidel Publishing Company.

Langness, L. L. and Turner, J. L. (1986) It wasn't fair: six years in the life of Larry B, in L. L. Langness and H. G. Levine (eds) *Culture and Retardation*. Kluwer: D. Reidel Publishing Company.

Lather, P. (1986) Research as praxis, *Harvard Educational Review*, 56(3): 257–77.

Lawson, M. (1991) A recipient's view, in S. Ramon (ed.) *Beyond Community Care: Normalisation and Integration Work*. London: Macmillan in association with MIND Publications.

Lawthom, R. (1996) 'You're just like my daughter': articulation of a feminist discourse. Paper presented at the Psychology of Women Conference, Bristol.

Le Bon, G. (1985) *The Crowd: A Study of the Popular Mind*. New York: Viking Press.

Lea, S. L. (1988) Mental retardation: social construction or clinical reality? *Disability, Handicap and Society*, 3(1): 63–9.

Levine, H. G. and Langness, L. L. (1986) Conclusions: themes in an anthropology of mild mental retardation, in L. L. Langness and H. G. Levine (eds) *Culture and Retardation*. Kluwer: D. Reidel Publishing Company.

Lincoln, Y. S. and Guba, E. G. (1985) *Naturalistic Inquiry*. Beverly Hills, CA: Sage.

Lindow, V. (1993) A vision for the future, in P. Beresford and T. Harding (eds) *A Challenge to Change: Practical Experiences of Building User-led Services*. London: National Institute for Social Work.

Lister, P. (1990) Women, economic dependency and citizenship, *Journal of Social Policy*, 19: 445–67.

Lofland, J. (1971) *Analyzing Social Situations: A Guide to Qualitative Observation and Analysis*. Belmont, CA: Wardsworth.

Longley, S. and Collins, G. J. (1994) The development of a non-verbal satisfaction measure for use with people who have severe or profound learning disabilities, *British Journal of Developmental Disabilities*, 40(2): 143–9.

Lowe, K. and de Paiva, S. (1988) Canvassing the views of people with a mental handicap, *Irish Journal of Psychology*, 9(2): 220–34.

Luckin, B. (1986) Time, place and competence: society and history in the writings of Robert B. Edgerton, *Disability, Handicap and Society*, 1: 89–102.

Lukes, S. (1974) *Power: a radical View*. London: Macmillan.

Lukes, S. (ed.) (1986) *Power*. Oxford: Blackwell.

Lyons, R. (1977) *Autobiography: A Reader for Writers*. New York: Oxford University Press.

McCarthy, I. C. (1994) Poverty: an invitation to colonial practice? *Feedback*, 3: 17–21.

McKenna, C. (1986) Self-advocacy in the lives of people with mental handicap. Unpublished MPhil, University of Manchester.

MacKenzie, D. M. and Langa, A. (1994) Quality of life measurement in learning disability: basic issues, *British Journal of Developmental Disabilities*, 40(78): 72–8.

Malinowski, B. (1922) *Argonauts of the Western Pacific*. London: Routledge.

March, J., Steingold, B., Justice, S. and Mitchell, P. (1997) Follow the yellow brick road! People with learning difficulties as co-researchers, *British Journal of Learning Disabilities*, 25: 77–80.

March, P. (1992) Do photographs help adults with severe mental handicaps to make choices? *British Journal of Mental Subnormality*, 28: 122–8.

Marks, G. (1994) 'Armed now with hope': the construction of the subjectivity of students within integration, *Disability and Society*, 9(1): 71–84.

Marsh, P., Rosser, E. and Harré, R. (1978) *The Rules of Disorder*. London: Routledge.

Marshall, H. and Rabbe, B. (1993) Political discourse: talking about nationalisation and privatisation, in E. Burman and I. Parker (eds) *Discourse Analytic Research: Repertoires and Readings of Texts in Action*. London: Routledge.

Martin, J., White, A. and Meltzer, H. (1989) *Disabled Adults: Services, Transport and Employment*. London: OPCS.

Marx, G. and McAdam, D. (1994) *Collective Behaviour and Social Movements*. Engelwood Cliffs, NJ: Prentice Hall.

Marx, K. (1845) *Theses on Feuerbach*, in K. Marx and F. Engels, *Selected Works*. London: Lawrence & Wishart.

Marx, M. and Engels, F. (1832/1962) *The German Ideology*. Moscow: Progress Publishers:

Marx, K. and Engels, F. (1962) *The Eighteen Brumaire of Louis Bonaparte*, in K. Marx and F. Engels, *Selected Works*. Moscow: Foreign Languages Publishing House.

Masson, J. (1990) *Against Therapy*. London: Fontana.

May, H. (1995) Access in social science research. Paper presented at the Graduate Research Training Programme, University of Sheffield.

Means, R. and Smith, R. (1994) *Community Care: Policy and Practice*. Basingstoke: Macmillan.

Menolascino, F. J. and Eaton, L. F. (1980) Future trends in mental retardation, *Child Psychiatry and Human Development*, 10(3): 156–68.

Mercer, J. R. (1973) *Labeling the Mentally Retarded: Clinical and Social System Perspectives on Mental Retardation*. Los Angeles: University of California Press.

Mesibov, G. B. (1976) Alternatives to the principle of normalization, *Mental Retardation*, 14(5): 30–2.

Miles, M. (1992) Concepts of mental retardation in Pakistan: toward cross-cultural and historical perspectives, *Disability, Handicap and Society*, 7(3): 235–55.

Miller, A. B. and Keys, C. B. (1996) Awareness, action, and collaboration: how the self-advocacy movement is empowering for persons with developmental disabilities, *Mental Retardation*, 34(5): 312–19.

Minehan, T. (1934) *Boy and Girl Tramps of America*. Chicago: University of Chicago Press.

Minkes, J., Robinson, C. and Weston, C. (1994) Consulting the children: interviews with children using residential care services, *Disability and Society*, 9(1): 47–57.

Mischler, E. G. (1986) The analysis of interview narratives, in T. R. Sarbin (ed.) *Narrative Psychology: The Storied Nature of Human Conduct*. New York: Praeger.

Mitchell, D. (1997) What about the workers? People with learning difficulties and their paid carers. Paper presented at the Social History of Learning Disability Conference on 'Inclusion and Exclusion', 10 December.

Mitchell, P. (1997) The impact of self-advocacy on families, *Disability and Society*, 12(1): 43–56.

Mitchell, P. (1998) *Self-advocacy and Families*. Unpublished PhD thesis, The Open University.

Mitroff, I. and Kilman, R. (1978) *Methodological Approaches to Social Science*. San Francisco: Jossey-Bass.

Mittler, P. (1984) Quality of life and services for people with disabilities, *Bulletin of the British Psychological Society*, 37 (July): 218–25.

Moffett, J. and McElheny, K. R. (1966) *Points of View: An Anthology of Short Stories*. New York: Signet.

Moore, M., Beazley, S. and Maelzer, J. (1998) *Researching Disability Issues*. Buckingham: Open University Press.

Moore, M. and Goodley, D. (1999) People with learning difficulties and performing arts: maximising the benefits of participation. Project report for Salford and Trafford Disability Arts Initiative, University of Sheffield, Sheffield.

Morris, J. (1991) *Pride Against Prejudice: Transforming Attitudes to Disability*. London: The Women's Press.

Morris, J. (1993a) Gender and disability, in J. Swain, V. Finkelstein, S. French and M. Oliver (eds) *Disabling Barriers – Enabling Environments*. London: Sage.

Morris, J. (1993b) *Independent Lives: Community Care and Disabled People*. London: Macmillan.

Morris, J. (ed.) (1996) *Encounters with Strangers: Feminism and Disability*. London: The Women's Press.

Morris, P. (1969) *Put Away: A Sociological Study of Institutions for the Mentally Retarded*. London: Routledge & Kegan Paul.

Nicholson, H. (1928) *The Development of Biography*. New York: Harcourt Brace.

Nisbet, R. (1976) *Sociology as an Art Form*. London: Heinemann.

Oakley, A. (1981) Interviewing women: a contradiction in terms, in H. Roberts (ed.) *Doing Feminist Research*. London: Routledge.

O'Brien, J. (1985) *Speaking Up and Speaking Out* (A report on the International Self-advocacy Leadership Conference, Tacoma, WA, USA) Eugene: University of Oregon.

O'Brien, J. (1987) A guide to life style planning: using the activities catalogue to integrate services and natural support systems, in B. W. Wilson and G. T. Bellamy (eds) *The Activities Catalogue: An Alternative Curriculum for Youth and Adults with Severe Disabilities*. Baltimore: Brookes.

O'Brien, J. and Lyle O'Brien, C. (1997) What do members want from people first? Article from Internet homepage of the center on Human Policy, Syracuse University, New York (http://soeweb.syr.edu/).

O'Brien, J. and Sang, B. (1984) *Advocacy: The UK and American Experiences*. London: King Edward's Hospital Fund.

O'Donnell, B. (1976) Resident rights interview, *Mental Retardation*, 14(6): 13–17.

Oliver, M. (1990) *The Politics of Disablement*. Basingstoke: Macmillan.

Oliver, M. (1992) Changing the social relations of research production, *Disability, Handicap and Society*, 7(2): 101–14.

Oliver, M. (1993) Conductive education: if it wasn't so bad it would be funny, in J. Swain, V. Finkelstein, S. French and M. Oliver (eds) *Disabling Barriers – Enabling Environments*. London: Sage.

Oliver, M. (1996) *Understanding Disability: From Theory to Practice*. London: Macmillan.

Oliver, M. (n.d.) Politics and Language: understanding the disability discourse in *Insider Perspectives: The Voice of Disabled People*. Sheffield: University of Sheffield, Division of Education, research module booklet.

Oliver, M. and Barnes, C. (1997) All we are saying is give disabled researchers a chance, *Disability and Society*, 12(5): 811–14.

Oliver, M. and Zarb, G. (1989) The politics of disability: a new approach, *Disability, Handicap and Society*, 4(3): 221–39.

Orne, M. T. (1962) The nature of hypnosis: artefact and essence, *Journal of Abnormal and Social Psychology*, 58: 277–99.

Oswin, M. (1991) *Am I Allowed to Cry? A Study of Bereavement amongst People Who Have Learning Difficulties*. London: Souvenir Press.

Paechter, C. (1996) Power, knowledge and the confessional in qualitative research, *Discourse: Studies in Cultural Politics of Education*, 17(1): 75–84.

Page, L. and Aspis, S. (1997) Special feature, *Viewpoint*, January: 6–7.

Parker, I. (1997) *Psychoanalytic Culture: Psychoanalytic Discourse in Western Society*. London: Sage.

Parker, I., Georgaca, E., Harper, D., McLaughlin, T. and Stowell-Smith, M. (1995) *Deconstructing Psychopathology*. London: Sage.

Parker, I. and Shotter, J. (eds) (1990) *Deconstructing Social Psychology*. London: Routledge.

Parker, I. and the Bolton Discourse Network (1999) *Critical Textwork: An Introduction to Varieties of Discourse and Analysis*. Buckingham: Open University Press.

Parker, T. (1963) *The Unknown Citizen*. London: Hutchinson.

Parker, T. (1990) *Life after Life: Interviews with Twelve Murderers*. London: Secker & Warburg.

Parker, T. (1994) Tony Parker – writer and oral historian: interviewed by Paul Thompson, *Oral History*, Autumn: 64–73.

Peberdy, A. (1993) Observing, in P. Shakespeare, D. Atkinson and S. French (eds) *Reflecting on Research Practice: Issues in Health and Social Welfare*. Buckingham: Open University Press.

People First Liverpool (1996) *Annual Report*. Liverpool: Liverpool People First, Merseyside Trade Union and Unemployment Resources Centre, 24 Hardman Street, Liverpool L1 9AX.

People First London (n.d.) *Black People First*. London: People First of London Borough, Instrument House, 207–215 Kings Cross Road, London WC1X 9DB.

People First London (n.d.) *Helping You to Get the Services You Want*. London: People First of London Borough.

People First London (n.d.) *Laws about Our Rights*. London: People First of London Borough.

People First London (n.d.) *Making It Easy First*. London: People First of London Borough.

People First London (n.d.) *Oi! It's My Assessment*. London: People First of London Borough.

People First London (n.d.) *Outside but Not Inside . . . Yet*. London: People First of London Borough.

People First London (n.d.) *Safer Sex Pack*. London: People First of London Borough.

People First London (n.d.) *Your Right to Housing and Support*. London: People First of London Borough.

People First of Washington State and University of Oregon (1984) *Speaking Up and Speaking Out* (A report on the First International Self-advocacy Leadership Conference, Tacoma, WA, USA). Eugene: University of Oregon.

Perske, R. (1996) Self-advocates on the move, in G. Dybwad and H. Bersani (eds) *New Voices: Self-advocacy by People with Disabilities*. Cambridge, MA: Brookline Books.

Phillips, P. (1990) A self-advocacy plan for high school students with learning disabilities: a comparative case study analysis of students', teachers' and parents' perceptions of program effects. *Journal of Learning Disabilities*, 23(8): 466–71.

Plummer, K. (1983) *Documents of Life: An Introduction to the Problems and Literature of a Humanistic Method*. London: George Allen & Unwin.

Plummer, K. (1995) Life story research, in J. A. Smith, R. Harré and L. V. Langenhove (eds) *Rethinking Methods in Psychology*. London: Sage.

Potter, J. and Collie, F. (1989) 'Community care' as persuasive rhetoric: a study of discourse. *Disability, Handicap and Society*, 4(1): 57–65.

Potter, J. and Wetherell, M. (1987) *Discourse and Social Psychology: Beyond Attitudes and Behaviour*. London: Sage.

Potts, M. and Fido, R. (1991) *A Fit Person to Be Removed: Personal Accounts of Life in a Mental Deficiency Institution*. Plymouth: Northcote House.

Potts, P. (1998) The ex-files. Paper presented at the Policy, Failure and Difference Seminar, Ranmoor Hall, Sheffield.

Powerhouse (1996) Power in the house: women with learning difficulties organising against abuse, in J. Morris (ed.) *Encounters with Strangers: Feminism and Disability*. London: The Women's Press.

Reason, P. (ed.) (1988) *Human Inquiry in Action: Developments in New Paradigm Research*. London: Sage.

Reason, P. (ed.) (1994) *Participation in Human Inquiry*. London: Sage.

Reason, P. and Hawkins, P. (1988) Storytelling as inquiry, in P. Reason (ed.) *Human Inquiry in Action: Developments in New Paradigm Research*. London: Sage.

Ricci, I. (1985) Mediator's notebook: reflections on promoting equal empowerment and entitlements for women, *Journal of Divorce*, 8: 49–61.

Roffman, A. J., Herzog, J. E. and Wershba-Gershon, P. M. (1994) Helping young adults understand their learning disabilities, *Journal of Learning Disabilities*, 27(7): 413–19.

Rosaldo, M. (1984) Toward an anthropology of self and feeling, in R. A. Schweder and R. A. Levine (eds) *Culture Theory: Essays on Mind, Self and Emotion*. Cambridge: Cambridge University Press.

Rosenhan, D. L. (1973) On being sane in insane places, *Science*, 179, January: 250–8.

Rosie, A. (1993) 'He's a liar, I'm afraid': truth and lies in a narrative account, *Sociology*, 27(1): 144–52.

Ross, R. (1972) Problems of advocacy. Paper presented at the American Orthopsychiatric Association, 5–8 April.

Rusch, R. G., Hall, J. C. and Griffin, H. C. (1986) Abuse provoking characteristics of institutionalised mentally retarded individuals, *American Journal of Mental Deficiency*, 90: 618–24.

Ryan, J. and Thomas, F. (1980) *The Politics of Mental Handicap*. London: Free Association Press (rev. edn 1987).

Safilios-Rothschild, C. (1981) Disabled persons' self-definitions and their implications for rehabilitation, in A. Brechin, P. Liddiard and J. Swain (eds) *Handicap in a Social World*. Kent: Hodder & Stoughton in Association with Open University Press.

Sang, B. (1989) The independent voice of advocacy, in A. Brack and C. Grimshaw (eds) *Mental Health in Crisis*. London: Pluto Press.

Sarason, S. B. and Doris, J. (1969) *Psychological Problems in Mental Deficiency*. New York: Harper & Row.

Sarbin, T. R. (ed.) (1986) *Narrative Psychology: The Storied Nature of Human Conduct*. New York: Praeger.

Schapiro, J. (1976) Senior advocacy program for the developmentally disabled. Paper presented at the 54th Annual International Convention of the Council for Exceptional Children, Chicago, 4–9 April.

Schatzman, L. and Strauss, A. L. (1973) *Field Research: Strategies for a Natural Sociology*. Englewood Cliffs, NJ: Prentice Hall.

Scheiner, A. and Abroms, I. (1980) *The Practical Management of the Developmentally Disabled Child*. St Louis: C. V. Mosby.

Schlaff, C. (1993) From dependency to self-advocacy: re-defining disability, *American Journal of Occupational Therapy*, 47(10): 943–8.

Schutz, A. (1964) *Collected Papers II: Studies in Social Theory*. The Hague: Martinus Nijhoff.

Shakespeare, P. (1993) Performing, in P. Shakespeare, D. Atkinson and S. French (eds) *Reflecting on Research Practice: Issues in Health and Social Welfare*. Buckingham: Open University Press.

Shakespeare, P., Atkinson, D. and French, S. (eds) (1993) *Reflecting on Research Practice: Issues in Health and Social Welfare*. Buckingham: Open University Press.

Shakespeare, T. (1993) Disabled people's self-organisation: a new social movement? *Disability, Handicap and Society*, 8(3): 249–64.

Shakespeare, T. (1997a) Cultural representation of disabled people: dustbins for disavowal? in L. Barton and M. Oliver (eds) *Disability Studies: Past Present and Future*. Leeds: The Disability Press.

Shakespeare, T. (1997b) Rules of engagement: changing disability research, in L. Barton and M. Oliver (eds) *Disability Studies: Past Present and Future*. Leeds: The Disability Press.

Shakespeare, T. and Watson, N. (1997) Defending the social model, *Disability and Society*, 12(2): 293–300.

Shakespeare, T. (ed.) (1998) *The Disability Reader: Social Science Perspectives*. London: Cassell.

Shaw, C. (1931) *The Natural History of a Delinquent Career*. Chicago: University of Chicago Press.

Shaw, C. R. (1930) *The Jack Roller: A Delinquent Boy's Own Story*. Chicago: The University of Chicago Press.

Shearer, A. (1972) *Our Life*. London: CMH/VIA.

Shearer, A. (1973) *Listen*. London: CMH/VIA.

Shearer, A. (1981a) *Disability: Whose Handicap?* Oxford: Blackwell.

Shearer, A. (1981b) A Framework for independent living, in A. Walker and P. Townsend (eds) *Disability Rights in Britain*. Oxford: Martin Robertson.

Sheppard, R. (1991) Awareness paper: sex therapy and people with learning difficulties, *Sexual and Marital Therapy*, 6(3): 307–16.

Shoultz, B. (1997a) More thoughts on self-advocacy: the movement, the group, and the individual. Article from Internet homepage of the Center on Human Policy, Syracuse University, New York (http://soeweb.syr.edu/).

Shoultz, B. (1997b) The self-advocacy movement. Article from Internet homepage of the Center on Human Policy, Syracuse University, New York (http://soeweb.syr.edu/).

Shoultz, B. (1997c) The self-advocacy movement: opportunities for everyone. Article from Internet homepage of the Center on Human Policy, Syracuse University, New York (http://soeweb.syr.edu/).

Sidell, M. (1989) How do we know what we think we know? in A. Brechin and J. Walmsley (eds) *Making Connections: Reflecting on the Lives and Experiences of People with Learning Difficulties*. London: Hodder & Stoughton in Association with The Open University.

Sidell, M. (1993) Interpreting, in P. Shakespeare, D. Atkinson and S. French (eds) *Reflecting on Research Practice: Issues in Health and Social Welfare*. Buckingham: Open University Press.

Siegel, J. F. and Kantor, O. (1982) Self-advocacy: change within the individual and professional, *Social Work*, 27(5): 451–3.

Siegel, P. S. and Ellis, N. R. (1985) Note on the recruitment of subjects for mental retardation research, *American Journal of Mental Deficiency*, 89(4): 431–3.

Sievert, A. L., Cuvo, A. J. and Davis, P. K. (1988) Training self-advocacy skills to adults with mild handicaps, *Journal of Applied Behaviour Analysis*, 21(3): 299–309.

Sigelman, C., Budd, E., Spanhel, C. and Schoenrock, C. (1981) When in doubt, say yes: acquiescence in interviews with mentally retarded persons, *Mental Retardation*, 19: 53–8.

Sigelman, C. K., Budd, E. C., Winer, J. L., Schoenrock, C. J. and Martin, P. W. (1982) Evaluating alternative techniques of questioning mentally retarded persons, *American Journal of Mental Deficiency*, 86(5): 511–18.

Sigelman, C. K., Schoenrock, C. J., Spanhel, C. L. *et al.* (1980) Surveying mentally retarded persons: responsiveness and response validity in three samples, *American Journal of Mental Deficiency*, 84(5): 479–86.

Simons, K. (1992) *'Sticking Up for Yourself': Self Advocacy and People with Learning Difficulties*. Community Care publication in association with the Joseph Rowntree Foundation.

Simons, K. (1994) Enabling research: people with learning difficulties, *Research, Policy and Planning*, 12(2): 4–5.

Skrtic, T. (ed.) (1995a) *Disability and Democracy: Reconstructing (Special) Education for Postmodernity*. New York: Teachers College Press.

Skrtic, T. (1995b) Power/knowledge and pragmatism: a postmodern view of the professions. In T. Skrtic (ed.) *Disability and Democracy: Reconstructing (Special) Education for Postmodernity*. New York: Teachers College Press.

Skrtic, T. (1995c) Special education and students disability as organizational pathologies: toward a metatheory of school organization and change, in T. Skrtic (ed.) *Disability and Democracy: Reconstructing (Special) Education for Postmodernity*. New York: Teachers College Press.

Sleeter, C. E. (1995) Radical structuralist perspectives on the creation and use of learning disabilities, in T. M. Skrtic (ed.) *Disability and Democracy: Reconstructing (Special) Education for Postmodernity*. New York: Teachers College Press.

Smiley, C. W. and Craik, M. C. (1972) Citizen advocacy in a mental retardation unit, *Canada's Mental Health*, 20(2): 18–22.

Smith, D. (1987) The limits of positivism in social work research, *British Journal of Social Work*, 17: 401–16.

Sparkes, A. C. (1994) Life histories and the issue of voice: reflections on an emerging relationship, *Qualitative Studies in Education*, 7(2): 165–83.

Speak for Ourselves of Newcastle (1993) *Start! How to Set Up and Run a Successful Self-advocacy Group*. Speak for Ourselves, c/o Skills for People, Haldane House, Tankerville Terrace, Jesmond, Newcastle upon Tyne NE2 3AH.

Spradley, J. P. (1979) *The Ethnographic Interview*. New York: Holt, Rinehart & Wilson.

Stanley, L. (1990) Feminist praxis and the academic mode of production: an editorial introduction, in L. Stanley (ed.) *Feminist Praxis: Research, Theory and Epistemology in Feminist Sociology*. London: Routledge.

Stanley, L. (1994) Sisters under the skin? Oral histories and autobiographies, *Oral History*, Autumn: 88–9.

Stanley, L. and Wise, S. (1993) *Breaking Out Again: Feminist Ontology and Epistemology*. London: Routledge

Stanovich, K. E. and Stanovich, P. J. (1979) Speaking for themselves: a bibliography of writings by mentally handicapped individuals, *Mental Retardation*, 17: 83–6.

Steele, R. S. (1986) Deconstructing histories: toward a systematic criticism of psychological narratives, in T. R. Sarbin (ed.) *Narrative Psychology: The Storied Nature of Human Conduct*. New York: Praeger.

Stott, W. (1973) *Documentary Expression and Thirties America*. New York: Oxford University Press.

Stratford, B. (1991) Human rights and equal opportunities for people with mental handicap – with particular reference to Down's syndrome, *International Journal of Disability, Development and Education*, 38(1): 3–13.

Stuart, M. (1997) Different voices, different communities: stories of the closure of a long stay convent home for women with learning difficulties. Paper presented at the Social History of Learning Disability Conference on 'Inclusion and Exclusion', 10 December.

Stuart, O. (1993) Double oppression: an appropriate starting point? in J. Swain, V. Finkelstein, S. French and M. Oliver (eds) *Disabling Barriers – Enabling Environments*. London: Sage.

Sullivan, A. (1996) *Virtually Normal: An Argument about Homosexuality*. London: Vintage Books.

Sutcliffe, J. (1990) *Adults with Learning Difficulties: Curriculum Choice and Empowerment*. Leicester: National Institute of Adult Continuing Education in Association with Open University Press.

Sutcliffe, J. and Simons, K. (1993) *Self-advocacy and Adults with Learning Difficulties: Contexts and Debates*. Leicester: National Institute of Adult Continuing Education.

Swain, J. (1995) Constructing participatory research: in principle and in practice, in P. Clough and L. Barton (eds) *Making Difficulties: Research and the Construction of SEN*. London: Paul Chapman Ltd.

Swain, J., Finkelstein, V., French, S. and Oliver, M. (eds) (1993) *Disabling Barriers – Enabling Environments*. London: Sage.

Swain, J. and French, S. (1998) Lessons from segregation. Paper presented at the Policy, Failure and Difference Seminar, Ranmoor Hall, Sheffield.

Taylor, S. J. and Bogdan, R. (1984) *Introduction to Qualitative Research Methods: The Search for Meanings*, 2nd edn. New York: John Wiley & Sons.

Taylor, S. J. and Bogdan, R. (1989) On accepting relationships between people with mental retardation and non-disabled people: towards an understanding of acceptance, *Disability, Handicap and Society*, 4(1): 21–37.

Taylor, S. J. and Bogdan, R. (1992) Defending illusions: the institution's struggle for survival, in P. M. Ferguson, D. L. Ferguson and S. J. Taylor (eds) *Interpreting Disability*. New York: Teachers Press College.

Thomas, D. (1982) *The Experience of Handicap*. London: Methuen.

Thomas, W. I. and Znaniecki, F. (1918–20) *The Polish Peasant in Europe and America*, 5 vols. Chicago: University of Chicago Press.

Thompson, P. (1988) *The Voice of the Past: Oral History*, 2nd edn. Oxford: Oxford University Press.

Todd, S. and Shearn, J. (1997) Family dilemmas and secrets: parents' disclosure of information to their adult offspring with learning disabilities, *Disability and Society*, 12(3): 341–66.

Todis, B. (1992) 'Nobody helps!': Lack of perceived support in the lives of elderly people with learning disabilities, in P. M. Ferguson, D. L. Ferguson and S. J. Taylor (eds) *Interpreting Disability: A Qualitative Reader*. New York: Teachers College Press.

Tomlinson, S. (1995) The radical structuralist view of special education and disability: unpopular perspectives on their origins and development, in T. M. Skrtic (ed.) *Disability and Democracy: Reconstructing (Special) Education for Postmodernity*. New York: Teachers College Press.

Townsend, P. (1969) Foreword, in P. Morris (ed.) *Put Away: A Sociological Study of Institutions for the Mentally Retarded*. London: Routledge & Kegan Paul.

Tremblay, M. (1959) The key informant technique: a non-ethnographic application. *American Anthropologist*, 59: 688–98.

Turner, B. S. (ed.) (1990) *Theories of Modernity and Postmodernity*. London: Sage.

Turner, J. L. (1980) Yes I am human: autobiography of a 'retarded career', *Journal of Community Psychology*, 8: 3–8.

Turner, M. (1991) Literature and social work: an exploration of how literature informs social work in a way social sciences cannot, *British Journal of Social Work*, 21: 229–43.

Tyne, A. (1994) Taking responsibility and giving power, *Disability and Society*, 9(2): 249–54.

Unzicker, P. (1988) Quoted in B. Burstow and D. Weitz (eds) *Shrink Resistant*. Vancouver: New Star Books.

UPIAS (1976) *Fundamental Principles of Disability*. London: Union of the Physically Impaired Against Segregation.

Usher, R. (1995) Textuality and reflexivity in educational research, in D. Scott and R. Usher (eds) *Understanding Educational Research*. London: Routledge.

Vincent, C. (1998) Class, race and collective action: African Caribbean parents' involvement in education. Paper presented at the Policy, Failure and Difference Seminar, Ranmoor Hall, Sheffield.

Vincent, C. and Warren, S. (1997) A 'different kind' of professional? Case studies of the work of parent-centred organizations, *International Journal of Inclusive Education*, 1(2): 143–61.

Vlachou, A. (1997) *Struggles for Inclusion: An Ethnographic Study*. Buckingham: Open University Press.

Walker, R. (1981) On the uses of fiction in educational research (and I don't mean Cyril Burt), in D. Smetherham (ed.) *Practising Evaluation*. Driffield: Nafferton.

Walmsley, J. (1991) 'Talking to top people': some issues relating to the citizenship of people with learning difficulties, *Disability, Handicap and Society*, 6(3): 219–31.

Walmsley, J. (1992) Opening doors: a role for open learning in developing valued social roles, *British Journal of Mental Subnormality*, 38(2): 135–42.

Walmsley, J. (1993) Explaining, in P. Shakespeare, D. Atkinson and S. French (eds) *Reflecting on Research Practice: Issues in Health and Social Welfare*. Buckingham: Open University Press.

Walmsley, J. (1995) Life history interviews with people with learning difficulties, *Oral History*, Spring: 71–7.

Warner, W. L. and Lunt, P. S. (1941) *The Social Life of a Modern Community*. New Haven, CT: Yale University Press.

Watson, N., Riddell, S. and Wilkinson, H. (eds) (2000) *Disability, Culture and Identity*. London: Longman.

Watson, W. (1996) Bad Samaritan: very cognitively disabled people and the sociological sensibility, *International Journal of Critical Sociology*, 37(3): 231–51.

Wendell, S. (1996) *The Rejected Body: Feminist Philosophical Reflections on Disability*. New York: Routledge.

Wertheimer, A. (1989) A Voice of Our Own: Now and in the Future. Report of the 1988 People First International Conference.

Wertheimer, A. (1990) Users speak out, *Community Care*, 28 June: 26–7.

Wetherell, M. (1996) Life histories/social histories, in M. Wetherell (ed.) *Identities, Groups and Social Issues*. London: Sage in association with The Open University.

Whittaker, A., Gardener, S. and Kershaw, J. (1991) *Service Evaluation by People with Learning Difficulties: Based on the People First Report*. London: King's Fund Centre.

Whittaker, A., Kershaw, J. and Spargo, J. (1993) Service evaluation by people with learning difficulties, in P. Beresford and T. Harding (eds) *A Challenge to Change: Practical Experiences of Building User-led Services*. London: National Institute for Social Work.

Whittemore, R., Langness, L. and Koegel, P. (1986) The life history approach to mental retardation, in L. Langness and H. Levine (eds) *Culture and Retardation*. Dordrecht: D. Reidel Publishing Company.

WHO (1992) *International Classification of Impairments, Disabilities and Handicaps*. Geneva: World Health Organization.

Whyte, W. F. (1943) *Street Corner Society*. Chicago: University of Chicago Press.

Widdicombe, S. (1993) Autobiography and change: rhetoric and authenticity of 'gothic style', in E. Burman and I. Parker (eds) *Discourse Analytic Research: Repertoires and Readings of Texts in Action*. London: Routledge.

Williams, F. (1973) *Workshop on Participation*. London: CMH/VIA.

Williams, F. (1989) *Social Policy: A Critical Introduction – Issues of Race, Gender and Class*. London: Polity Press.

Williams, P. (1982) Participation and self-advocacy, *CMH Newsletter*, 20 (Spring): 3–4.

Williams, P. and Shoultz, B. (1982) *We Can Speak for Ourselves*. London: Souvenir Press.

Wilson, E. (1992) Contemporary issues in choice making for people with a learning disability. Part I: underlying issues in choice making, *Mental Handicap*, 20 (March): 31–3.

Wise, H. D. (1973) Is teacher advocacy compatible with professionalism? *Today's Education*, 62(6): 4–5.

Wolfensberger, W. (1972a) *Citizen Advocacy for the Handicapped, Impaired and Disadvantaged: an Overview*. Washington, DC: President's Committee on Mental Retardation.

Wolfensberger, W. (1972b) *Normalization: The Principle of Normalization in Human Services*. Toronto: Leanord Crainford.

Wolfensberger, W. (1981) The extermination of handicapped people in World War II Germany, *Mental Retardation*, 19: 1–7.

Wolfensberger, W. (1987) Values in the funding of social services (a commentary paper), *American Journal of Mental Deficiency*, 92(2): 141–3.

Woolgar, S. (1993) Epistemological issues in scientific explanations. Paper presented at the Qualitative Research Methods for Psychologists, Brunel University.

Worrell, B. (1987) Walking the fine line: the people first advisor, *Entourage*, 2(2): 30–5.

Worrell, B. (1988) *People First: Advice for Advisors*. Ontario Canada: National People First Project.

Worsley, P. (ed.) (1991) *The New Modern Sociology Readings*. London: Penguin.

Wright, D. and Digby, A. (1996) *From Idiocy to Mental Deficiency: Historical Perspectives on People with Learning Disabilities*. London: Routledge.

Yarmol, K. (1987) Pat Worth – self-advocate par excellence, *Entourage*, 2(2): 26–9.

Zarb, G. (1992) On the road to Damascus: first steps towards changing the relations of disability research, *Disability, Handicap and Society*, 7: 125–38.

Zarb, G. and Oliver, M. (1993) *Ageing with a Disability: What Do They Expect After All These Years?* Greenwich: University of Greenwich.

Zetlin, A. G. and Turner, J. L. (1985) Transition from adolescence to adulthood: perspectives of mentally retarded individuals and their families, *American Journal of Mental Deficiency*, 89(6): 570–9.

Index